PRINCIPLES
of MATHEMATICS
Workbook **12**

PRINCIPLES
of MATHEMATICS
12
Workbook

Series Authors and Consultants
Cathy Canavan-McGrath, Hay River, Northwest Territories
Serge Desrochers, Calgary, Alberta
Hugh MacDonald, Edmonton, Alberta
Carolyn Martin, Edmonton, Alberta
Michael Pruner, Vancouver, British Columbia
Hank Reinbold, St. Albert, Alberta
Rupi Samra-Gynane, Vancouver, British Columbia
Carol Shaw, Winnipeg, Manitoba
Roger Teshima, Calgary, Alberta
Darin Trufyn, Edmonton, Alberta

NELSON EDUCATION

NELSON / EDUCATION

Principles of Mathematics 12 Workbook

Lead Educator
Chris Kirkpatrick

Series Authors
Cathy Canavan-McGrath
Michael Pruner
Carol Shaw
Darin Trufyn

Workbook Author
First Folio Resource Group Inc.

Editorial Director
Linda Allison

Publisher, Mathematics
Colin Garnham

Managing Editor, Development
Erynn Marcus

Product Manager
Linda Krepinsky

Program Manager
Colin Bisset

Senior Content Editor
Tom Gamblin

Developmental Editor
First Folio Resource Group Inc.

Director, Content and Media Production
Linh Vu

Content Production Editor
Joe Zingrone

Copyeditor
Julia Cochrane

Proofreader
Gerry Jenkison

Production Manager
Helen Jager Locsin

Design Director
Ken Phipps

Interior Design
VisutronX
Eugene Lo

Cover Design
Eugene Lo

Cover Image
Veer/Corbis

Asset Coordinator
Suzanne Peden

Illustrators
MPS Limited

Compositor
MPS Limited

Cover Research
Debbie Yea

Printer
Webcom

Table of Contents

Getting Started

1. Match each number system with the letter that represents it and the numbers that best match it. The first number system is given as an example.

a) whole numbers $\underline{\text{W}}$ $\underline{\text{iii}}$ N, W, I, Q, R

b) integers ___ ___

c) rational numbers ___ ___

d) real numbers ___ ___

e) natural numbers ___ ___

i) ..., $-2, -1, 0, 1, 2,...$

ii) e.g., $\dfrac{1}{2}, -\dfrac{2}{3}, -5, 7$

iii) $0, 1, 2, 3,...$

iv) $1, 2, 3,...$

v) e.g., $\pi, 5, -\dfrac{5}{7}, \sqrt{2}$

2. Place letter labels on the Venn diagram in the correct positions.

natural numbers   rational numbers

real numbers   integers

whole numbers

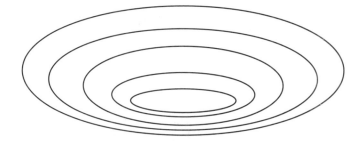

3. List all the number systems to which each number belongs. Choose from N, W, I, Q, and R.

a) -14.723 **c)** $\sqrt[3]{-27}$ **e)** $\cos 30°$

b) $\dfrac{45}{6}$ **d)** $2 \sin 30°$ **f)** $3 - \sqrt{9}$

4. Decide whether each statement is true or false. If it is false, provide a counterexample.

   a) The positive square root of a number is less than or equal to the number itself.

   b) If all of the side lengths in a polygon are equal, then all of the angle measures are equal.

   c) On Monday nights, Jana does less than 1 h of homework. On a given night, Jana did 2 h of homework, so that night was not a Monday.

5. State whether each conjecture is supported or disproved by the given evidence.

   a) The square of a rational number is also a rational number:

   $$(-2)^2 = 4, \left(\frac{4}{5}\right)^2 = \frac{16}{25}$$

   b) All right triangles have two acute angles: a triangle with side lengths 3 cm, 4 cm, and 5 cm

   c) If the mean of two numbers is positive, then both the numbers must be positive: $\dfrac{7 + (-2)}{2} = 2.5$

   d) All prime numbers are odd: 13, 41, 89

6. Use deductive reasoning to write the logical conclusion for each situation.

   a) Each exterior angle of a triangle equals the sum of the two opposite interior angles. In $\triangle ABC$, $\angle A = 95°$ and $\angle B = 52°$.

   conclusion: _____

   b) In Québec, cars must be equipped with snow tires in winter by law.

   Pascal lives in Québec.

   It is January.

   Pascal's car is legal to drive.

   conclusion: _____

1.1 Types of Sets and Set Notation

Keep in Mind

▶ You can represent a set of elements by

- listing the elements; for example, $A = \{6, 7, 8, 9\}$
- using words or a sentence; for example, $A = \{$all integers greater than 5 and less than 10$\}$
- using set notation; for example, $A = \{x \mid 5 < x < 10, x \in I\}$

▶ You can show how sets and their subsets are related using Venn diagrams. Venn diagrams do not usually show the relative sizes of the sets.

▶ Sets are equal if they contain exactly the same elements, even if the elements are listed in different orders.

▶ You can indicate the number of elements in Set A using the notation $n(A)$. You may not be able to count all the elements in a very large or infinite set, such as the set of real numbers.

▶ The sum of the number of elements in a set and its complement is equal to the number of elements in the universal set: $n(A) + n(A') = n(U)$.

▶ When two sets are disjoint, they contain no common elements.

Example

Indicate the multiples of 4 and 8 from 1 to 400 inclusive, using set notation and noting any subsets. Also represent the sets and subsets in a Venn diagram.

Solution

Step 1. I defined U as the universal set of natural numbers from 1 to 400.

$$U = \{1, 2, 3, ..., 398, 399, 400\}$$

$$U = \{x \mid 1 \leq x \leq 400, x \in N\}$$

Step 2. I defined F as the set of multiples of 4 from 1 to 400.

$$F = \{4, 8, 12,..., 392, 396, 400\}$$

$$F = \{f \mid f = 4x, 1 \leq x \leq 100, x \in N\}$$

Step 3. I defined E as the set of multiples of 8 from 1 to 400.

$$E = \{8, 16, 24,..., 384, 392, 400\}$$

$$E = \{e \mid e = 8x, 1 \leq x \leq 50, x \in N\}$$

Step 4. I considered the sets and subsets, including the complement of *F*.

> *E* is a subset of *F* and of *U* because they both contain all the elements of *E*.
>
> Likewise, *F* is a subset of *U* because *U* contains all the elements of *F*.
>
> $$E \subset F \subset U$$
>
> $F' = \{\text{non-multiples of 4 from 1 to 400}\}$

Step 5. I represented this information in a Venn diagram.

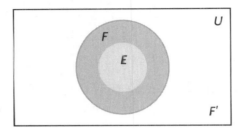

Practice

1. a) Draw a Venn diagram to represent these sets:

- the universal set: $U = \{\text{natural numbers from 1 to 50 inclusive}\}$
- $S = \{\text{multiples of 6}\}$
- $T = \{\text{multiples of 12}\}$
- $X = \{\text{multiples of 15}\}$
- $Y = \{\text{multiples of 17}\}$

b) List the disjoint subsets, if there are any.

c) Is each statement true or false? If it is false, correct it. Explain your answer.

i) $S \subset T$

ii) $Y \subset U$

iii) $S \subset S$

iv) $Y' = \{\text{even numbers from 1 to 50}\}$

> **TIP**
> The notation { } means a set that contains no elements. This is called the empty set.

v) In this example, the set of natural numbers from 51 to 60 equals { }.

2. Brazil (*B*) and British Columbia (*C*) have the following species:

$B = \{\text{owl, eagle, cougar}\}$

$C = \{\text{owl, eagle, cougar, sea lion, bighorn sheep, minke whale}\}$

a) Illustrate these sets of species in a Venn diagram.

b) Is either set a subset of the other? Explain.

3. a) Draw a Venn diagram to show

- the universal set: $U = \{\text{integers from } -20 \text{ to } 20\}$
- $E = \{\text{multiples of 4}\}$
- $S = \{\text{multiples of 9}\}$

b) List the disjoint subsets, if there are any.

4. Make a list of different machines and technology around your home. Organize these items into sets using a Venn diagram. Explain what the sets represent.

5. Consider this universal set:

$$U = \{A, B, C, D, E, F, G, 1, 2, 3, 4, 5, 6, 7, 8, 9, 0\}$$

a) List the following subsets:

- $S = \{$characters formed with straight lines only$\}$

- $C = \{$characters formed with curves only$\}$

b) Is the statement $C = S'$ true or false?

Provide your reasoning.

MULTIPLE CHOICE

6. Which choice describes the Venn diagram best?

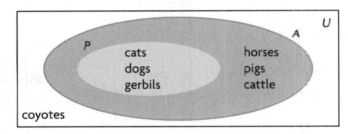

A. $U = \{$four-legged animals$\}$, $A = \{$animals kept by humans$\}$, $P = \{$pets$\}$

B. $U = \{$animals kept by humans$\}$, $A = \{$pets$\}$, $P = \{$animals kept by humans$\}$

C. $U = \{$all animals$\}$, A or $P = \{$animals kept by humans$\}$

D. $U = \{$farm animals$\}$, C and $I = \{$pets$\}$

7. Determine $n(U)$, the number of elements in the universal set, given $n(X) = 47$ and $n(X') = 156$.

A. 156 **B.** 109 **C.** 203 **D.** 47

> **TIP**
> Keep in mind that a set and its complement are disjoint.

WRITTEN RESPONSE

8. The library contains many kinds of books, audio books, CDs, DVDs, and so on. Create a Venn diagram to organize these items, with a few sample elements in each set. Explain what you did.

1.2 Exploring Relationships between Sets

Keep in Mind

▸ Sets that are not disjoint share common elements.

▸ When drawing or looking at a Venn diagram, keep the following in mind:

- Each region of the diagram represents something different.
- Each element in a universal set appears only once.
- An element that occurs in more than one set goes in the region where the sets containing the element overlap.
- To count the elements in non-disjoint sets, count the elements in each region just once.

Example

Chantal asked 36 people at a senior citizens' residence what types of movies they liked, with the results shown. She wants to use the data to answer these questions:

- How many people like mystery or comedy or both?
- How many people like mystery only or comedy only?

Draw a Venn diagram to show the data.

Type	Number of People Who Like
mystery	20
comedy	15
neither	6

Solution

Step 1. I defined appropriate sets for the situation:

$$U = \{\text{all people asked}\}$$

$$M = \{\text{people who like mystery}\}$$

$$C = \{\text{people who like comedy}\}$$

Step 2. I thought about whether there was any overlap.

$$20 + 15 + 6 = 41$$

Since Chantal asked 36 people, then there must be some overlap—some people must like both genres.

Step 3. I determined the number of people who liked at least one genre.

Number of people asked − number who liked neither genre = 36 − 6, or 30

30 people like mystery or comedy or both.

But from the table, up to 20 + 15 = 35 people like mystery or comedy or both, so it must be that 35 − 30 = 5 people like both mystery and comedy.

20 − 5 = 15, so 15 people like mystery only.

15 − 5 = 10, so 10 people like comedy only.

Step 4. I drew a Venn diagram to confirm my results.

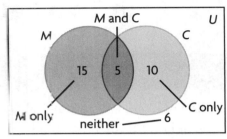

Practice

1. Giselle asked 35 people what flowers they had bought for Mother's Day, with these results.

   a) How many people bought roses and geraniums?

   b) How many people bought only roses?

   c) Draw a Venn diagram to show the data.

Flower	Number of People Asked
roses	17
geraniums	17
neither	6

NUMERICAL RESPONSE

2. There are 90 guests at a winter resort in Manitoba. Of these guests, 64 plan to go dog sledding and 51 plan to go snowshoeing. There are 16 guests who do not plan to do either activity.

   _____ guests plan to do both activities.

   _____ guests plan to go dog sledding but not snowshoeing.

   _____ guests plan to go snowshoeing but not dog sledding.

WRITTEN RESPONSE

3. In all, 940 students attend Mapleton Veterinary College. Of these, 580 have a dog, 480 have a cat, and 40 have neither kind of pet. Show in a Venn diagram how many students have **a)** a cat and a dog; **b)** a cat but not a dog; and **c)** a dog but not a cat. Explain what you did.

1.3 Intersection and Union of Two Sets

Keep in Mind

▸ The union of sets A and B, $A \cup B$, consists of all of the elements in A or B or both. It is represented by the entire region of these sets on a Venn diagram.

▸ The intersection of sets A and B, $A \cap B$, consists of all of the elements shared by both sets. It is represented by the region of overlap on a Venn diagram.

▸ The Principle of Inclusion and Exclusion states that
$n(A \cup B) = n(A) + n(B) - n(A \cap B)$ or
$n(A \cup B) = n(A \setminus B) + n(B \setminus A) + n(A \cap B)$, where "$A \setminus B$" indicates elements that are in Set A but not in Set B.

▸ If sets A and B are disjoint (contain no common elements), then $n(A \cap B) = 0$ and $n(A \cup B) = n(A) + n(B)$.

Example

The following produce is sold at a farmers' market.

| corn | apples | onions | beets | carrots |
| parsnips | tomatoes | asparagus | beans | watermelon |

Determine the number of food types with each quality.

a) round

b) grows underground

c) either round or grows underground

d) is neither round nor grows underground

Solution

Step 1. I defined the universal set and the subsets I would use.

U = {all the produce at the farmers' market}

R = {all the produce that is round}

G = {all the produce that grows underground}

Step 2. I wanted to use an organized approach, to be sure to account for each food, so I made these lists:

round: apples, onions, beets, tomatoes, watermelon

grows underground: onions, beets, carrots, parsnips

both: onions, beets

Step 3. I created a Venn diagram that included the overlap.

Step 4. I used the Venn diagram to determine each quantity.

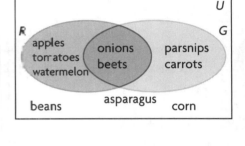

a) number of round foods that do not grow underground:

$$n(R \setminus G) = n(R) - n(R \cap G)$$

$$n(R \setminus G) = 5 - 2, \text{ or } 3$$

b) number of foods that grow underground and are not round:

$$n(G \setminus R) = n(G) - n(R \cap G)$$

$$n(G \setminus R) = 4 - 2, \text{ or } 2$$

c) number of foods that are either round or grow underground:

$$n(R \cup G) = n(R) + n(G) - n(R \cap G)$$

$$n(R \cup G) = 5 + 4 - 2, \text{ or } 7$$

d) number of foods that are neither round nor grow underground:

$$n((R \cup G)') = n(U) - n(R \cup G)$$

$$n((R \cup G)') = 11 - 7, \text{ or } 4$$

Practice

1. Consider the Venn diagram shown.

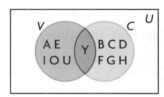

a) Determine $V \cup C$.   _____

b) Determine $n(V \cup C)$.   _____

c) Determine $V \cap C$.   _____

d) Determine $n(V \cap C)$.   _____

2. Consider the following two sets:

$A = \{-5, -3, -1, 1, 3, 5\}, B = \{1, 2, 3, 4, 5, 6\}$

a) Determine $A \cup B$, $n(A \cup B)$, $A \cap B$, and $n(A \cap B)$.

b) Draw a Venn diagram to show these two sets.

3. Angelo asked 85 people if they liked chocolate or cherry frozen yogurt.

   - 6 people did not like either flavour.
   - 16 people liked both flavours.
   - 42 people liked only chocolate.

   Determine how many people liked only cherry.

4. Fraser asked 65 people at the mall if they liked to listen to audio books or read printed books.

   - 9 people did not like either.
   - 39 people liked audio books.
   - 31 people liked printed books.

   Determine how many people liked both types, how many liked only audio books, and how many liked only printed books.

5. Dariya keeps track of the people who attend fitness classes at the local exercise club. In one week, 600 people used the club.

   - 41 people did not do cardio or weight classes.
   - 437 people did cardio classes.
   - 268 people did weight classes.

   Determine how many people did both cardio and weight classes.

6. On an ocean liner, 741 passengers were asked if they would like fish or vegetable stew for dinner.

   - All passengers liked at least one of these choices.
   - 100 liked fish and stew equally.
   - 239 preferred fish.

   Determine how many passengers preferred the stew.

7. At Saskatoon's John G. Diefenbaker International Airport, Claude asked 103 people if they had visited Regina or Winnipeg within the past year.

   - 8 people had not been to either city.
   - 55 people had been to Winnipeg.
   - 70 people had been to Regina.

   Determine how many people had been to both cities.

8. Becky is a travel agent. She has kept track of why all of her 948 clients have travelled the past year.

   - 569 people travelled for pleasure.
   - 398 people travelled for business.
   - 29 people travelled for neither business nor pleasure.

   Determine how many people travelled for business and pleasure.

MULTIPLE CHOICE

9. Jie asked 111 people what type of television shows they like.

   - 61 people like police dramas.
   - 78 people like comedies.
   - 14 people like neither type of show.

   Determine how many people like both types of shows.

   A. 42   **B.** 19   **C.** 36   **D.** 50

WRITTEN RESPONSE

10. Rocco reads the following report from an employee:

    "I interviewed 100 people about whether they like orange juice with or without pulp: 63 like it with pulp, 69 like it without pulp, and 10 people do not drink orange juice."

    Should Rocco believe this report? Explain, with the aid of a diagram.

1.4 Applications of Set Theory

Keep in Mind

▸ To represent three intersecting sets with a Venn diagram, use three intersecting circles. In the Venn diagram shown,

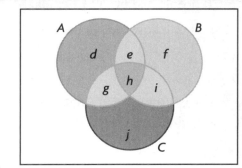

- $A \cap B \cap C$ is represented by region h,
- $A \cap B$ is represented by the union of regions e and h,
- $A \cap C$ is represented by the union of regions g and h, and
- $B \cap C$ is represented by the union of regions h and i.

▸ You can use the Principle of Inclusion and Exclusion to determine the number of elements in the union of three sets.

$$n(A \cup B \cup C) = n(A) + n(B) + n(C) - n(A \cap B) - n(A \cap C) - n(B \cap C) + n(A \cap B \cap C)$$

Example

Use the following clues to answer the questions below:
In a Grade 12 math class,

- 25 students have a tablet, an MP3 player, or a cellphone.
- 15 students have a tablet.
- 14 students have an MP3 player.
- 13 students have a cellphone.
- 5 students have a tablet and an MP3 player.
- 4 students have a tablet and a cellphone.
- 2 students have an MP3 player and a cellphone.

a) How many students have all three devices?

b) How many students have only one device?

Solution

a) **Step 1.** I defined the sets in this situation.

D = {students who have electronic devices} T = {students who have a tablet}

M = {students who have an MP3 player} C = {students who have a cellphone}

Let x represent the number of students who have all three electronic devices.

Step 2. I drew a Venn diagram to show how the numbers of elements in the four sets are related.

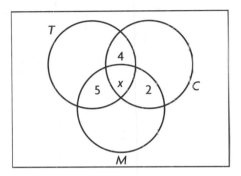

Step 3. I determined a relationship involving x using the Principle of Inclusion and Exclusion.

$$n(T) + n(M) + n(C) - n(T \cap M) - n(T \cap C) - n(M \cap C) + n(T \cap M \cap C) = n(T \cup M \cup C)$$

$$15 + 14 + 13 - (x + 5) - (x + 4) - (x + 2) + x = 25$$

$$42 - x - 5 - x - 4 - x - 2 + x = 25$$

$$31 - 2x = 25$$

$$-2x = -6$$

$$x = 3$$

TIP

To determine the number of elements, x, in a region of a Venn diagram,

- write down the algebraic form of the Principle of Inclusion and Exclusion;
- substitute any numbers you know;
- substitute expressions involving x;
- solve for x.

Therefore, 3 students have all three electronic devices.

b) **Step 1.** I subtracted the number of students who have more than one device from the total number of students.

students with one device $= 25 - (2 + 3 + 4 + 5)$

students with one device $= 25 - 14$

students with one device $= 11$

Therefore, 11 students have only one device.

Practice

1. The three circles in the Venn diagram (X, Y, and Z) contain the same number of elements. Determine one set of values for x, y, and z.

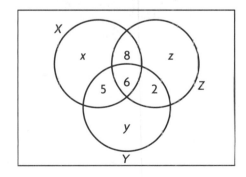

2. Creative Cupcakes sells vanilla, chocolate, and lemon cupcakes. On Monday, customer sales were as shown in the Venn diagram. Determine each amount.

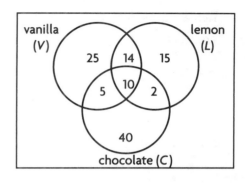

a) $n((V \cup C) \setminus L)$

b) $n((L \cup V) \setminus C)$

c) $n((V \cup C) \cup (V \cup L))$

d) $n(L \setminus V \setminus C)$

3. Barney is planning a tree-trekking holiday in British Columbia. Give four words or phrases that Barney might use to search for information on the Internet. Use set theory to explain how quotation marks and the word "and" could help him refine his search.

4. Terence is trying to increase sales at his pizza store. He is trying to decide whether he should offer a package deal to customers who buy pizzas and chicken wings. He hires a survey company to research consumer preferences. A survey of 500 people provides the following information:

- 100 buy wings.
- 450 buy pizza.
- 80 buy neither.

What percent of Terence's customers might use a package deal? Use set notation in your answer.

5. A total of 81 students attended a three-day information session on working in developing countries. The three countries featured were Mali, India and Vietnam. One country was featured per day.

- 45 attended the session on Mali, 40 on India, and 35 on Vietnam.
- 10 attended the session on Mali and India only.
- 15 attended the session on Mali and Vietnam only.
- 12 attended the session on India and Vietnam only.
- All students attended at least one session.

How many students attended all three sessions?

NUMERICAL RESPONSE

6. The yearbook committee consists of three photographers and five editors. Two members are both photographers and editors. There are _____ members on the committee.

7. The school ski club consists of four alpine skiers and six Nordic skiers. Two of the members are both alpine skiers and Nordic skiers. There are _____ members in the club.

WRITTEN RESPONSE

8. There are 155 Grade 12 students at Westdale High. The number of students enrolled in the following courses is shown.

- 78 in biology
- 70 in chemistry
- 40 in physics
- 2 in all three sciences

- 20 in biology and chemistry
- 10 in chemistry and physics
- 10 in biology and physics

a) Complete the Venn diagram to illustrate the situation.

b) How many students do not take any of the three science courses? Explain.

Complete the following to summarize the important ideas from this chapter.

Q: What are the different ways of representing sets?

NEED HELP?
- See Lesson 1.1

A: • By _____ the elements; for example, {7, 14, 21,...}.

    • By _____ the set; for example, the set of all positive multiples of 7.

    • By using set _____; for example, $\{7x \mid x > 0, x \in I\}$.

    • By using a _____ diagram.

    • The _____ of a Set A can be written as A'. It contains all the

      elements in the _____ set that are _____ in the Set A.

Q: What is important about the different regions of a Venn diagram involving non-disjoint sets?

NEED HELP?
- See Lesson 1.2

A: • Each _____ represents a _____ set or combination of sets.

    • Each _____ in a universal set appears _____.

    • An element that occurs in more than one _____ goes in the

      _____ where the sets containing the element _____.

Q: How can you determine the number of elements in different regions of a Venn diagram?

NEED HELP?
- See Lessons 1.1, 1.2, 1.3, and 1.4

A: • For a set and its _____, $n(A) + n(A') = $ _____.

    • For two disjoint sets, $n(A \cup B) = $ _____ and $n(A \cap B) = $ ___.

    • For two non-_____ sets, the _____ states

    $n(A \cup B) = $ _____ $ + n(B) - $ _____

    or $n(A \cup B) = n(A \setminus B) + $ _____ $ + n(A \cap B)$.

    • For three non-_____ sets, the _____ states

    $n(A \cup B \cup C) = n(A) + $ _____ $ + $ _____ $ - n(A$ _____ $B) - $ _____

        $ - $ _____ $ + n(A$ _____ B _____ $C)$.

MULTIPLE CHOICE

1. Determine $n(U)$, the universal set, given $n(X) = 21$ and $n(X') = 400$.

   A. 421   **B.** 389   **C.** 21   **D.** 401

2. Which choice describes the Venn diagram and the sets best?

   A. $U =$ {instruments in orchestra}, $S =$ {strings}, $W =$ {woodwinds}; $S = U'$

   B. $U =$ {strings}, $S =$ {brass}, $U' =$ {percussion}; $W = S'$

   C. $U =$ {instruments in orchestra }, $S =$ {strings}, $W =$ {woodwinds}; $S \subset U$, $W \subset U$, S and W are disjoint.

   D. $U =$ {instruments in orchestra}, $S =$ {woodwinds}; S and U are disjoint.

3. Marcel asked some students if they liked liquorice or popcorn.

   • 17 students like liquorice only.

   • 31 students like popcorn only.

   • 40 students like both types of food.

   • 6 students like neither type of food.

   Determine how many students Marcel asked.

   A. 98   **B.** 94   **C.** 66   **D.** 17

4. A total of 140 students went to a conference on future careers. In addition to an exhibit, three sessions were offered on being an electrician, a plumber, or a carpenter.

   • 19 just attended the exhibit.

   • 60 went to electricity, 57 went to plumbing, and 64 went to carpentry.

   • 14 went to electricity and plumbing, but not carpentry.

   • 22 went to plumbing and carpentry, but not electricity.

   • 14 went to electricity and carpentry, but not plumbing.

   How many students attended all three sessions?

   A. 55   **B.** 129   **C.** 5   **D.** 19

5. A total of 195 people went to the library one day.

   • 26 patrons did not borrow any items.

   • 100 patrons borrowed DVDs, 90 borrowed books, and 71 borrowed CDs.

   • 16 borrowed books and CDs, but not DVDs.

   • 21 borrowed CDs and DVDs, but not books.

   • 19 borrowed books and DVDs, but not CDs.

   How many patrons borrowed all three types of media?

   A. 18   **B.** 182   **C.** 74   **D.** 32

NUMERICAL RESPONSE

6. There are 64 passengers on a morning bus. Of these passengers, 35 need transfers and 39 are going to work. There are 12 passengers who do not need transfers and are not on their way to work.

   _____ passengers need transfers and are going to work.

   _____ passengers need transfers but are not going to work.

   _____ passengers are going to work but do not need transfers.

7. The number of elements in the universal set, $n(U)$, given $n(X) = 58$ and $n(X') = 219$, is _____.

8. At a university, 339 first-year students need to think about which option to take in their second year.

   • 20 students are interested in teaching only.

   • 183 students are interested in computer science.

   • 194 students are interested in finance.

   _____ students are interested in computer science only.

   _____ students are interested in finance only.

   _____ students are interested in computer science and finance.

9. The school athletic team consists of 6 runners and 3 high jumpers. Two team members are high jumpers and runners. There are _____ members on the team.

10. The local beauty salon has a total staff of 8 manicurists and 9 hairdressers. Three of these are manicurists and hairdressers. There are _____ people on staff.

WRITTEN RESPONSE

11. A department store offers shirts and pants on sale for one day. Of the 748 customers who go to the store, 561 buy shirts, 552 buy pants, and 60 buy neither. Show in a Venn diagram how many customers bought

a) shirts and pants;

b) shirts, but not pants; and

c) pants, but not shirts. Explain what you did.

12. There are 122 students who have signed up for after-school clubs. Of these, 79 signed up for the drama club, 66 signed up for the band club, and 14 signed up for other activities. Show in a Venn diagram how many students signed up for **a)** both drama and band; **b)** drama but not band; and **c)** band but not drama.

13. A car dealer conducted a survey of 230 customers about three options: power steering (*S*), power windows (*W*), and automatic headlights (*H*).

- 126 like the steering.
- 87 like the windows.
- 105 like the headlights.

- 23 like the steering and windows, but not the headlights.
- 22 like the windows and headlights, but not the steering.
- 31 like the headlights and steering, but not the windows.
- 12 like all three options.

How many customers did not like any of the three options? Explain your answer.

Getting Started

1. Match each term with the best picture or description.

   a) the intersection of two sets

   b) two disjoint sets

   c) outcome table

   d) tree diagram

   i)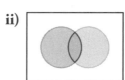

   ii)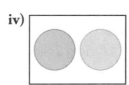

   iii)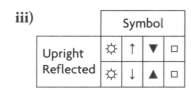

   iv)

2. Create a Venn diagram to represent each relationship.

   a) Universal set U: whole numbers; E: set of even numbers; P: set of prime numbers

   b) Universal set W: all 52 cards in a standard deck; A: set of all aces; B: set of all black cards

3. Determine $n(A \cup B)$ for each pair of sets described.

   a) $n(A) = 14$, $n(B) = 9$, $n(A \cap B) = 7$

   b) $n(A) = 22$, $n(B) = 17$, $n(A \cap B) = 0$

4. There are 563 visitors to a water-cycle exhibit at a school's eco day.

- 245 visitors participate in the hands-on activity.
- 437 visitors watch the multimedia documentary.
- 96 visitors neither participate in the activity nor watch the documentary.

a) How many visitors experience at least one of the activity and documentary?

b) How many visitors experience both?

5. List the elements of each set.

a) R, the set of red face cards in a standard deck of playing cards

b) D, the set of different two-digit numbers using the digits 1, 2, 3, and 4

c) P, the set of all possible products when a pair of standard dice are rolled

6. List the subsets of each set. Include the empty set as a subset.

a) $\{\square, \diamond, \bigcirc\}$ **b)** $\{25\}$ **c)** $\{A, B, C, D\}$

7. Consider these sets: A, even integers; B, odd integers; C, integers divisible by 6.

a) Create a Venn diagram to show how all three sets of numbers are related.

b) Which two of these three sets of integers are not disjoint?

8. Let S be the set of natural numbers less than or equal to 16.
Let $A = \{1, 5, 8, 13, 16\}$, and let B be the set of even numbers in S.

a) List the elements of A', B', $A \cup B$, and $A \cap B$.

b) List the elements of $A' \cup B'$ and $A' \cap B'$.

c) Create a Venn diagram showing S, A, and B.

Include each number in S in the correct place in your diagram.

2.1 Counting Principles

YOU WILL NEED
• calculator

Keep in Mind

▶ The Fundamental Counting Principle says the following:

- If one task can be performed in a ways AND another task can be performed in b ways, then both tasks can be performed in $a \cdot b$ ways.

- If a series of tasks can be performed in a ways AND b ways AND c ways and so on, then all these tasks can be performed in $a \cdot b \cdot c \dots$ ways.

▶ For OR situations, the Fundamental Counting Principle does not apply:

- If the tasks are mutually exclusive, they involve disjoint sets A and B, and $n(A \cup B) = n(A) + n(B)$.

- If the tasks are *not* mutually exclusive, they involve non-disjoint sets C and D, and $n(C \cup D) = n(C) + n(D) - n(C \cap D)$ (the Principle of Inclusion and Exclusion).

▶ Outcome tables, organized lists, and tree diagrams are useful to help solve counting problems when you need to display all the possible outcomes.

Example 1

Kim is choosing a new cellphone. She can choose the 300, 400, or 500 model, in green, pink, indigo, orange, or taupe trim. Kim is also deciding whether or not to get a data plan for her phone.

a) How many different choices does Kim have altogether, accounting for model, colour, and data plan or not?

b) The store agent advises Kim not to choose the 300 model if she wants a data plan. Also, the 500 model is not available in indigo or taupe trim. How many choices does Kim have now?

Solution

a) Kim must choose a model AND a colour AND whether to get a data plan. I applied the Fundamental Counting Principle.

Number of ways to choose a model: $a = 3$

Number of ways to choose a colour: $b = 5$

Number of ways to choose a data plan or not: $c = 2$

Total number of ways to choose a phone: $a \cdot b \cdot c = 3 \cdot 5 \cdot 2$, or 30 ways

Kim has 30 different choices.

b) This is a more complicated situation, so I used a tree diagram.

When there are more than two tasks, a tree diagram is a better strategy than an outcome table.

There are 21 branches, so Kim now has 21 ways to choose a phone.

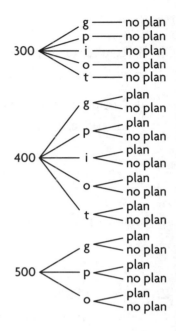

Example 2

From a standard deck of cards, how many possibilities are there for drawing
a) a two or a face card?   **b)** a spade or a queen?

Solution

Step 1. I recognized that both parts of the problem were OR situations.

Step 2. I let *A* represent the event of drawing a two and *B* represent the event of drawing a face card (jacks, queens, and kings). I knew that a card could either be a two or a face card, but not both, so the events are mutually exclusive.

$$n(A \cup B) = n(A) - n(B)$$

$$n(A \cup B) = 4 + 12, \text{ or } 16$$

a) There are 16 possibilities for drawing a two or a face card.

Step 3. I let *S* represent the event of drawing a spade, *Q* represent the event of drawing a queen, and *U* represent all possible draws of one card from a standard deck. I drew a Venn diagram to visualize how the two events are related.

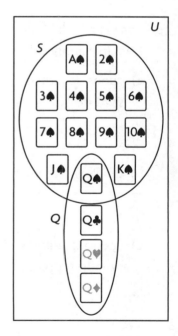

Step 4. I could see that I needed the number of cards in the union of the two sets. I applied the Principle of Inclusion and Exclusion, to make sure I did not count the queen of spades twice.

$$n(S \cup Q) = n(S) + n(Q) - n(S \cap Q)$$

$$n(S \cup Q) = 13 + 4 - 1, \text{ or } 16$$

b) There are 16 possibilities for drawing a spade or a queen.

Practice

1. Bryce likes to vary the way he takes his coffee. He can have it black, with milk, or with cream, and he can also decide whether or not to have sugar.

   a) Create an outcome table to count the total number of ways Bryce can take his coffee.

   b) Use the Fundamental Counting Principle to verify your response to part a).

2. Marie and Sitka are in charge of repainting their homeroom. They have a choice of mauve, lime green, or pale gold paint, with either a gloss or a matte finish, and they can go with either an ivory or a cream trim.

   a) Complete this tree diagram to count all of Marie and Sitka's choices.

   b) Use the Fundamental Counting Principle to verify your response to part a).

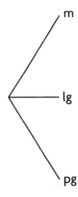

3. For each of the following situations, state whether the Fundamental Counting Principle applies. Explain how you know.

   a) choosing either a keypad or touch-screen phone from one of 4 providers, with or without a data plan

   b) drawing either a red card or a face card from a standard deck of cards

   c) choosing a pizza with regular, deep, or thin crust; pepperoni, mushroom, or ham topping; and mozzarella or cheddar cheese

   d) rolling a sum of 8 on two standard dice

4. Count the number of possibilities for each situation in question 3.

   a) ___   c) ___

   b) ___   d) ___

5. A combination lock uses the letters A through H on the first dial and the digits 0 through 9 on the second and third dials.

   a) How many possible combinations are there for this lock?

   b) How many combinations do not use the same digit twice?

6. a) How many ways are there to draw either a red number card (2 through 10) or a face card from a standard deck of cards?

   b) How many ways are there to draw either a red number card or a 7?

7. A set of cards contains 8 triangle cards, 5 circle cards, 7 kite cards, and 3 rectangle cards. Four of the cards are shown. If Peter draws one card from the whole set, how many possibilities are there? Explain how you know.

MULTIPLE CHOICE

8. In a set of 13 distinct natural numbers, 3 of the numbers are prime numbers, and 4 of them are even. The number 2 is in the set. Sondra wants to choose an odd prime number from the set. Which of the following applies?

   A. the Fundamental Counting Principle   C. both principles

   B. the Principle of Inclusion and Exclusion   D. neither principle

WRITTEN RESPONSE

9. Misha is ordering a customized salad from a deli counter. He can create his salad from the choices on the right.

   a) How many different salads could Misha create altogether? Show your reasoning.

   - Boston, romaine, or baby spinach leaves
   - cucumber or tomato but not both
   - croutons, bacon bits, both, or neither
   - ranch, thousand island, balsamic, or French dressing

   b) Misha does not like cucumber. Also, he has decided to have either croutons or bacon bits but not both. How many different salads could he create to meet these requirements? Show your reasoning.

YOU WILL NEED
• calculator

Keep in Mind

▸ The number of permutations, or ordered arrangements, of a set of n different objects is given by the expression $n! = n(n - 1)(n - 2)...(3)(2)(1)$, called n factorial. In this context, the expression is defined for natural numbers.

Example 1

A six-digit secret code number uses the digits 1 through 6 exactly once each. If the first digit of the code number is 3 and the last digit is 2, how many possibilities are there for the code number?

Solution

I knew that the first digit was 3 and the last digit was 2, so the middle four digits of the

3					2

code number could be any permutation of the set {1, 4, 5, 6}. There are 4 different digits in this set, so the number of permutations is $4! = (4)(3)(2)(1)$, or 24. There are 24 possibilities.

Example 2

a) Simplify $\dfrac{(n + 3)(n + 2)!}{(n + 1)!}$.

b) Solve $\dfrac{(n + 3)(n + 2)!}{(n + 1)!} = 30$

where $n \in N$.

Solution

a) I wrote each factorial as a product and then looked for common factors in the numerator and denominator.

$$\frac{(n + 3) \cdot (n + 2)!}{(n + 1)!} = \frac{(n + 3)(n + 2)(n + 1)(n) \ldots (3)(2)(1)}{(n + 1)(n) \ldots (3)(2)(1)}$$

$$= \frac{(n + 3)(n + 2)(n + 1)!}{(n + 1)!}$$

$$= (n + 3)(n + 2)$$

$$= n^2 + 5n + 6$$

b) I used the simplified expression from part a) to write a quadratic equation. I then solved this equation by factoring.

TIP

When $n = -8$, the expressions $(n + 2)! = (-6)!$ and $(n + 1)! = (-7)!$ are undefined. So, $n = -8$ could not be a solution in any case.

$$n^2 + 5n + 6 = 30$$

$$n^2 + 5n - 24 = 0$$

$$(n + 8)(n - 3) = 0$$

$$n + 8 = 0 \quad \text{or} \quad n - 3 = 0$$

$$n = -8 \qquad\qquad n = 3$$

I knew that n must be a natural number, so the solution is $n = 3$.

Practice

1. a) How many arrangements are possible using all of the letters in WHISTLER?

b) How many arrangements of the letters in WHISTLER end with a W?

2. Evaluate the following expressions.

a) $5! = $ ___

b) $7 \cdot 6! = $ ___

c) $\dfrac{6!}{3!} = $ ___

d) $\dfrac{7!}{3!2!} = $ ___

3. Simplify the following expressions, where $n \in I$.

a) $\dfrac{(n + 1)!}{n!}$

b) $n(n - 1)(n - 2)!$

c) $\dfrac{(n + 4)!}{(n + 2)!}$

d) $\dfrac{(n - 1)!}{(n + 1)!}$

NUMERICAL RESPONSE

4. Solve the equation $\dfrac{n!}{(n - 2)(n - 3)!} = 20$, where $n \in I$.

TIP

Check each possible solution for n to decide whether all the factorials are defined.

$$\dfrac{n!}{(n - 2)(n - 3)!} = \dfrac{n(n - 1)(\underline{\hspace{1cm}})!}{(\underline{\hspace{1cm}})!}$$

So,

$$n(\underline{\hspace{1cm}}) = 20$$

$$\underline{\hspace{1cm}}^2 - \underline{\hspace{1cm}} = 20$$

$$\underline{\hspace{2cm}} = 0$$

$$(\underline{\hspace{1cm}})(\underline{\hspace{1cm}}) = 0$$

$$n - \underline{\hspace{1cm}} = 0 \quad \text{or} \quad n + \underline{\hspace{1cm}} = 0$$

$$n = \underline{\hspace{1cm}} \quad \text{or} \quad n = \underline{\hspace{1cm}}$$

2.3 Permutations When All Objects Are Distinguishable

YOU WILL NEED
• calculator

Keep in Mind

▸ When order matters in a counting problem, then permutations are involved.

▸ The number of permutations of r objects chosen from a set of n different objects is $_nP_r = \dfrac{n!}{(n-r)!}$, where $0 \le r \le n$. A consequence of this formula is that $0! = 1$.

▸ When all n objects are used in an arrangement, there are $_nP_n = n!$ permutations.

▸ If repetition is allowed, the number of permutations that can be created from a set of n different objects is n^r.

Example 1

How many different permutations are there of 5 objects from a set of 7 different objects, if repetition is not allowed?

Solution

Step 1. I needed to determine $_nP_r$ when $n = 7$ and $r = 5$.

$$_nP_r = \frac{n!}{(n-r)!}$$

$$_7P_5 = \frac{7!}{(7-5)!}$$

$$_7P_5 = \frac{7!}{2!}$$

Step 2. I simplified the expression using the fact that $\dfrac{2!}{2!} = 1$.

$$_7P_5 = \frac{7 \cdot 6 \cdot 5 \cdot 4 \cdot 3 \cdot 2!}{2!}$$

$$_7P_5 = 7 \cdot 6 \cdot 5 \cdot 4 \cdot 3$$

$$_7P_5 = 2520$$

Example 2

Marta is writing a science fiction story in which the serial number of a starship can have one, two, or three different letters, followed always by four different numerals. How many different starship serial numbers are possible?

Solution

Step 1. I decided to consider three separate cases.

Case 1: 1 letter plus 4 numerals

Case 2: 2 letters plus 4 numerals

Case 3: 3 letters plus 4 numerals

Step 2. For Case 1, there are 26 ways to choose the letter and $_{10}P_4$ ways to choose the numerals. I used the Fundamental Counting Principle.

$$\text{Number of 1-letter serial numbers} = 26 \cdot _{10}P_4$$

$$= 26 \cdot \frac{10!}{(10-4)!}$$

$$= 26 \cdot \frac{10!}{6!}$$

$$= 26 \cdot 10 \cdot 9 \cdot 8 \cdot 7, \text{ or } 131\,040$$

TIP

Try making a permutation problem simpler by splitting it into mutually exclusive cases. Then, add the number of ways for each case for the total number of ways.

Step 3. For Cases 2 and 3, I used $_{26}P_2$ and $_{26}P_3$ in place of 26 for the number of letters.

$$\text{Number of 2-letter serial numbers} = _{26}P_2 \cdot _{10}P_4$$

$$= \frac{26!}{(26-2)!} \cdot \frac{10!}{(10-4)!}$$

$$= \frac{26!}{24!} \cdot \frac{10!}{6!}$$

$$= 26 \cdot 25 \cdot 10 \cdot 9 \cdot 8 \cdot 7, \text{ or } 3\,276\,000$$

$$\text{Number of 3-letter serial numbers} = _{26}P_3 \cdot _{10}P_4$$

$$= \frac{26!}{23!} \cdot \frac{10!}{6!}$$

$$= 26 \cdot 25 \cdot 24 \cdot 10 \cdot 9 \cdot 8 \cdot 7, \text{ or } 78\,624\,000$$

Step 4. Since the cases are mutually exclusive, I added the numbers for each. There are $131\,040 + 3\,276\,000 + 78\,624\,000 = 82\,031\,040$ serial numbers in total.

Example 3

A set of 6 numbered symbol cards includes 3 cards with circles, 2 cards with squares, and 1 card with a kite. How many ways are there to lay out the cards in a single row so that the circle cards are 2nd, 4th, and 6th from the left?

Solution

Step 1. I created a diagram to visualize the cards laid out in a row.

Step 2. There are 3 ways to place a circle card in Position P2, 2 ways for Position P4, and 1 way for Position P6. There are $_3P_3$ ways to place the circle cards altogether.

Step 3. The remaining 3 cards could be placed in any permutation into the positions P1, P3, and P5. There are $_3P_3$ ways to do this.

Step 4. Using the Fundamental Counting Principle, there are $_3P_3 \cdot _3P_3 = 3! \cdot 3!$, or $6 \cdot 6 = 36$ ways to lay out the cards with circle cards in P2, P4, and P6.

Practice

1. How many permutations are there in each case?

   a) 3 objects from 5 different objects   b) 3 objects from 7 different objects

2. How many permutations of 4 objects are there from

   a) 5 objects?   b) 6 objects?   c) 7 objects?

3. In how many ways can you draw each number of marbles, one by one, without replacement, out of a bag of 8 different marbles? For each number, state the number of permutations in the form $_nP_r$.

   a) 8 marbles   b) 5 marbles   c) 3 marbles   d) 1 marble

4. In how many ways can Adam, Benoit, Carys, Dilip, and Eva be appointed to a student committee with 5 different positions under each set of conditions?

   a) Carys is to be president.

   b) Neither Benoit nor Carys will be president.

5. State the values of n for which each expression is defined, where $n \in I$.

   a) $\dfrac{n!}{(n-2)!}$; $n \geq$ ___   b) $(n+1)n(n-1)!$; $n \geq$ ___   c) $\dfrac{2(n+2)!}{(n+3)!}$; $n \geq$ ___

6. The 4th, 5th, and 6th digits of a phone number such as 403-555-1234 are called the exchange. How many exchanges are possible

   a) if each of the digits 0 to 9 are used at most once?

   b) if the only exchange NOT allowed is 555? (This fake exchange is often used in films and TV programs—and math books!)

7. At a child's birthday party, prizes are awarded for best costume, best craft, and best-decorated cookie. In how many different ways can prizes be awarded to the 15 guests at the party under each of these conditions?

   a) Each guest receives at most one prize.

   b) Each guest may receive any or all of the prizes.

8. Could the expression $\dfrac{n!}{(n + 1)!}$, where $n \geq 1$, represent a permutation problem?

a) Explain why or why not, in terms of the value of the expression.

b) Explain why or why not, in terms of the possible meaning of the expression.

9. Neil is creating an 8-character password. More than half of the characters will be upper- or lowercase letters, and the rest will be digits from 0 to 9. Neil will use at least one digit and will not use any character more than once. The digits will follow the letters.

a) Describe three different cases for this problem.

b) How many passwords are possible if in each password the digits follow the letters?

NUMERICAL RESPONSE

10. Solve each equation. State any restrictions on the variable.

a) $_{n-1}P_2 = 12$

b) $_5P_r = 60$

_____

_____

WRITTEN RESPONSE

11. Without calculating, predict which is larger: $_9P_6$ or $_8P_5$. Explain your prediction.

2.4 Permutations When Objects Are Identical

• calculator

Keep in Mind

▶ When n objects are arranged in different orders, there are fewer than $n!$ permutations if some of the objects are identical.

▶ For a set of n objects, if a objects are identical, another b are identical, another c are identical, and so on, then the number of permutations is

$$\frac{n!}{a!\,b!\,c!\,\ldots}.$$

Example 1

The figures to the right are to be arranged in a single row.

a) How many different arrangements are possible?

b) How many arrangements are possible if the end figures must both be stars?

Solution

a) There are 10 figures altogether, with 2 identical ✕ figures, 3 identical ♣ figures, and 5 identical ☆ figures. So the number of permutations is

$$\frac{10!}{2!3!5!} = \frac{10 \cdot 9 \cdot 8 \cdot 7 \cdot 6 \cdot 5!}{2 \cdot 1 \cdot 3 \cdot 2 \cdot 1 \cdot 5!}$$

$$= \frac{10 \cdot 9 \cdot (4 \cdot 2) \cdot 7}{2}$$

$$= 10 \cdot 9 \cdot 4 \cdot 7, \text{ or } 2520$$

There are 2520 permutations.

b) In this case, I needed to think only about the middle 8 figures: 2 identical ✕s, 3 identical ♣s, and $5 - 2 = 3$ identical ☆s.

$$\frac{8!}{2!3!3!} = \frac{8 \cdot 7 \cdot 6 \cdot 5 \cdot 4 \cdot 3!}{2 \cdot 1 \cdot 3 \cdot 2 \cdot 1 \cdot 3!}$$

$$= \frac{8 \cdot 7 \cdot 5 \cdot (2 \cdot 2)}{2}$$

$$= 8 \cdot 7 \cdot 5 \cdot 2, \text{ or } 560$$

There are 560 permutations.

Example 2

Ricardo jumps into a taxi to travel 8 blocks west and 3 blocks north across town. Assuming there are no one-way streets, how many routes could the taxi driver take, travelling only west or north?

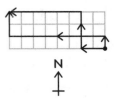

Solution

Step 1. I thought about the problem in terms of permutations.

Whichever route the taxi driver chose, I knew that the taxi would have to go 8 blocks west and 3 blocks north. So the "objects" would be the blocks travelled west, a, and the blocks travelled north, b.

Step 2. I determined the values of the variables for this problem:

$a = 8$ and $b = 3$, so $n = 8 + 3$, or 11.

Step 3. The number of routes, R, is given by

$$R = \frac{11!}{8! \cdot 3!}$$

$$R = \frac{11 \cdot 10 \cdot 9 \cdot 8!}{8! \cdot 3 \cdot 2 \cdot 1}$$

$$R = \frac{11 \cdot (5 \cdot 2) \cdot (3 \cdot 3)}{3 \cdot 2 \cdot 1}$$

$$R = 11 \cdot 5 \cdot 3, \text{ or } 165$$

There are 165 possible routes the taxi could take.

Practice

1. Evaluate the following expressions.

    a) $\dfrac{7!}{4! \cdot 3!}$ b) $\dfrac{7!}{3! \cdot 2! \cdot 2!}$ c) $\dfrac{8!}{3! \cdot 3!}$ d) $\dfrac{10!}{5! \cdot 3!}$

2. These figures are to be arranged in a single row.

    a) How many different arrangements are possible?

    b) How many arrangements are possible if the middle figure must be a star?

    c) How many arrangements are possible if the middle figure is NOT a star?

3. How many different arrangements can be made using all of the letters in the word REARRANGE?

4. Complete the following alternative solution of Example 2 on the previous page.

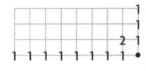

a) As shown, there are 2 routes to get to the intersection one block north and one block west of Ricardo's starting point. Complete the pattern to show the number of routes to get to all the intersections in the row one block north of the start.

b) Suppose there are x routes to Intersection A and y routes to Intersection B shown in this diagram. How many routes are there to Intersection C?

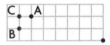

c) Complete the diagram in part a), and determine the total number of routes Ricardo's taxi could take.

5. How many routes are there from A to B in each map, if you only travel south and west?

a)

b)

6. Gareth works at a video rental store. He has 6 copies each of 3 different new DVD releases to put on a shelf.

a) In how many different ways can he arrange the DVDs on the shelf?

b) In how many different ways can the DVDs be arranged if the copies of each one must be grouped together?

7. a) In a set of n objects, there is one subset of 3 identical objects, and the rest are all different. Investigate the pattern of the numbers of arrangements of these n objects. Make a statement about the pattern as n increases.

Number of Objects, n	3	4		
Number of Arrangements	1			

b) In a set of n objects, there are two subsets of 3 identical objects, and the rest are all different. Investigate the pattern of the numbers of arrangements of these n objects. Make a statement about the pattern as n increases.

Number of Objects, n	6	7		
Number of Arrangements	20			

MULTIPLE CHOICE

8. A ball bearing is about to roll down a pegged board, as shown. Viewing the possible routes as a permutation of n objects, what is the best value of n?

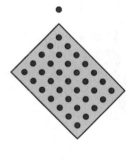

   A. 5   **B.** 7   **C.** 11   **D.** 35

9. Which of these expressions represents the number of permutations of 3 identical objects plus 2 other, different objects?

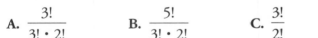

   A. $\dfrac{3!}{3! \cdot 2!}$ **B.** $\dfrac{5!}{3! \cdot 2!}$ **C.** $\dfrac{3!}{2!}$ **D.** $\dfrac{5!}{3!}$

NUMERICAL RESPONSE

10. A teacher is creating a true-false test with 10 questions.

   a) The answers can have _____ different permutations if there are exactly 3 true answers.

   b) _____ different permutations have exactly 3 false answers.

   c) _____ different permutations have at least 3 true answers and at least 3 false answers.

WRITTEN RESPONSE

11. Create a counting problem that can be solved using the expression $\dfrac{7!}{3! \cdot 2!}$.

2.5 Exploring Combinations

YOU WILL NEED
• calculator

Keep in Mind

▶ In combinations of objects or outcomes, order does not matter. So when r objects are chosen from a set of n different objects, there are always fewer combinations than permutations.

Example

All the diamonds from a standard deck of playing cards are shuffled, and 4 of these 13 cards are dealt out in a row.

a) How many different permutations of 4 diamonds could be dealt?

b) Suppose the order does not matter. How many different combinations could be dealt?

Solution

a) I knew that the number of permutations of 4 cards from a set of 13 is

$$_{13}P_4 = \frac{13!}{(13 - 4)!}$$

$$_{13}P_4 = \frac{13 \cdot 12 \cdot 11 \cdot 10 \cdot 9!}{9!}$$

$$_{13}P_4 = 17\ 160$$

There are 17 160 different permutations.

b) I reasoned that for each subset of 4 diamonds, there are $4! = 24$ possible orders. So, given that order does not matter, there is only 1 combination for each 24 permutations. Therefore, there are $17\ 160 \div 24 = 715$ different combinations.

Practice

1. a) How many different permutations are there of 3 objects chosen from a set of 5 different objects?

   b) How many different ways are there of arranging each subset of 3 objects?

   c) How many different combinations are there of 3 objects chosen from a set of 5 different objects?

2. **a)** How many permutations can be formed using all 5 of the symbols shown?

   b) How many combinations can be formed using all 5 symbols?

   c) Explain your answer to part b).

3. **a)** Write out all the permutations of 3 letters chosen from the set {a, b, c, d}. How many are there?

   b) Write out all the combinations of 3 letters chosen from the same set, writing each combination in alphabetical order. How many are there?

   c) How many times more permutations than combinations are there in this case? What does this factor mean?

4. At a restaurant, 12 friends are ordering dessert. Everyone wants the strawberry pavlova, but there are only 4 left. In how many ways can the 4 strawberry pavlovas be distributed, if no one is willing to share?

5. **a)** Write an expression for the number of permutations of 4 objects chosen from 7 different objects in factorial notation. Do not simplify your expression.

   b) Write an expression for the number of ways to arrange each subset of 4 objects.

   c) Use your answers to parts a) and b) to write an expression for the number of combinations of 4 objects chosen from 7 different objects in factorial notation.

2.6 Combinations

YOU WILL NEED
• calculator

> **Keep in Mind**
>
> ▸ When order does not matter, use combinations to solve counting problems.
>
> ▸ The number of combinations of r objects chosen from a set of n different objects is given by
>
> $$\binom{n}{r} \text{ or } {}_nC_r = \frac{n!}{r!(n-r)!}, \text{ where } 0 \leq r \leq n.$$

Example 1

How many subcommittees of 4 students can be formed from a student council consisting of 7 students?

Solution

Step 1. Only the students chosen matter, not the order in which they are chosen.
So I knew I needed to use combinations.

Step 2. I calculated ${}_nC_r$ using the appropriate values for n and r.

$$_7C_4 = \frac{7!}{4!(7-4)!}$$

$$_7C_4 = \frac{7!}{4! \cdot 3!}$$

$$_7C_4 = \frac{7 \cdot 6 \cdot z \cdot 5 \cdot 4!}{4! \cdot 3 \cdot 2 \cdot 1}$$

$$_7C_4 = 7 \cdot 5, \text{ or } 35$$

Example 2

At Karina's birthday party, there are 7 boys and 9 girls. Karina has to choose 6 children to start off a party game, including at least one boy and at least one girl. In how many ways can she do this?

Solution 1

Step 1. I broke the problem into cases.

Case 1: 1 boy and 5 girls	Case 4: 4 boys and 2 girls
Case 2: 2 boys and 4 girls	Case 5: 5 boys and 1 girl
Case 3: 3 boys and 3 girls	

Step 2. I used these cases to write down and evaluate an expression for the number of ways to pick 6 children with at least one boy and at least one girl.

$$_7C_1 \cdot {}_9C_5 + {}_7C_2 \cdot {}_9C_4 + {}_7C_3 \cdot {}_9C_3 + {}_7C_4 \cdot {}_9C_2 + {}_7C_5 \cdot {}_9C_1$$
$$= 882 + 2646 + 2940 + 1260 + 189, \text{ or } 7917 \text{ ways}$$

Solution 2

Step 1. I chose an indirect reasoning strategy. I decided to determine

- the number of ways to choose any 6 children from 16,
- the number of ways to choose 6 boys from 7, and
- the number of ways to choose 6 girls from 9.

TIP

Consider using indirect reasoning if it reduces the number of cases you need to consider.

Step 2. I used my reasoning to write down and evaluate an expression for the number of ways to pick 6 children with at least one boy and at least one girl.

$$\binom{16}{6} - \binom{7}{6} - \binom{9}{6} = 8008 - 7 - 84, \text{ or } 7917 \text{ ways}$$

Practice

1. **a)** List all of the permutations of 3 symbols chosen from the symbols $\bigcirc, \square, \diamond,$ and $\triangle$.

   b) List all of the combinations of 3 symbols chosen from the same list.

   c) How is the number of permutations of 3 symbols related to the number of combinations of 3 symbols? Explain.

2. Evaluate the following.

   a) $_5C_2 = \dfrac{5!}{3! \cdot 2!},$ or ___

   c) $_{10}C_5 = \dfrac{\square}{\square \cdot \square},$ or ___

   b) $\dbinom{7}{3} = \dfrac{\square}{\square \cdot \square},$ or ___

   d) $\dbinom{13}{1} = \dfrac{\square}{\square \cdot \square},$ or ___

3. **a)** In how many ways can a set of 6 cards be dealt from just the hearts in a standard deck?

   b) In how many ways can a set of 6 cards be dealt from just the hearts in a standard deck if the set of 6 cards includes no face cards?

4. A committee is to be chosen from a set of 11 students, of whom Tomas is one. The committee has a chair and 4 other members. In how many ways can the committee be selected

   a) if Tomas is the chair?

   b) if Tomas is on the committee, but someone else is the chair?

   c) if Tomas is on the committee, and he may or may not be the chair?

5. **a)** Write an expression for $\binom{n}{n-r}$ in terms of factorials.

   b) By simplifying your expression, show that $\binom{n}{n-r} = \binom{n}{r}$.

6. An improv team has spots for 3 women and 2 men, and 14 women and 8 men audition. How many different combinations of people could be chosen for the team?

TIP

Decide whether a problem involves the Fundamental Counting Principle or mutually exclusive cases.

7. Suppose you are choosing three of the symbols $+$, $-$, $\times$, $\div$, and $\sqrt{}$.

   a) Write an expression in the form $_nC_r$ for the total number of combinations.

   b) You decide to break this into two cases:
      - choose 2 symbols from $+$, $-$, $\times$, and $\div$; and also choose the symbol $\sqrt{}$, or
      - choose 3 symbols from $+$, $-$, $\times$, and $\div$. Write expressions in the same form for the total number of combinations for the two cases.

Pascal's triangle

$$1$$
$$1 \quad 1$$
$$1 \quad 2 \quad 1$$
$$1 \quad 3 \quad 3 \quad 1$$
$$1 \quad 4 \quad 6 \quad 4 \quad 1$$

   c) Complete these equations relating your expressions from parts a) and b).
   $$\underline{}C\underline{} = \underline{}C\underline{} + \underline{}C\underline{} = \underline{} + \underline{}$$

   d) The start of Pascal's triangle is shown on the right. Circle the numbers in the triangle that correspond to your equation from part c).

8. Solve each equation. State any restrictions on the variable.

   a) $_nC_2 = 21$ b) $\binom{n+1}{3} = 4\binom{n}{2}$ c) $_8C_r = 28$

MULTIPLE CHOICE

9. Roger is counting the number of 5-card hands that can be dealt from a standard deck and contain at least 2 black cards. Which of these expressions applies?

   A. $\binom{26}{0}\binom{26}{5} + \binom{26}{1}\binom{26}{4}$ C. both expressions

   B. $\binom{26}{0}\binom{26}{5} + \binom{26}{1}\binom{26}{4} + \binom{26}{2}\binom{26}{3}$ D. neither expression

WRITTEN RESPONSE

10. How many ways are there to divide a committee of 12 students into

   a) 3 groups of 4?   b) 4 groups of 3?

> ## Keep in Mind
>
> ▶ In counting problems, use permutations when order is important and use combinations when it is not.
>
> ▶ Look for specific features of the problem.
>
> • If there is a repetition of r out of n objects, you should usually divide by $r!$.
>
> • If multiple tasks or stages are linked by the word "and," apply the Fundamental Counting Principle (use multiplication).
>
> • If multiple tasks or stages are linked by the word "or," the problem can usually be broken down into mutually exclusive cases (use addition).

Example 1

How many sequences can be formed using each of the digits 0 through 9 exactly once, if

• the final digit in the sequence is 0,

• a multiple of 4 is the first digit in the sequence, and

• another multiple of 4 is either 5th, 6th, or 7th in the sequence?

Solution

Step 1. Order is important, so I knew this problem involves permutations. I also realized that the problem involves both "and" and "or," so I would have to consider multiple cases but also multiple stages.

Step 2. I decided to use the third condition to determine three cases.

Case 1: multiples of 4 in 1st and 5th positions with 0 as the final digit

Case 2: multiples of 4 in 1st and 6th positions with 0 as the final digit

Case 3: multiples of 4 in 1st and 7th positions with 0 as the final digit

I realized that each case would have the same number of permutations, so I would have to determine only the number of permutations for Case 1.

Step 3. I realized that each sequence can be formed by

• placing the 0 in 10th spot,

• then the 4 in the 1st or 5th spot,

• then the 8 in the remaining spot out of 1st and 5th, and

• then all the remaining digits in the remaining 7 spots.

I used the Fundamental Counting Principle:

Number of sequences for Case 1 = $1 \cdot 2 \cdot 1 \cdot 7!$, or 10 080

Step 4. The total number of sequences for all three cases is $3 \cdot (10\ 080)$, or 30 240

Example 2

How many different 4-card hands containing at least 1 heart can be dealt to one person from a standard deck of playing cards?

Solution

Step 1. The order of the cards does not matter, so I knew that the problem involved combinations. I decided to use indirect reasoning because I realized this would involve fewer calculations.

Step 2. I chose a strategy of subtracting the number of 4-card hands with no hearts from the total number of 4-card hands.

Total number of 4-card hands $= {}_{52}C_4$

Number of 4-card hands with no hearts $= {}_{39}C_4$

Number of 4-card hands with at least 1 heart:

$$
{}_{52}C_4 - {}_{39}C_4 = \frac{52 \cdot 51 \cdot 50 \cdot 49 \cdot 48!}{4! \cdot 48!} - \frac{39 \cdot 38 \cdot 37 \cdot 36 \cdot 35!}{4! \cdot 35!}
$$

$$
= 270\ 725 - 82\ 251
$$

$$
= 188\ 474
$$

There are 188 474 different 4-card hands with at least 1 heart.

Practice

1. Identify whether each situation involves permutations or combinations. Explain how you know.

   a) appointing a chair, vice chair, and secretary from a committee of 9 students

   b) choosing any 3 of 5 flavours of fruit juice

   c) forming a sequence of $+$ and $\times$ symbols using 5 $+$ symbols and 4 $\times$ symbols

2. How many possibilities are there for a five-digit combination using the digits from 0 to 9

 a) if each digit can be used many times?

 b) if each digit can be used only once?

3. Darryn wants to count the number of sequences he could form using all the spades in a standard deck, with the conditions that

 • the king is the final card in the sequence,

 • the first card in the sequence is also a face card, and

 • the final face card must be 5th or 9th in the sequence.

 a) Does this problem involve permutations or combinations? Explain.

 b) How many sequences are possible with these conditions?

4. The 16 members of a soccer team are travelling to a match in 3 vehicles, which have room for 7, 5, and 4 passengers, respectively.

 a) Does this situation involve permutations or combinations? Explain.

 b) Does this situation involve either the Fundamental Counting Principle or the Principle of Inclusion and Exclusion? Explain.

 c) In how many ways can the team be seated in the vehicles?

5. Keith is creating a collage using 6 separate prints of an image of Mt. Robson, British Columbia, each print in a different monochrome colour. How many collages using at least 4 of the prints can Keith create?

6. How many unordered collections of 3 letters and 4 digits are possible if no characters are repeated?

7. In backgammon, counters are placed on points marked by long triangles. You cannot land your counter on a point where your opponent has two or more counters, but you can jump over that point. For example, in the position shown, black can move past the two points held by white with a roll of 1 and 6, but not with a roll of 2 and 5. How many rolls with two standard dice allow black to move past both white points in this position? Count (1, 6) and (6, 1) as different rolls.

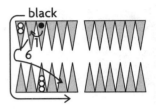

NUMERICAL RESPONSE

8. Katie likes to wear odd socks. She can choose two non-matching socks from a drawer with six different, separated pairs of socks in _____ ways.

9. How many arrangements are there of the letters in the word ANAGRAM

a) with no conditions?

_____ arrangements

b) if the arrangements cannot start with an A?

_____ arrangements

WRITTEN RESPONSE

10. How many different 5-card hands containing at most 2 red cards can be dealt to one person from a standard deck of playing cards?

a) Would you use direct or indirect reasoning for this problem? Explain.

b) Determine the number of possible hands with these conditions.

Complete the following to summarize the important ideas from this chapter.

Q: What meaning do the words AND and OR often have in counting problems?

A: • AND often indicates two or more separate tasks. If one task can be performed in *a* ways and another can be performed in *b* ways, then by the _____, both tasks can be performed in

 _____ ways.

 • OR often indicates tasks or sets that may or may not be _____

 _____.

NEED HELP?
• See Lesson 2.1

Q: What expressions can you use to determine numbers of permutations, either of a whole set of *n* different objects or of *r* objects chosen from that set?

A: • The number of permutations of *n* _____ objects is ___.

 • The number of permutations of ___ objects chosen from ___

 _____ objects is

$$ \_\_P\_\_ = \frac{\boxed{}}{\boxed{}}. $$

NEED HELP?
• See Lessons 2.2 and 2.3

Q: What type of expression could you use to determine the number of permutations of a set of objects, some of which are identical?

A: • For a set of *n* objects of which *a* are _____, another *b* are

 _____, another ___ are identical, and so on, the number of permutations is given by

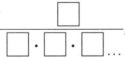

NEED HELP?
• See Lesson 2.4

Q: When should you use combinations to solve counting problems? What expression can you use to determine numbers of combinations?

A: • Use combinations in situations where order *does/does not* matter (circle one).

 • The number of combinations of ___ objects chosen from ___

 _____ objects is

$$ \_\_C\_\_ = \left(\frac{\boxed{}}{\boxed{}} \right) = \frac{\boxed{}}{\boxed{}}. $$

NEED HELP?
• See Lessons 2.5 and 2.6

MULTIPLE CHOICE

1. How many possibilities are there for drawing either a club or a face card from a standard deck of cards?

   A. 16   **B.** 19   **C.** 22   **D.** 25

2. Identify the solutions of $\dfrac{(n + 5)!}{(n + 3)(n + 2)!} = 12$, where $n \in I$.

   A. $n = -1$ and $n = -8$ **B.** $n = -1$ **C.** $n = -4$ and $n = -5$ **D.** $n = 4$ and $n = 5$

3. Which situation could give rise to the expression $\dfrac{12!}{(12 - 5)!}$?

   A. counting arrangements of 12 objects, 5 of which are identical

   B. counting arrangements of 5 objects chosen from 12 different objects

   C. choosing a basketball team of 5 from a starting line-up of 12 players

   D. forming a sequence using 5 different symbols followed by 7 different digits

4. Raychelle is determining the number of arrangements of n marbles in a row, of which a marbles are white and the other b marbles are blue. Which formula applies to this problem?

   A. $_nC_a$ **C.** The formulas are equivalent and both apply.

   B. $\dfrac{n!}{a! \cdot b!}$ **D.** Neither formula applies.

5. Which of the following is NOT a useful step in solving the equation $4\,_nC_2 = {}_{n+2}C_3$?

   A. writing algebraic expressions for $_nC_2$ and $_{n+2}C_3$

   B. removing a factor of n from both sides

   C. factoring to solve a quadratic equation in n

   D. subtracting to get 0 on one side of the equal sign

6. Four players are each dealt a 13-card hand from a standard deck of playing cards. Which of the following does this situation involve?

   A. permutations and the Fundamental Counting Principle

   B. permutations and the Principle of Inclusion and Exclusion

   C. combinations and the Principle of Inclusion and Exclusion

   D. combinations and the Fundamental Counting Principle

7. How many four-digit codes are possible using the digits 0 through 9

    a) if digits can be repeated? _____ codes   **b)** with no repeated digits? _____ codes

8. Simi draws a single card from a standard deck of playing cards. How many possibilities does she have to draw

    a) either an ace or a red face card?

    _____ possibilities

    b) either a heart or a 9?

    _____ possibilities

9. a) A president, vice-president, and secretary from a council of 10 students can be chosen in _____ ways.

    b) A subcommittee of 4 from the remaining 7 students can be chosen in _____ ways.

10. _____ different arrangements of the letters in the word SEQUENCES are possible.

11. The number of possible sequences of all the hearts from a standard deck, given that the ace and king cannot be next to each other and that the 13 cards are dealt in a single row, is _____.

12. In Oscar Wilde's play *The Importance of Being Earnest*, there are 5 male roles and 4 female roles. However, one of the female roles, Lady Bracknell, is sometimes played by a male actor. Suppose 8 men and 6 women audition for a production of this play. After all the roles have been cast, _____ different groups of unsuccessful auditioners are possible.

13. Suppose 7 points are arranged in a circle.

    a) Triangles can be formed by joining sets of three of the points, for example as shown. _____ different triangles can be formed by joining these points.

    b) If different pairs of points are joined by straight lines, for example as shown, a pattern of straight lines is formed. _____ different patterns of straight lines can be formed from the 7 points.

14. Yelena rolls a die and tosses two coins, a loonie and a toonie.

    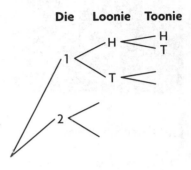

    a) Complete the tree diagram and use it to determine the total number of outcomes Yelena could achieve.

    b) Use the Fundamental Counting Principle to verify your answer to part a). Show your work.

    c) Based on the tree diagram, how many outcomes are possible for which Yelena rolls a multiple of 3 or gets at least one tail?

    d) Use the Principle of Inclusion and Exclusion to verify your answer to part b). Show your work.

15. Two 3-by-3 grids are joined in two different ways, as shown to the right.

    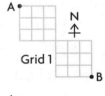

    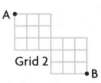

    a) Predict which combined grid has the greater number of routes from Point A to Point B, moving only east or south. Give reasons, but do not calculate.

    b) Check your prediction by calculating the number of routes for each grid.

16. How many different 6-card hands with at least 2 aces can be dealt from a standard deck of cards?

Chapter 3 · Probability

Getting Started

1. Use one of the following terms to complete each statement.

   sample space   intersection   permutation   combination

   experimental   theoretical   Fundamental Counting Principle

   a) If two sets are mutually exclusive, then they have no elements in

      their _____.

   b) An arrangement of a set of objects in which order does not matter is a

      _____.

   c) The _____ consists of all the possible outcomes of an experiment.

   d) Mira rolled a standard die seven times and got a 3 twice. She states that
      the probability of rolling a 3 is $\frac{2}{7}$. This is an example of _____
      probability.

   e) The _____ determines that
      when there are four ways to do one thing and three ways to do another
      thing, then both things can be done in $4 \cdot 3 = 12$ ways.

   f) A set of objects arranged in a definite order is a _____.

   g) The _____ probability of rolling a five with a standard die
      is $\frac{1}{6}$.

2. Complete the sample space for the outcomes of rolling a four-sided die and
   tossing two coins.

3. Evaluate each expression.

   a) $_6P_6$

   b) $_7C_5$

   c) $\dfrac{8!}{5!}$

   d) $_{10}P_7$

   e) $\dbinom{5}{2}$

   f) $_{113}C_1$

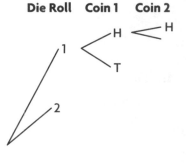

Die Roll   Coin 1   Coin 2

4. a) Complete the sample space for the difference of the rolls of two standard dice.

b) Determine the probability of getting a difference of 2 when rolling two standard dice.

c) Determine the probability of rolling a 6 and then a 4 when rolling a standard die twice.

Difference of the Rolls of Two Standard Dice						
−	1	2	3	4	5	6
1	0				4	
2				2		
3	2					
4						
5						
6						

d) Determine the probability of rolling a 6 and a 4, in either order, when rolling a standard die twice.

5. Shade the indicated region in each Venn diagram.

a) $A \cap B$

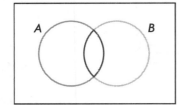

b) $A \cup B$

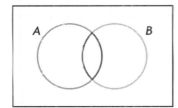

c) $(A \cap B)'$

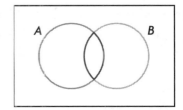

6. A group of 13 friends are travelling to a concert in 3 cars. One of the cars can carry 5 people and the other cars can carry 4 people each. Any of the friends can drive any of the vehicles. In how many ways can the friends choose which vehicles to travel in?

7. In how many distinct ways can the letters of the word PROBABILITY be arranged?

Exploring Probability

Keep in Mind

- An event is a set of outcomes. For example, with a standard die, the event "throw an even number" is the set of outcomes 2, 4, and 6.

- The probability of an event can range from 0 (impossible) to 1 (certain).

- The experimental probability of Event A is $P(A) = \dfrac{n(A)}{n(T)}$, where $n(A)$ is the number of times Event A occurred and $n(T)$ is the total number of trials, T, in the experiment.

- The theoretical probability of Event A is $P(A) = \dfrac{n(A)}{n(S)}$, where $n(A)$ is the number of favourable outcomes for Event A and $n(S)$ is the total number of outcomes in the sample space S, where all outcomes are equally likely.

- Probability is helpful for making decisions, because you can use it to determine the likelihood of an event.

Example

Consider Game A. Is it fair? If it is not fair, how could you make it fair?

Game A: Eli and Eloise put 7 rubber bracelets in a bag: 4 are blue, 1 is pink, 1 is yellow, and 1 is striped. Eli takes a bracelet without looking. If he takes a blue bracelet, then he wins. Otherwise, Eloise wins.

Solution

Step 1. I considered all of the possible events.

Eli wins if he takes a blue bracelet. I called this Event A. It can happen in 4 ways.

Eloise wins if Eli takes a pink, yellow, or striped bracelet. I called this Event B. It can happen in 3 ways.

Step 2. I determined the probabilities of either Eli or Eloise winning.

$$P(\text{Eli winning}) = \frac{n(A)}{n(S)} \qquad\qquad P(\text{Eloise winning}) = \frac{n(B)}{n(S)}$$

$$P(\text{Eli winning}) = \frac{4}{7}, \text{ or } 0.571\ldots, \text{ or } 57.142\ldots\% \qquad P(\text{Eloise winning}) = \frac{3}{7}, \text{ or } 0.428\ldots, \text{ or } 42.857\ldots\%$$

Step 3. The probability that Eli will win is greater than 50%, so Game A is unfair.

Step 4. I think I could make the game fair by removing one blue bracelet from the bag.

I determined the probabilities of Eli and Eloise winning with 3 blue, 1 pink, 1 yellow, and 1 striped bracelets.

$P(\text{Eli winning}) = \dfrac{3}{6}$ $P(\text{Eloise winning}) = \dfrac{3}{6}$

$P(\text{Eli winning}) = \dfrac{1}{2}$, or 0.5, or 50% $P(\text{Eloise winning}) = \dfrac{1}{2}$, or 0.5, or 50%

Eli is likely to win half the time. Eloise is likely to win half the time. Each player has an equal chance of winning, so Game A is now fair.

Practice

1. Suggest a second way that Game A can be made fair.

2. Consider each game. Is it fair? If it is not fair, which player has the advantage? Explain briefly.

   a) **Game B:** Angelique and Marco each toss a 4-sided die, numbered from 1 to 4. Angelique wins if the sum is 4. Marco wins if the sum is 6. Otherwise, neither wins.

   b) **Game C:** Jill and Sabrina each toss a 4-sided die, numbered from 1 to 4. If the sum of the dice is 2, 4, 6, or 8, then Jill wins. If the sum is 5, then Sabrina wins. If the sum is 3 or 7, no one wins.

MULTIPLE CHOICE

3. Which one of the following choices would make Game B in question 2 unfair?

   A. Angelique wins if the sum is 5; Marco wins if the sum is 4.

   B. Angelique wins if the difference is 1; Marco wins if the difference is 2 or 3.

   C. Angelique wins if the sum is odd; Marco wins if the sum is even.

   D. None of the above; Game B is already unfair.

3.2 Probability and Odds

> ## Keep in Mind
>
> ▸ $P(A')$ is the probability of the complement of A, where $P(A') = 1 - P(A)$.
>
> ▸ Odds express a level of confidence about the occurrence of an event.
>
>   • The odds in favour of Event A occurring are given by the ratio $\dfrac{P(A)}{P(A')}$, or $P(A) : P(A')$.
>
>   • The odds against Event A occurring are given by the ratio $\dfrac{P(A')}{P(A)}$, or $P(A') : P(A)$.
>
> ▸ If the odds in favour of Event A occurring are $m : n$, then
>
>   • the odds against Event A occurring are $n : m$
>
>   • $P(A) = \dfrac{m}{m + n}$

Example 1

Two brown-eyed parents are told that there is a 25% probability that their baby will have blue eyes. What are the odds in favour of such parents having a baby with blue eyes? What are the odds against?

Solution

Step 1. I wrote the probability as a part-to-whole ratio.

$$P(\text{blue eyes}) = 25\%, \text{ or } \frac{1}{4}$$

So the ratio of blue-eyed babies to babies with any eye colour is 1 : 4.

Step 2. I determined the complement of $P(\text{blue eyes})$ and wrote it as a part-to-whole ratio.

$$P(\text{not blue eyes}) = 75\%, \text{ or } \frac{3}{4}$$

So the ratio of not-blue-eyed babies to babies with any eye colour is 3 : 4.

Step 3. I wrote the odds in favour of having blue eyes as a part-to-part ratio. The first term is the number of favourable outcomes. The second term is the number of unfavourable outcomes.

The ratio of babies who have blue eyes to those who do not is 1 : 3.

The odds in favour of a baby having blue eyes are 1 : 3.

Step 4. To determine the odds against, I simply switched the terms.

The ratio of babies who do not have blue eyes to those who do is 3 : 1.

The odds against a baby having blue eyes are 3 : 1.

Example 2

Hali has gone to the store to buy a pair of jeans. From experience, she knows the odds against the store having her style of jeans in her size are 10 : 32. Determine the probability that the store will have jeans in her size.

Solution

Step 1. I determined the total number of outcomes:

number of unfavourable outcomes + number of favourable outcomes = 10 + 32, or 42

Step 2. I determined the probability that the store would have jeans in the correct size.

For every 42 times Hali went to the store, it had her size 32 times and did not have it 10 times.

$$P(\text{have size}) = \frac{\text{number of favourable outcomes}}{\text{total number of outcomes}}$$

$$P(\text{have size}) = \frac{32}{42}$$

$$P(\text{have size}) = 0.761..., \text{ or } 76.190...\%$$

The probability that the store will have jeans in Hali's size is 76.2%.

Practice

Answer all questions with percents to the nearest tenth. Express all odds in lowest possible terms.

1. The odds in favour of an event happening are given. Determine the probability that each event will happen.

   a) 3 : 5   **b)** 4 : 1   **c)** 7 : 5   **d)** 100 : 1

2. The odds against an event happening are given. Determine the probability that each event will happen.

   a) 4 : 7   **b)** 10 : 9   **c)** 22 : 3   **d)** 2 : 1

TIP

The sum of the terms in an odds ratio can be used to represent the total number of outcomes.

3. The probability that an event will happen is given. Determine the odds against each event happening.

  a) $P(A) = 35\%$ **b)** $P(B) = 50\%$ **c)** $P(C) = 10\%$ **d)** $P(D) = 85\%$

4. Determine the odds in favour of, and the odds against, each event, based on the data.

  a) The next traffic light is green; 12 of the last 16 lights were green.

  b) Tomorrow it will be sunny; 5 of the last 8 days were sunny.

  c) The next book Austin reads will be a biography; the last 10 of 12 books he read were biographies.

5. Determine the probability of each event in question 4.

  a)   **b)**   **c)**

6. Were the probabilities in the events in question 4 experimental or theoretical?

7. The odds in favour of Arianne passing her driver's test are 4 : 3.

  a) Determine the odds against Arianne passing her driver's test.

  b) Determine the probability that she will pass her driver's test.

8. Sergei has 16 coins in his pocket, and 4 of these coins are quarters. He reaches into his pocket and pulls out a coin at random.

   a) Determine the probability of the coin being a quarter.

   b) Determine the odds against the coin being a quarter.

9. Aisha draws a card at random from a deck with 52 standard playing cards and 4 jokers. A joker can be any card you choose it to be. for instance, if red is the favourable outcome and you draw a joker, you can choose it to be red.

   a) Determine the probability that the card is red.

   b) Determine the odds in favour of the card being red.

   c) Determine the probability that the card is a face card.

   d) Determine the odds in favour of the card being a face card.

10. Ear buds are on sale at the local electronics store. The last 7 times ear buds were on sale, they were in stock only 3 times.

   a) Determine the odds in favour of ear buds being in stock this time.

   b) Determine the odds against ear buds being in stock this time.

11. About 0.5% of women see no difference between the colours red and green. These people are often useful in the military because they can detect khaki camouflage much better than people who do see a difference between red and green. What are the odds in favour of Monique being able to detect camouflage?

12. Geocaching is a sport in which you use a global positioning system (GPS) to look for hidden "treasure" using coordinates posted on the Internet. Dasha has found 6 of the last 11 geocaches she was searching for. In 2 of those cases, she was the first to find the geocache.

   a) Determine the probability that Dasha will find the next geocache she looks for.

   b) Determine the odds against her finding it.

   c) Determine the odds in favour of her finding it first.

13. Roger has been awarded a penalty shot in a hockey game. Carlo is the goalie. Roger has scored 7 times in his last 20 penalty shots. Carlo has blocked 9 of the last 10 penalty shots that he has faced.

   a) Determine the odds in favour of Roger scoring, using his data only.

   b) Determine the odds in favour of Roger scoring, using Carlo's data only.

MULTIPLE CHOICE

14. A survey in a Western Canadian city determined that the odds in favour of a person between 18 and 35 using a social networking site are 42 : 16. Determine the probability of a randomly selected person between 18 and 35 from that city using a social networking site.

   A. 2.6%   B. 38%   C. 72.4%   D. 51.4%

Questions 15 and 16 relate to the following scenario.

Ratings for the TV program *Gotta Sing! Gotta Dance!* indicate that 45% of the viewers are male, 10% are under 18, 20% are 19 to 29 years old, 20% are 30 to 45 years old, and 50% are older than 45. Suppose that someone is watching *Gotta Sing! Gotta Dance!*

15. What are the odds in favour of this person being female?

   A. $9:11$ **B.** $11:9$ **C.** $9:20$ **D.** $20:9$

16. What are the odds against this person being 45 or younger?

   A. $1:1$ **B.** $2:1$ **C.** $1:2$ **D.** $5:1$

WRITTEN RESPONSE

17. Witold plays soccer. He has scored 6 times in 20 shots on goal. He says the odds in favour of him scoring are 3 to 10. Is he correct? Explain.

18. Lei is in a diving competition.

- If she gets a score of 5 on her next dive, she will be tied with another competitor and will have to do another dive.
- If she gets more than 5, she will win this round.
- If she does a front pike perfectly, she will score 5.
- If she does a backward somersault tuck perfectly, she will score 7.
- She did 4 of her last 6 pikes perfectly, and 3 of her last 5 backward tucks perfectly.

Which dive should Lei perform next? Explain.

3.3 Probabilities Using Counting Methods

> ### Keep in Mind
>
> ▶ You may be able to use the Fundamental Counting Principle and techniques involving permutations and combinations to solve probability problems with many possible outcomes. The context of each problem will determine which techniques to use.

Example 1

Gwen, Morgan, Arthur, and Kay are volunteering along with five other students to be on their school's math team. All the students have equal ability. Determine the probability that Gwen, Morgan, Arthur, and Kay along with one other student will be chosen to fill the five spots on the team.

Solution

Step 1. I determined the number of ways in which Gwen, Morgan, Arthur, Kay, and one other student can be chosen to fill the five positions.

Gwen, Morgan, Arthur, and Kay must be on the team. There are $_4C_4$ ways this can happen.

There are five students who can fill the last spot on the team. There are $_5C_1$ ways this can happen.

> **TIP**
> Use combinations when order is not important in the outcomes.

$$\text{Ways that G, M, A, K, and 1 other can be chosen} = {_4C_4} \cdot {_5C_1}$$

$$= \frac{4!}{4!(4-4)!} \cdot \frac{5!}{1!(5-1)!}$$

$$= 1 \cdot \frac{5!}{1!4!}$$

$$= 5$$

Step 2. I determined the total number of ways in which five students can be chosen from nine students. There are $_9C_5$ ways:

$$_9C_5 = \frac{9!}{5!(9-5)!}$$

$$_9C_5 = \frac{9!}{5!4!}$$

$$_9C_5 = \frac{9 \cdot 8 \cdot 7 \cdot 6 \cdot 5!}{5!4!}$$

$$_9C_5 = \frac{9 \cdot 8 \cdot 7 \cdot 6}{24}$$

$$_9C_5 = 126$$

There are 126 possible ways to choose 5 students.

Step 3. I determined the probability.

$$P(\text{G, M, A, K, and 1 other chosen}) = \frac{_5C_4 \cdot _5C_1}{_9C_5}$$

$$P(\text{G, M, A, K, and 1 other chosen}) = \frac{5}{126}$$

The probability that Gwen, Morgan, Arthur, and Kay, and one other student will be chosen is $\frac{5}{126}$, or about 3.9%.

Example 2

Nigel spells out COOKBOOK with letter tiles. Then he turns the tiles face down and mixes them up. He asks Kendra to arrange the tiles in a row and turn them face up. If the row of tiles spells COOKBOOK, Kendra will win a book of recipes. Determine the probability that Kendra will win.

Solution

Step 1. I examined the letters in the word. Since the order must be correct, this problem involves permutations. There are 8 letters in total: 4 Os, 2 Ks, and 2 other letters.

Step 2. I thought about how the letters could be arranged.

I could arrange the 8 letters in 8! ways if they were all different. But since there are 4 Os and 2 Ks, I have to divide by 4! and by 2! to eliminate the arrangements that would be the same.

Step 3. I calculated the total number of ways in which I can arrange the letters, represented by L.

$$L = \frac{8!}{4! \cdot 2!}$$

$$L = 840$$

840 different arrangements are possible.

Step 4. I thought about the number of ways to spell COOKBOOK

There is only one correct way to spell the word.

The probability of winning is $\frac{1}{840}$.

> **TIP**
> Use permutations when order is important in the outcomes.

Practice

1. A financial institution randomly generates temporary three-digit security codes for the backs of credit cards. Tisa is expecting her credit card to arrive in the mail. Determine the probability that her security code will consist of three different even digits.

2. In the card game Crazy Eights, players are dealt 8 cards from a standard deck of 52 playing cards. Determine the probability that a hand will contain exactly 7 hearts.

3. From a committee of 10 people, 3 are randomly chosen to be president, secretary, and treasurer. Determine the probability that Kamal, Eli, and Salama will be chosen.

4. Access to a particular online game is password protected. Every player must create a password that consists of 3 capital letters followed by 2 digits. For each condition below, determine the probability that a password chosen at random will contain the letters A, B, and C.

   a) Repetitions are not allowed in a password.

   b) Repetitions are allowed in a password.

5. Jarrod's teacher has packs of 9 different colours of construction paper available: red, orange, yellow, green, blue, purple, pink, brown, and turquoise. She distributes 5 sheets of construction paper, each a different colour, to each student. Determine the probability that Jarrod will receive red, purple, and blue construction paper, along with two other colours.

6. Rachelle has letter tiles that spell BOOKKEEPER. She turns the tiles face down and mixes them up. She asks Chris to arrange the tiles in a row and then turn them face up. If the row of tiles spells BOOKKEEPER, Chris will win a car. Determine the probability that Chris will win.

NUMERICAL RESPONSE

7. A high-school athletics department is forming a beginners' curling team to play in a social tournament. For the 4 positions of skip, third, second, and lead, 12 students, including 4 friends, have signed up. Every student has an equal chance of being chosen for any position.

   a) The probability that the 4 friends will be chosen is _____.

   b) If 14 students had signed up, the probability in (a) would be _____.

WRITTEN RESPONSE

8. There are nine players on a baseball team, all with equal athletic ability. The coach has decided to choose randomly the players who will play the three outfield positions (left field, centre field, and right field). Giselle and Jo are on the team. Determine the odds in favour of these two being chosen to play in the outfield. Explain your answer.

Keep in Mind

▶ The probability that either of two mutually exclusive events, *A* and *B*, will occur is the sum of the individual probabilities:

$$P(A \cup B) = P(A) + P(B)$$

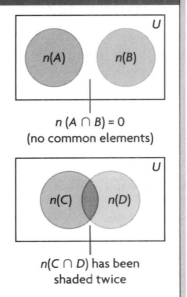

$n(A \cap B) = 0$
(no common elements)

▶ The probability that either of two non-mutually exclusive events, *C* and *D*, will occur is the sum of the individual probabilities minus the probability that both events will occur:

$$P(C \cup D) = P(C) + P(D) - P(C \cap D)$$

or $P(C \cup D) = P(C\backslash D) + P(D\backslash C) + P(C \cap D)$

$n(C \cap D)$ has been shaded twice

▶ You can use the Principle of Inclusion and Exclusion to determine the probability of non-mutually exclusive events.

Example 1

Jennifer rolls two 4-sided dice. Determine the probability that she will roll a sum that is either 6 or an odd number.

Solution

Step 1. I considered whether these events were mutually exclusive or not.

They are mutually exclusive, because both events cannot occur together since 6 is not odd.

Step 2. I made a table of the possible sums.

I shaded the sums that were 6 and circled the odd sums.

Step 3. I determined the individual probabilities in the table.

I let *A* represent rolling a sum of 6 and *B* represent rolling a sum that is odd.

$$P(A) = \frac{3}{16}; P(B) = \frac{8}{16}$$

Possible Sums When a Pair of 4-Sided Dice Are Rolled				
+	1	2	3	4
1	2	③	4	⑤
2	③	4	⑤	6
3	4	⑤	6	⑦
4	⑤	6	⑦	8

Step 4. I calculated the probability.

$$P(A \cup B) = P(A) + P(B)$$

$$P(A \cup B) = \frac{3}{16} + \frac{8}{16}$$

$$P(A \cup B) = \frac{11}{16}, \text{ or } 0.6875$$

Jennifer has a 68.75% chance of rolling a sum that is either 6 or an odd number.

Example 2

Xavier rolls two 4-sided dice. Determine the probability that he will roll a sum that is either even or greater than 5.

Solution

Step 1. I considered whether these events were mutually exclusive or not.

They are non-mutually exclusive events, because it is possible for both events to occur simultaneously since 6 and 8 are both even and greater than 5.

Step 2. I used the table of sums from Example 1.

I shaded the even sums and circled the sums greater than 5.

Step 3. I determined the individual probabilities in the table.

I let C represent rolling an even sum and D represent rolling a sum greater than 5.

Possible Sums When a Pair of 4-Sided Dice Are Rolled				
+	1	2	3	4
1	2	3	4	5
2	3	4	5	⑥
3	4	5	⑥	⑦
4	5	⑥	⑦	⑧

$$P(C) = \frac{8}{16}; P(D) = \frac{6}{16}; P(C \cap D) = \frac{4}{16}$$

Step 4. I calculated the probability:

$$P(C \cup D) = P(C) + P(D) - P(C \cap D)$$

$$P(C \cup D) = \frac{8}{16} + \frac{6}{16} - \frac{4}{16}$$

$$P(C \cup D) = \frac{10}{16}, \text{ or } 0.625$$

Xavier has a 62.5% chance of rolling a sum that is even or greater than 5.

Practice

1. Are the two events in each scenario mutually exclusive or not? Explain.

   a) Oleg rolls two 4-sided dice. He can move if the product is even or greater than 6.

   b) Tovah rolls one standard 6-sided die and one 4-sided die. She can move if the sum is even or 7.

   c) Hector rolls two standard dice, one red and one blue. He divides the number on the red die by the number on the blue die. He can move if the quotient is either a whole number or a terminating decimal less than 1.

   d) Paloma rolls two 4-sided dice. She can move if the difference between them is even or less than 3.

2. Determine the probability that each player in question 1 can move.

   a)   **c)**

   b)   **d)**

3. Salim is about to draw a card at random from a standard deck of 52 playing cards. If he draws a face card or a red card, he will win a point.

   a) Draw a Venn diagram to represent the two events.

   b) Are the events mutually exclusive? Explain.

   c) Determine the probability of drawing a face card or a red card.

4. The Venn diagram shows the declared population of Aboriginal Peoples in Canada, including First Nations, Inuit, and Métis, where

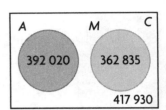

   A = {Aboriginal Peoples in Alberta, British Columbia, and Yukon}

   M = {Aboriginal Peoples in Manitoba, Saskatchewan, Northwest Territories, and Nunavut}, and

   C = {Aboriginal Peoples in Canada}.

   An Aboriginal person who lives in Canada is chosen at random.

   a) Determine the probability that this person lives in British Columbia, Alberta, or Yukon. Round your answer to the nearest tenth.

   b) Determine the probability that this person lives in Manitoba, Saskatchewan, Northwest Territories, or Nunavut.

MULTIPLE CHOICE

Questions 5 and 6 refer to the following scenario.
The probability that Mohammed will go to the swimming pool on Tuesday night is 0.75. The probability that he will buy groceries on Tuesday night is 0.5. The probability that he will do neither is 0.1.

5. Which Venn diagram models this scenario?

A. 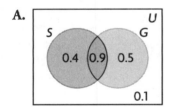 B. 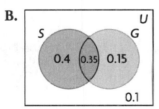 C. 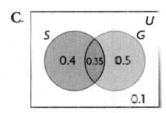 D.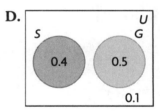

6. Determine the odds in favour of Mohammed doing at least one of these activities on Tuesday evening.

   A. $9 : 1$ **B.** $1 : 9$ **C.** 0.9   **D.** 0

WRITTEN RESPONSE

7. The probability that Kryztina will study on Sunday night is 0.5.
   The probability that she will practise her guitar on Sunday night is 0.4.
   The probability that she will do at least one of these activities is 0.7.
   Determine the probability that she will do both activities.

3.5 Conditional Probability

YOU WILL NEED
• calculator

Keep in Mind

▶ If the probability of one event depends on the probability of another event, then these events are called dependent events. For example, drawing a heart from a standard deck of 52 playing cards and then drawing another heart from the same deck without replacing the first card are dependent events.

▶ Suppose Event B depends on Event A occurring.

• The conditional probability that Event B will occur, given that Event A has occurred, can be represented as $P(B \mid A) = \dfrac{P(A \cap B)}{P(A)}$.

• The probability that both events will occur can be represented as $P(A \cap B) = P(A) \cdot P(B \mid A)$.

▶ A tree diagram is often useful for modelling problems that involve dependent events.

Example

A jam manufacturer knows that in a box of 48 jars, 5 will contain less jam than shown on the label. Determine the probability that 2 jars drawn at random will contain less jam.

Solution

Step 1. I drew a tree diagram to represent the ways 2 jars could be drawn from the box.

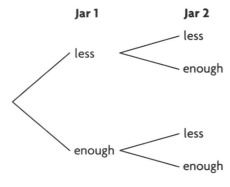

Step 2. I analyzed the diagram. There are 4 possible outcomes:

- W: Both jars have less jam than stated.
- Y: Jar 1 has less jam and Jar 2 has enough.
- X: Both jars have enough jam.
- Z: Jar 1 has enough and Jar 2 has less.

I am concerned only with outcome W.

Step 3. I determined the probability of outcome W

Let A represent the event that Jar 1 will have less jam.

There are 5 jars with less jam in the box of 48 jars: $P(A) = \dfrac{5}{48}$.

Step 4. I determined the conditional probability of the second dependent event.

Let B represent the event that Jar 2 will have less jam. If Jar 1 has less jam, then the

box now holds 47 jars, 4 of which have less jam. So, $P(B \mid A) = \dfrac{4}{47}$.

Step 5. I determined the probability of drawing 2 jars with less jam.

$$P(A \text{ and } B) = P(A) \cdot P(B \mid A)$$

$$P(A \text{ and } B) = \left(\frac{5}{48}\right) \cdot \left(\frac{4}{47}\right)$$

$$P(A \text{ and } B) = \frac{20}{2256} \text{ or } \frac{5}{564}$$

There are 5 chances in 564 that both jars will have less jam than stated on the label.

A Venn diagram is also a good way to organize data when determining probability.

Practice

1. Connie spins a spinner with equal sections numbered 1 to 8. She rolls a standard die. If the spinner lands on 3 and the sum of the two numbers is greater than 6, Connie wins a point.

   a) Are the two events dependent or independent?

   b) Determine the probability that Connie will win a point.

2. Tony draws a card from a well-shuffled standard deck of 52 playing cards. Then he draws another card from the deck without replacing the first card.

   a) Are these two events dependent or independent?

   b) Determine the probability that both cards are jacks.

Copyright © 2012 by Nelson Education Ltd.

3.5 Conditional Probability **71**

3. There are 75 males and 90 females in the graduating class in a Calgary school. Of these students, 40 males and 55 females plan to attend the University of Alberta (U of A) next year.

a) Determine the probability that a randomly selected student plans to attend U of A.

b) A randomly selected student plans to attend U of A. Determine the probability that the selected student is male.

4. Jason remembers to set the oven timer 70% of the time when he bakes banana bread. When he does remember to set the timer, the probability that he will burn the banana bread is 0.15. When he does not remember to set it, the probability that he will burn the banana bread is 0.75. Jason burned the banana bread today. What is the probability that he remembered to set the timer?

5. Eileen likes to go for daily jogs with her dog, BaiLee. If the weather is nice, she is 95% likely to jog for 5 km. If the weather is rainy, she is only 50% likely to jog for 5 km. The weather forecast for tomorrow indicates a 35% chance of rain. Determine the probability that Eileen will jog for 5 km.

6. Cellphone users were surveyed about their phone plan, with these results:
   - 85% of all users have call display.
   - 50% of users have a data plan.
   - 70% of users with a data plan also have call display.

   A cellphone user, who is selected at random, has call display. Determine the probability that this person also has a data plan.

7. The probability that a plane will leave Saskatoon on time is 0.85. The probability that a plane will leave Saskatoon on time and arrive in Vancouver on time is 0.70. The probability that a plane will arrive in Vancouver on time, given that it left Saskatoon on time, is _____.

8. The probability that a lawn trimmer battery will last for 5 years is 0.75. The probability that a battery will last for 6 years is 0.5. Suppose that your battery has lasted for 5 years. The probability that the battery will last for 6 years is _____.

WRITTEN RESPONSE

9. Your school football team is playing a game against another school tomorrow. Based on the team's record, it has a 50% chance of winning on rainy days and a 70% chance of winning on sunny days. Tomorrow, there is a 25% chance of rain. The football league does not allow ties.

a) Determine the probability that your school team will win tomorrow.

b) Determine the probability that your school team will lose tomorrow.

3.6 Independent Events

YOU WILL NEED
• calculator

Keep in Mind

▶ Events are independent when the probability of one does not depend on the probability of the other. For example, drawing a heart from a standard deck of 52 playing cards, replacing the card, and then drawing another heart from the same deck are independent events.

▶ Drawing an item and then drawing another item, after replacing the first item, results in a pair of independent events.

▶ The probability that two independent events, A and B, will both occur is the product of their individual probabilities:

$$P(A \cap B) = P(A) \cdot P(B)$$

▶ A tree diagram is often useful for modelling problems with independent events.

Example

Alin rolls two 4-sided dice and tosses one coin. Determine the probability that the product of the dice is an odd number and the coin lands tails.

Solution

Step 1. I defined the two events and considered whether they were dependent or ndependent.

Let O represent rolling an odd product.

Let T represent tossing tails with the coin.

Since these events do not depend on each other, they are independent.

Step 2. I already knew $P(T) = \dfrac{1}{2}$. I determined $P(O)$ using a table.

There are 16 possible products, of which 4 are odd.

$$P(O) = \frac{4}{16}, \text{ or } \frac{1}{4}$$

Product of Two 4-Sided Dice				
·	**1**	**2**	**3**	**4**
1	1	2	3	4
2	2	4	6	8
3	3	6	9	12
4	4	8	12	16

Step 3. I multiplied to determine the probability that both events will occur.

$$P(O \cap T) = P(O) \cdot P(T)$$

$$P(O \cap T) = \frac{1}{4} \cdot \frac{1}{2}$$

$$P(O \cap T) = \frac{1}{8}$$

There is a $\dfrac{1}{8}$ chance that the product will be odd and the coin will land tails.

Practice

1. Classify the events in each situation as independent or dependent.

   a) A spinner with 5 equal coloured sections—red, blue, green, yellow, and white—is spun twice in a row. The first event is spinning red, and the second event is also spinning red.

   b) Two marbles are drawn, without being replaced, from a bag containing 7 red marbles and 3 blue marbles. The first event is drawing a red marble, and the second event is drawing a blue marble.

   c) A coin is tossed and a standard die is rolled. The first event is tossing tails, and the second event is rolling a 3 on the die.

   d) There are 12 cards, one for each month, in a box. A card is drawn from the box and replaced, then a second card is drawn. The first event is drawing a month with only 4 letters, and the second event is drawing a month that contains an R.

2. For each situation described in question 1, determine the probability that both events will occur.

   a)   c)

   b)   d)

3. Marcel works two shifts a week at a coffee shop, one on a weekday and one on the weekend. He is available during the week from Tuesday to Thursday and on both days on the weekend. His boss randomly chooses which shifts Marcel will work.

   a) Does choosing the two shifts for one week involve dependent or independent events?

   b) Determine the probability that Marcel will work on Tuesday and Saturday.

4. Martina also works at the coffee shop. She is available to work two shifts from Monday to Thursday.

a) Are the two shifts dependent or independent events?

b) Determine the probability that Martina will work on Monday and Tuesday.

5. Two standard dice, one red and one green, are rolled. Harris scores a point if an odd number is rolled on the red die, and a point if a multiple of 3 is rolled on the green die.

a) Draw a tree diagram that shows all the possible outcomes.

b) Determine the probability of Harris scoring 2 points.

c) Determine the probability of Harris scoring 1 point.

6. Design a spinner so that when you roll a standard die and spin the spinner, the probability of rolling a multiple of 3 and spinning red is $\frac{1}{24}$.

MULTIPLE CHOICE

Questions 7 to 9 refer to the following scenario.

Ronnie is going on a cruise off the coast of Newfoundland. The travel brochure says the probability of seeing a whale is $\frac{9}{10}$ and the probability of seeing a puffin is $\frac{3}{5}$.

7. What is the probability that Ronnie will see a whale and a puffin?

   A. 0.30   **B.** 0.46   **C.** 0.54   **D.** 1.50

8. What is the probability that Ronnie will not see either sight?

   A. 0.04   **B.** 0.08   **C.** 0.40   **D.** 0.30

9. What is the probability that Ronnie will see only one of these sights?

   A. 0.30   **B.** 0.42   **C.** 0.50   **D.** 0.54

Questions 10 and 11 refer to the following scenario.

A 4-sided die, numbered 1 to 4, and an 8-sided die, numbered 1 to 8, are rolled.

10. What is the probability that the number on the 8-sided die is double the number on the 4-sided die?

   A. 0   **B.** $\dfrac{1}{4}$ **C.** $\dfrac{1}{8}$ **D.** $\dfrac{1}{16}$

11. What is the probability that the sum is odd?

   A. $\dfrac{1}{2}$ **B.** $\dfrac{1}{4}$ **C.** $\dfrac{1}{8}$ **D.** $\dfrac{1}{16}$

NUMERICAL RESPONSE

12. Two 8-sided dice, numbered 1 to 8, are rolled.

   a) The probability of rolling a sum of 12 is _____.

   b) The probability of rolling a sum of 1 is _____.

   c) The probability of rolling doubles is _____.

13. A paper bag contains 5 prize tickets for a movie pass, 10 prize tickets for an album download, and 15 prize tickets for a keychain. Suppose that a ticket is randomly drawn from the bag and replaced, and then a ticket is drawn again from the bag. You win the prize only if the same type of ticket is drawn both times.

   a) The probability of winning a movie pass is _____.

   b) The probability of winning any prize is _____.

   c) The probability of not winning a prize is _____.

Complete the following to summarize the important ideas from this chapter.

Q: How are the odds in favour of or against an event expressed?

A: • The odds in favour of an Event A with _____ $P(A)$ are expressed

as a _____, _____ : $1 -$ _____, or $P(\_\_\_) : P(_____)$.

• The odds _____ the same Event A are expressed as

$1 -$ _____ _____ : _____, or $P(_____) : P(_____)$.

• If the odds in favour of an Event A are $m : n$, its probability is

$P(A) = \dfrac{\boxed{}}{\boxed{}}$.

Q: How does the probability of either of two events occurring depend on whether they are mutually exclusive?

A: • If Events A and B are mutually exclusive, then the probability of either of

them occurring is $P(A \cup B) = $ _____.

• If the events are not mutually exclusive, then

$P(A \cup B) = P(A) + $ _____ $-$ _____.

Q: What are dependent events and how are their probabilities related?

A: • Two events are dependent if the _____ of one depends on the

_____ of the other.

• The _____ probability that Event B will occur, given that Event A

has occurred, is $P\left(\boxed{}\right) = \dfrac{\boxed{}}{\boxed{}}$.

• The probability that both events will occur is $P(A \cap B) = P(A) \cdot P(_____)$.

Q: What does it mean for two events to be independent?

A: • If two events are independent, then the _____ of one event does

not affect the _____ of the other.

• $P(_____) = P(B)$ and $P(A \mid B) = P(\_\_\_)$

• $P(A \cap B) = $ _____

MULTIPLE CHOICE

1. Ivanna and Diego play a game in which they roll an 8-sided die and a standard die. Ivanna wins a point if she rolls a sum that is a multiple of 2 or a multiple of 3. Diego wins a point if he rolls a sum that is a multiple of 2 or is greater than 9. Is the game fair? Why?

   A. Fair; both players have an equal chance of winning a point.

   B. Unfair; Ivanna has a better chance of winning a point.

   C. Unfair; Diego has a better chance of winning a point.

   D. Unfair; neither player can win a point.

2. The odds in favour of an event are 6 : 2. Determine the probability that the event will happen.

   A. 75%   **B.** 300%   **C.** 100%   **D.** 33%

3. The probability that an event will happen is 12%. Determine the odds against the event happening.

   A. 100 : 12   **B.** 12 : 100   **C.** 25 : 3   **D.** 22 : 3

4. Letter tiles spell SUCCESS. Determine the probability that when they are turned over, mixed up, and selected at random, they will spell SUCCESS.

   A. $\dfrac{1}{42}$ **B.** $\dfrac{1}{420}$ **C.** $\dfrac{1}{5040}$ **D.** $\dfrac{1}{1260}$

5. The probability that Gina will do cardio-kick-boxing on Monday is 0.6. The probability that she will read a book on Monday night is 0.5. The probability that she will do neither is 0.2. Determine the odds in favour of Gina doing both of these activities on Monday.

   A. 3 : 1   **B.** 3 : 7   **C.** 0.9   **D.** 0

6. The probability that a train will leave Vancouver on time is 0.9. The probability that a train will leave Vancouver on time and arrive in Kamloops on time is 0.8. Determine the probability that a train will arrive in Kamloops on time, given that it left Vancouver on time.

   A. 88.9%   **B.** 72.0%   **C.** 112.5%   **D.** 0%

7. Lei is going for a cruise along the northern coast of British Columbia. There is a $\frac{95}{100}$ probability of seeing a glacier calving and a $\frac{5}{6}$ probability of seeing a polar bear. What is the probability that Lei will see a glacier calving and a polar bear?

A. 87.7% **B.** 50% **C.** 79.2% **D.** 9 : 1

NUMERICAL RESPONSE

8. Ida enjoys competitive snowboarding. She placed in the top 10 of the last 25 races she entered. She won 3 of those races.

   a) The probability that Ida will place in the top 10 of her next race is _____%.

   b) The odds against Ida placing in the top 10 are _____.

   c) The odds in favour of Ida winning are _____.

9. Kira plays the balloon pop game at a carnival. There are 40 balloons, with the name of a prize inside each balloon. The prizes are 8 stuffed bears, 6 dolls, 14 toy trucks, 8 hula-hoops, and 4 rings. Kira pops a balloon with a dart. The odds against her winning either a doll or a ring are _____.

10. The probability that a certain light bulb will last for 6 years is 0.6. The probability that it will last for 8 years is 0.4. Suppose that a light bulb has lasted for 6 years. To the nearest tenth of a percent, the probability that it will last for 8 years is _____%.

11. Two 8-sided dice, numbered 1 to 8, are rolled. Answer in fraction form.

   a) The probability of rolling a sum of 10 is _____.

   b) The probability of rolling a sum that is a multiple of 3 is _____.

   c) The probability of rolling a sum that is a multiple of 5 or 6 is _____.

WRITTEN RESPONSE

12. The probability that Nathan will study on Monday night is 0.75. The probability that he will practise his violin on Monday night is 0.3. The probability that he will do at least one of these activities is 0.6. Determine the probability that he will do both activities. Explain what you did.

13. Winston plays basketball. He has scored on 12 of his last 20 free throws. He says the odds in favour of him scoring are 3 to 5. Is he right? Explain.

14. Feather and Jane each have 20 marbles: 15 red and 5 blue.
- Feather places 6 red marbles and 4 blue marbles in Bag 1.
- She places the rest of her marbles in Bag 2.
- Jane places all of her marbles in Bag 3.
- Feather then draws 1 marble from bag 1 and 1 marble from Bag 2.
- Jane draws 2 marbles from Bag 3.

a) Are Feather and Jane equally likely to draw 2 blue marbles from their bags? Explain.

b) Determine the probability that Feather and Jane will both draw 1 red marble and 1 blue marble. Explain what you did.

MULTIPLE CHOICE

1. Consider these sets:

   - $U = \{$the months of the year$\}$
   - $A = \{$the months of the school year$\}$
   - $B = \{$the months that begin with the letter J$\}$
   - $C = \{$the months that end with the letter r$\}$

   Which of these statements is true?

   A. $A \subset B$ **C.** $A' = B$

   B. $C \subset A$ **D.** $n(A) + n(B) + n(C) = n(U)$

2. An arts centre offers Saturday craft classes in scrapbooking, glassblowing, and painting. There are 45 students. Of these,

   - 23 are taking scrapbooking, 26 glassblowing, and 21 painting
   - 10 are taking scrapbooking and glassblowing
   - 11 are taking scrapbooking and painting
   - 12 are taking painting and glassblowing

   How many students are taking all three craft classes?

   A. 8   **B.** 10   **C.** 12   **D.** 14

3. Which of the following statements is false?

   A. $10! = 3\,628\,800$ **C.** $_5P_5 = 1$

   B. $_{10}P_6 = 151\,200$ **D.** $_{10}C_6 = 210$

4. The recycling club has 12 members. Which of the following statements is false?

   A. There are $479\,001\,600$ ways that all the members be arranged in a row for a yearbook photo.

   B. There are 1320 ways that the club can choose a president, a vice-president, and a treasurer.

   C. There are 495 ways that the club can choose 4 members to sell T-shirts during the Green Fair.

   D. There are 60 ways that 2 people can be chosen to buy snacks for the next meeting.

5. A hockey columnist claims at the start of this season that the odds in favour of the Winnipeg Jets winning the Stanley Cup are 2:5.

If the columnist is correct, which of the following statements are true?

A. The odds at the start of this season against the Winnipeg Jets winning the Stanley Cup are 5:2.

B. The probability at the start of this season that the Winnipeg Jets will win the Stanley Cup is $\frac{2}{7}$.

C. The probability at the start of this season that Winnipeg Jets will not win the Stanley Cup is $\frac{5}{7}$.

D. All of the above.

6. Joyce rolls two standard dice. Which of the following statements is false?

A. The probability that the sum is even or 11 is $\frac{5}{9}$.

B. The probability that the sum is greater than 10 is $\frac{1}{6}$.

C. The probability that the sum is odd given that the first die is a 2 is $\frac{1}{12}$.

D. The probability that the first die is less than 4 and the second die is greater than 4 is $\frac{1}{6}$.

NUMERICAL RESPONSE

7. Erynn surveyed 30 students about their favourite sport. She recorded her results. Some students chose more than one sport.

a) How many students like hockey or volleyball? _____

b) How many students like only hockey or only volleyball? _____

c) How many students like both hockey and volleyball? _____

Favourite Sport	Number of Students
hockey	15
volleyball	16
not hockey or volleyball	10

8. A secure password for an online bank account requires 4 characters using letters and digits.

a) How many different passwords are possible if upper- and lowercase letters are permitted and repetition is allowed? _____

b) How many different passwords are possible if only lowercase letters are permitted and repetition is not allowed? _____

9. A soccer team has a record of 8 wins and 4 losses. In how many different ways could this record have been compiled? _____

10. Sid has created a card game. He removes the 12 face cards from a standard deck of playing cards and draws 2 cards from the remaining cards. Determine the probability that both drawn cards are black

  a) if the first card drawn is replaced   _____

  b) if the first card drawn is not replaced   _____

WRITTEN RESPONSE

11. List five elements in each of the following sets.

  a) A = {Canadian cities west of Winnipeg}

  b) $B = \{b \mid b = 4x, x \in N\}$

12. Annie rolls two four-sided dice and observes the sum of the numbers on both dice.

  a) Create an outcome table for this situation.

  b) Display the following sets in a Venn diagram:

  • rolls that result in an even sum

  • rolls that result in a sum greater than 5

c) In how many ways can Annie roll the dice and get an even sum that is greater than 5?

d) What is the probability that on any roll the sum will be odd?

13. You flip a coin and roll this spinner.

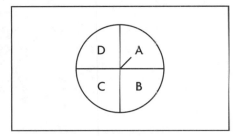

a) Draw a tree diagram to show all possible outcomes.

b) Verify that you have listed all possible outcomes using the Fundamental Counting Principle.

c) Determine the probability that you flip heads and spin D.

14. Determine the number of different arrangements that are possible using all the letters in each word.

    a) KELOWNA   **b)** CALGARY   **c)** TORONTO

15. Solve.

$$\frac{(n + 2)!}{n!} = 30$$

16. Twelve horses are running in a race. Suppose that each horse is equally likely to win the race. What is the probability that the number 5 horse will finish in the top three?

17. In the game of bridge, four players are dealt 13 cards from a shuffled standard deck of 52 cards. Determine the probability that a player

    a) is dealt only red cards

    b) is dealt all the cards of a suit

18. The quality control supervisor at a light bulb manufacturer knows that in a case of 500 light bulbs, 3 will be defective. A quality control worker draws 2 light bulbs at random from a case of 500. Determine the probability that the worker draws

a) 2 defective bulbs

b) 2 non-defective bulbs

c) exactly 1 defective bulb

Chapter 4

Rational Expressions and Equations

Getting Started

1. Match each term with the most appropriate description or example.

a) lowest common denominator ___

b) binomial ___

c) quotient ___

d) common factor ___

e) equivalent rational numbers ___

f) factored expression ___

g) denominator ___

i) $5x(x^2 + x + 3)$

ii) $2x^2 - 5$

iii) $\dfrac{3}{-5}$ and $\dfrac{-21}{35}$

iv) the least number into which the denominators of two or more rational numbers all divide

v) the result of dividing one quantity by another

vi) the bottom of a fraction

vii) an integer that divides into two or more other integers

2. Evaluate each product or quotient.

a) $\dfrac{3}{10} \cdot \dfrac{5}{4}$

b) $\dfrac{2}{9} \cdot 3$

c) $\dfrac{2}{21} \div \dfrac{4}{7}$

d) $\dfrac{\dfrac{4}{3}}{\dfrac{5}{12}}$

3. Evaluate each sum or difference.

a) $\dfrac{2}{7} + \dfrac{6}{7}$

b) $\dfrac{1}{3} + \dfrac{3}{5}$

c) $\dfrac{4}{5} - \dfrac{3}{10}$

d) $\dfrac{5}{4} - \dfrac{5}{6}$

4. Solve each quadratic equation.

a) $x^2 + 4x = 0$

b) $4x^2 - 9 = 0$

c) $x^2 + 9 = 6x$

5. Solve for x.

a) $\dfrac{5x}{3} = \dfrac{7}{12}$

b) $x(x + 8) = 14 + 3x$

6. Two rectangles are joined side to side. Each rectangle has a width of $1\frac{1}{3}$ in. One rectangle is $\dfrac{7}{8}$ in. long and the other is $2\frac{1}{4}$ in. long.

What is the exact area of the composite figure? Use a sketch to help you.

7. Marin is solving the following problem: For a party, take-out pizzas were ordered and delivered pre-cut into $\dfrac{1}{8}$ portions. If exactly $2\frac{5}{8}$ pizzas are left, how many portions remain?

Without solving the problem, explain in your own words how it involves dividing rational numbers.

8. In a sprint triathlon, Gillian swims 750 m in 19 min 15 s, cycles 20 km in 42 min 45 s, and runs 5 km in 23 min 30 s. What is her average speed over the whole event

a) as an exact value in kilometres per minute?

b) to the nearest tenth of a kilometre per hour?

4.1 Equivalent Rational Expressions

Keep in Mind

▶ A rational expression is the ratio of two polynomials, such as $\dfrac{5x + 2}{x + 3}$, $x \neq -3$.

▶ All rational expressions are undefined for the non-permissible values of a variable that make the denominator equal to zero.

   • To ensure that a rational expression is defined, you must state all non-permissible values of the variable.

   • If the denominator contains a binomial, you can determine the non-permissible values by factoring the binomial.

▶ You can use substitution to determine if two rational expressions are *not* equivalent, but not to determine if they *are* equivalent.

Example 1

Ajiv has run 2 mi of a half-marathon (13 mi) in 10 min. He wants to finish the race with an average speed of 0.2 mi/min. Determine the time, in minutes, in which Ajiv must run the remaining 11 mi.

Solution

Step 1. I used the formula $\text{speed} = \dfrac{\text{distance}}{\text{time}}$ to write a rational expression for Ajiv's average speed. I let x represent the time in which Ajiv will finish the race.

$$\text{Average speed} = \frac{13}{10 + x} \text{ mi/min}$$

Step 2. Ajiv wants an average speed of 0.2 mi/min. I expressed this as a fraction. Then I wrote an equivalent fraction with 13 in the numerator, so I could compare the denominators of the equivalent fractions.

$$0.2 \text{ mi/min} = \frac{1}{5} \text{ mi/min}$$

$$0.2 \text{ mi/min} = \frac{1}{5} \cdot \frac{13}{13} \text{ mi/min, or } \frac{13}{65} \text{ mi/min}$$

Step 3. I compared the two expressions for average speed: $\dfrac{13}{10 + x} = \dfrac{13}{65}$

Step 4. Since the numerators are equal and the fractions are equal, then the denominators must be equal. I solved for x.

$$10 + x = 65$$

$$x = 55$$

Ajiv needs to run the remaining 11 mi in 55 min.

> **TIP**
>
> You can use similar strategies to write equivalent forms of a rational expression as you do when writing equivalent forms of a rational number, including
>
> • multiplying the numerator and the denominator by the same factor, and
>
> • dividing the numerator and the denominator by a common factor.

Example 2

Identify which rational expression, if any, is equivalent to $\dfrac{6x^2 + 9x}{3x}$.

A. $\dfrac{2x + 3}{3x}$ **B.** $\dfrac{2x^2 + 3x}{x}$ **C.** $\dfrac{12x + 18}{6}$

Solution

Step 1. I determined the non-permissible values for the expressions.

For $\dfrac{6x^2 + 9x}{3x}$, the non-permissible value occurs when $3x = 0$, or $x = 0$.

In expression C, 0 is a permissible value for x, so C is not equivalent to $\dfrac{6x^2 + 9x}{3x}$.

Expressions A and B do have the same non-permissible value, $x = 0$, so they may be equivalent to $\dfrac{6x^2 + 9x}{3x}$.

Step 2. I multiplied Expressions A and B by a form of 1.

> **TIP**
> Multiplying by 1 does not change a value.

A

$$\frac{2x + 3}{3x} = \frac{2x + 3}{3x} \cdot \frac{3x}{3x}$$
$$= \frac{6x^2 + 9x}{9x^2}$$

The numerator is the same, but the denominator is different, so A is not equivalent to $\dfrac{6x^2 + 9x}{3x}$.

B

$$\frac{2x^2 + 3x}{x} = \frac{2x^2 + 3x}{x} \cdot \frac{3}{3}$$
$$= \frac{6x^2 - 9x}{3x}$$

Both the numerator and the denominator are the same, so B is equivalent to $\dfrac{6x^2 + 9x}{3x}$.

Step 3. I verified my result by substituting the same permissible value, $x = 1$, into both expressions and evaluating.

Given expression: $\dfrac{6(1)^2 + 9(1)}{3(1)} = \dfrac{6 + 9}{3}$, or 5   B: $\dfrac{2(1)^2 + 3(1)}{(1)} = \dfrac{2 + 3}{1}$, or 5

The values are the same, so Expression B is equivalent to $\dfrac{6x^2 + 9x}{3x}$.

Practice

1. Write an equivalent rational expression for each of the following expressions.

a) $\dfrac{x}{x + 5}$

b) $\dfrac{3x^2 - 2x}{3x}$

c) $\dfrac{5y + 10y^2}{10y}$

d) $\dfrac{4x - 8}{3x}$

2. Define a variable and write a rational expression to describe each situation. State any non-permissible values.

    a) the speed of a car that has travelled 60 km

    b) the speed of a jet that has flown 150 km

    c) the speed of a submarine that has sailed 20 000 leagues under the sea (about 111 000 km)

    d) the rate of growth of a beanstalk that grows for 20 days

3. Determine all of the non-permissible values of the variable, if any, in each rational expression. Then write an equivalent rational expression.

    a) $\dfrac{4x - 2}{3x^2 + 1}$

    d) $\dfrac{1}{(6x - 6)(x + 2)}$

    b) $\dfrac{x - 2}{x^2 + x - 6}$

    e) $\dfrac{1}{x^2 + 2x + 1}$

    c) $\dfrac{x - 5}{x^2 - 25}$

    f) $\dfrac{x + 3}{x^2 - x - 12}$

4. Determine all of the non-permissible values for $\dfrac{2-x}{(3x-2)(x+2)}$.

A. $x=-2$ B. $x=\dfrac{2}{3}, x=-2$ C. $x=0$ D. $x=6, x=0$

5. Identify the rational expression that is NOT equivalent to $\dfrac{16-4x}{12x^2+4x}$.

A. $\dfrac{4-x}{x(3x+1)}$ B. $\dfrac{(16-4x)2x}{2x(12x^2+4x)}$ C. $\dfrac{16(1-x)}{4x(3x+1)}$ D. $\dfrac{4(4-x)}{4x(3x+1)}$

6. Identify the rational expression that is equivalent to $\dfrac{2x^2-15x+18}{x^2-36}$.

A. $\dfrac{3+2x}{x-6}$ B. $\dfrac{3x+2}{1-6x}$ C. $\dfrac{(6x+9)(x+6)}{(3x+18)(x-6)}$ D. $\dfrac{6x+4x^2}{3x^2-12x}$

WRITTEN RESPONSE

7. A combine harvester can harvest a row of corn in x hours. A newer combine harvester can harvest a row of corn 30 min faster.

   a) Write a rational expression for the fraction of the row of corn harvested by the newer combine harvester in 1 h.

   b) What are the restrictions on the variables? Explain.

8. Jamia is riding her new bike along a familiar route. She rode the 7 km route 20 min faster than usual.

   a) Write a rational expression for Jamia's speed.

   b) Determine the non-permissible values, and explain why they are non-permissible.

   c) State the restrictions on the expression you wrote for part a).

4.2 Simplifying Rational Expressions

> ### Keep in Mind
>
> ▶ To simplify a rational expression, factor the numerator and the denominator; then divide both by their greatest common factor (GCF).
>
> ▶ A rational expression is in simplified form when the GCF of the numerator and the denominator is 1.
>
> ▶ The non-permissible values must be stated before the rational expression is simplified to ensure that all restrictions for the variable are included.

Example 1

Simplify $\dfrac{-36a}{12a^2}$.

Solution

Step 1. I determined the non-permissible value of the variable and wrote the restriction.

$$\frac{-36a}{12a^2},\ a \neq 0$$

Step 2. I factored to identify common factors in the numerator and denominator.

$$\frac{-36a}{12a^2} = \frac{-3(12a)}{a(12a)}$$

Step 3. I simplified so that the numerator and denominator had no common factor.

$$= \frac{-3}{a},\ a \neq 0$$

> **TIP**
>
> When the numerator and denominator of a rational expression are identical, the expression has a value of 1 for all permissible values. For example,
>
> $$\frac{12a}{12a} = 1$$

Example 2

Simplify $\dfrac{4y^3 - 12y^2}{6y^2 + 16y}$.

Solution

Step 1. I determined the non-permissible values, which occur when the denominator is equal to 0. I stated these as restrictions.

$$6y^2 + 16y = 0$$

$$2(y)(3y + 8) = 0$$

$$y = 0 \ \text{ or } \ 3y + 8 = 0$$

$$y = -\frac{8}{3}$$

$$y \neq 0, y \neq -\frac{8}{3}$$

Step 2. I factored the numerator and denominator.

$$\frac{4y^3 - 12y^2}{6y^2 + 16y} = \frac{(y - 3)(2y)(2y)}{(3y + 8)(2y)}$$

Step 3. I used the fact that $\frac{2y}{2y} = 1$, $y \neq 0$, to simplify.

$$= \frac{(y - 3)(2y)(2y)}{(3y + 8)(2y)}$$

$$= \frac{2y^2 - 6y}{3y + 8}, y \neq 0, -\frac{8}{3}$$

In simplified form, the expression is $\frac{2y^2 - 6y}{3y + 8}$, $y \neq 0$, $y \neq -\frac{8}{3}$.

Practice

For all questions, state any non-permissible values of the variable as restrictions.

1. Determine the non-permissible values for each rational expression, state these values as restrictions, and simplify.

   a) $\dfrac{3x}{4x - 2x^3}$

   b) $\dfrac{4x + 8}{28x}$

   c) $\dfrac{x + 3}{x^2 - 9}$

   d) $\dfrac{x + 6}{(x + 6)(x + 6)}$

2. Simplify each rational expression.

   a) $\dfrac{-28y}{21y^3}$

   b) $\dfrac{-35x}{28x^3}$

   c) $\dfrac{8y^4}{2y^2}$

   d) $\dfrac{81s^2}{36s}$

   e) $\dfrac{27x^3}{36x}$

   f) $\dfrac{111s^3}{(3s + 6)}$

3. Simplify each rational expression.

a) $\dfrac{14x^2}{36x + 12}$

c) $\dfrac{(x - 3)(x + 1)}{(x - 3)^2}$

b) $\dfrac{18x}{2x^3 + 2x}$

d) $\dfrac{6x + 12}{(x + 2)(3x - 1)}$

4. Simplify each rational expression.

a) $\dfrac{-35x}{28x^3}$

d) $\dfrac{27x^3}{36x}$

b) $\dfrac{48r^2}{-36r^3}$

e) $\dfrac{56t^2}{35t^3}$

c) $\dfrac{105x^2}{33x^3}$

f) $\dfrac{121u^2}{-55u}$

5. Simplify each rational expression.

a) $\dfrac{8 - 2x^2}{2x^2 + 16x}$

d) $\dfrac{63x^3}{9x^2 - 45x}$

b) $\dfrac{12x^2 - 6}{(4x^2 - 2)x}$

e) $\dfrac{(15x + 45)(x + 3)}{15(x + 3)(x - 3)}$

c) $\dfrac{x^3(6 - 2x)}{x^2(2 - x)}$

f) $\dfrac{21x^2 + 3x}{9x^2 + 6x}$

6. Simplify each rational expression.

a) $\dfrac{16x^2}{x^2(4x^2 + 2)}$

c) $\dfrac{3x^2 + 6x}{3x^2 - 12x}$

b) $\dfrac{105x^2}{33x^3}$

d) $\dfrac{23c^2 + 2c + 123}{23c^2 + 2c + 123}$

MULTIPLE CHOICE

7. Which of the following rational expressions are in their simplest form?

i) $\dfrac{x}{16x + 14x^3}$

ii) $\dfrac{9x}{2x^2 + 1}$

iii) $\dfrac{5x + 16x^2}{10x}$

A. i) and ii)   **B.** ii) only   **C.** i) and iii)   **D.** i) only

8. Which of the following rational expressions are in their simplest form?

i) $\dfrac{x + 12}{9x^2 + 1}$

ii) $\dfrac{8x^3}{4x^2 + 20x}$

iii) $\dfrac{13y}{y^2 + 2}$

A. i) only   **B.** ii) and iii)   **C.** iii) only   **D.** i) and iii)

9. Determine all of the non-permissible values for $\dfrac{4x}{3x - 2x^2}$.

A. $x = 0, x = \dfrac{3}{2}$ **B.** $x = 0$ **C.** $x = 0, x = \dfrac{2}{3}$ **D.** $x = \dfrac{3}{2}$

10. Determine all of the non-permissible values for $\dfrac{5(x + 1)}{10x^2 - 20x}$.

A. $x = 0, x = -1$ **B.** $x = 0$ **C.** $x = 0, x = 2$ **D.** $x = -2$

WRITTEN RESPONSE

11. Liquid chlorine is added to a pool to sanitize the water. After t hours, the concentration of chlorine in the pool can be expressed as $\dfrac{21t}{12 + 4t}$ mg/L. Determine the concentration of chlorine in the pool after 3 h. Explain your response.

4.3 Multiplying and Dividing Rational Expressions

Keep in Mind

▸ Rational expressions can be multiplied and divided in the same way as rational numbers. That is, if A, B, C, and D are polynomials, then

$$\frac{A}{B} \cdot \frac{C}{D} = \frac{AC}{BD}, B, D \neq 0$$

$$\frac{A}{B} \div \frac{C}{D} = \frac{A}{B} \cdot \frac{D}{C} \quad \text{or} \quad \frac{AD}{BC}, B, D, \text{ and } C \neq 0$$

▸ To determine any non-permissible values of the variable, determine all the values that make the denominators equal to zero in the factored quotient or product. For division, remember to consider both the numerator and the denominator of the divisor.

Example 1

Simplify $\dfrac{3x^2 + 9x}{14x} \cdot \dfrac{7x}{x + 3}$.

Solution

Step 1. I identified the non-permissible values. The denominator is 0 when $x = 0$ and $x = -3$.

Step 2. I factored and then multiplied the numerators and multiplied the denominators.

$$\frac{3x^2 + 9x}{14x} \cdot \frac{7x}{x + 3} = \frac{3(x)(x + 3)}{14(x)} \cdot \frac{7x}{x + 3}$$

$$= \frac{3(x + 3)}{14} \cdot \frac{7x}{x + 3}$$

$$= \frac{3(x + 3)(7x)}{2 \cdot 7(x + 3)}$$

Step 3. I wrote the product in simplified form.

$$= \frac{3x}{2}, x = 0, -3$$

> **TIP**
> To multiply rational expressions:
> 1. Factor the numerators and denominators, if possible.
> 2. Identify all non-permissible values.
> 3. Multiply the numerators and multiply the denominators. Write as a single rational expression.
> 4. Simplify using common factors.
> 5. Write the product, stating the non-permissible values of the variable.

Example 2

Simplify $\dfrac{20x^2 - 5x}{2x - 2} \div \dfrac{4x^3 + x^2}{2x^2 + 2x}$.

Solution

Step 1. I factored to determine the non-permissible values and wrote these as restrictions.

$$\frac{20x^2 - 5x}{2x - 2} \div \frac{4x^3 + x^2}{2x^2 - 2x} = \frac{5(x)(4x - 1)}{2(x - 1)} \div \frac{x^2(4x + 1)}{2(x)(x - 1)}, \qquad x \neq 0, x \neq 1$$

Step 2. I multiplied the first expression by the reciprocal of the second expression. For this step to be valid, $x \neq -\dfrac{1}{4}$.

$$= \frac{5(x)(4x - 1)}{2(x - 1)} \cdot \frac{2(x)(x - 1)}{x^2(4x + 1)}$$

Step 3. I simplified, removing the common factors from the numerator and denominator.

$$= \frac{5(x)(4x - 1)(2)(x)(x - 1)}{2(x - 1)(x)(x)(4x + 1)}$$

$$= \frac{5(4x - 1)}{4x + 1}, \qquad x \neq 0, 1, -\frac{1}{4}$$

Practice

For all questions, state any non-permissible values of the variable as restrictions.

1. Determine the non-permissible values of the variable, if any.

   a) $\dfrac{5x}{x - 5} \cdot \dfrac{3x(x + 2)}{2x - 1}$

   b) $\dfrac{4x^3}{x + 4} \div \dfrac{x}{x - 1}$

   c) $\dfrac{5x}{6} \cdot \dfrac{3x(x + 4)}{7}$

   d) $\dfrac{3}{x - 3} \div \dfrac{x + 2}{x}$

2. Simplify each expression.

   a) $\left(\dfrac{4x^2}{12x}\right)\left(\dfrac{4}{12x^3}\right)$

   b) $16x^2 \div \dfrac{3x}{8}$

   c) $\dfrac{-4x^2}{24} \div x$

   d) $\left(\dfrac{18x^2}{12x}\right)\left(\dfrac{3x}{3x}\right)$

3. Simplify each expression.

a) $\dfrac{6x}{x + 2} \cdot \dfrac{x(x + 2)}{3x - 1}$

c) $\dfrac{x - 4}{x} \cdot \dfrac{x + 2}{2x - 1}$

b) $\dfrac{4x^3(x + 2)}{x + 2} \cdot \dfrac{2x}{2x + 1}$

d) $\dfrac{x + 3}{x - 5} \cdot \dfrac{4x(x - 2)}{x + 3}$

4. Simplify each expression.

a) $\dfrac{5x}{x - 5} \div \dfrac{3x(x + 2)}{2x - 1}$

c) $\dfrac{5x - 2}{x + 1} \div \dfrac{x + 2}{x - 1}$

b) $\dfrac{4x}{2x - 3} \div \dfrac{x + 5}{4x - 6}$

d) $\dfrac{4x(x + 1)}{x + 2} \div \dfrac{x + 1}{x + 2}$

5. Simplify each expression.

a) $\dfrac{1}{2x + 10} \cdot \dfrac{x + 5}{4x + 1}$

b) $\dfrac{7x^2}{x + 7} \cdot \dfrac{x + 7}{14x}$

c) $\dfrac{9x(x + 7)}{2x(x - 3)} \cdot \dfrac{x + 1}{x - 1}$

6. Simplify the expression $\dfrac{9x(x+7)}{2x(x-3)} \div \dfrac{x+1}{x-1}$.

7. State the non-permissible values of the variable, if any, for each expression.

a) $\dfrac{3x}{x-3} \cdot \dfrac{2x(x+2)}{4x-1}$ non-permissible values: _____

b) $\dfrac{x}{9} \cdot \dfrac{x(x+5)}{16}$ non-permissible values: _____

c) $\dfrac{6x^3}{x+2} \div \dfrac{x}{x-2}$ non-permissible values: _____

d) $\dfrac{4}{x-2} \div \dfrac{x+4}{x}$ non-permissible values: _____

8. Fatouma tried to simplify an expression, as shown below. In which step did she make an error? Explain. Write the correct solution.

$\dfrac{45x - 15x^2}{6x^3 - 12x^2} = \dfrac{5(3x)(3-x)}{2x(3x)(x-3)}$ Step 1: Factor.

$= \dfrac{5(3x)[-(x-3)]}{2x(3x)(x-3)}$ Step 2: Write $3 - x$ as $-(x-3)$.

$= \dfrac{5(3x)[-(x-3)]}{2x(3x)(x-3)}$ Step 3: Eliminate common factors.

$= \dfrac{5}{2x}$ Step 4: Write in simplified form.

4.4 Adding and Subtracting Rational Expressions

YOU WILL NEED
• calculator

> **Keep in Mind**
>
> ▸ You can add or subtract rational expressions only when they have a common denominator.
>
> $$\frac{A}{B} + \frac{C}{D} = \frac{AD + CB}{BD} \quad \text{and} \quad \frac{A}{B} - \frac{C}{D} = \frac{AD - CB}{BD} \text{ with } B, D \neq 0$$
>
> ▸ The non-permissible values of the variable in the simplified expression are the combination of the non-permissible values of the original expressions.

Example 1

Simplify $\dfrac{4y}{3y - 2} - \dfrac{6}{y + 2}$.

Solution

Step 1. I identified the restrictions of the variable: $y \neq \dfrac{2}{3}, y \neq -2$

Step 2. I noticed that the binomials in the denominator of each term did not have a common factor. Therefore, the lowest common denominator (LCD) must be $(3y - 2)(y + 2)$.

I multiplied each term by a form of 1, to write an equivalent expression with the LCD, and then simplified.

$$\frac{4y}{3y - 2} - \frac{6}{y + 2} = \frac{4y(y + 2)}{(3y - 2)(y + 2)} - \frac{6(3y - 2)}{(3y - 2)(y + 2)}$$

$$= \frac{4y(y + 2) - 6(3y - 2)}{(3y - 2)(y + 2)}$$

$$= \frac{4y^2 + 8y - 18y + 12}{(3y - 2)(y + 2)}$$

$$= \frac{4y^2 - 10y + 12}{(3y - 2)(y + 2)}, y \neq \frac{2}{3}, y \neq -2$$

> **TIP**
>
> To add or subtract rational expressions:
> 1. Factor both numerators and both denominators, if possible.
> 2. State the non-permissible values.
> 3. Determine the lowest common denominator (LCD).
> 4. Rewrite each rational expression as an equivalent expression with the LCD as the denominator.
> 5. Add or subtract the numerators.
> 6. Write the simplified rational expression. Restate the non-permissible values of the variable.

Example 2

Simplify $\dfrac{10}{x^2 - 25} + \dfrac{12}{x + 5}$.

Solution

Step 1. I noticed that I could factor the denominator in the first term. The non-permissible values are $x = 5$ and $x = -5$.

$$\frac{10}{x^2 - 25} + \frac{12}{x + 5} = \frac{10}{(x + 5)(x - 5)} + \frac{12}{x + 5}$$

> **TIP**
>
> The LCD is the product of all the common factors and all the unique factors of the denominators. The LCD is not always the product of all the denominators.

Step 2. I multiplied the second term by a form of 1, so both terms would have the same denominator.

$$\frac{10}{x^2 - 25} + \frac{12}{x + 5} = \frac{10}{(x + 5)(x - 5)} + \frac{12(x - 5)}{(x + 5)(x - 5)}$$

Step 3. I simplified further.

$$= \frac{10 + 12(x - 5)}{(x + 5)(x - 5)}$$

$$= \frac{10 + 12x - 60}{(x + 5)(x - 5)}$$

$$= \frac{12x - 50}{(x + 5)(x - 5)}, x \neq -5, x \neq 5$$

Practice

1. Determine the lowest common denominator for each pair of rational expressions.

   a) $\dfrac{3x}{x^2(x - 2)}, \dfrac{5}{2x - 4}$

   c) $\dfrac{1}{x^2 - 6x + 9}, \dfrac{1}{x^3 - 9x}$

   b) $\dfrac{-2}{8x^3}, \dfrac{6y}{12x}$

   d) $\dfrac{16}{2(x - 3)(x + 1)}, \dfrac{-x}{(x + 1)(x - 1)}$

2. Determine the non-permissible values for each pair of rational expressions in question 1 and write them as restrictions.

   a) $x \neq$ _____   **b)** $x \neq$ _____   **c)** $x \neq$ _____   **d)** $x \neq$ _____

For questions 3 to 6, state any non-permissible values of the variables as restrictions.

3. Simplify each expression.

   a) $\dfrac{14x^2}{6x} - \dfrac{2x^2}{6x}$

   c) $\dfrac{1}{y^2 + 2y} - \dfrac{5y + 3}{y^2 + 2y}$

   b) $\dfrac{5x - 1}{x + 1} + \dfrac{2x - 1}{x + 1}$

   d) $\dfrac{7z + 3}{z^2(z - 1)} - \dfrac{4 - 2z}{z^2(z - 1)}$

4. Simplify each expression.

a) $\dfrac{-5a + 4}{2a^2} + \dfrac{2}{5a}$

c) $\dfrac{12}{11x} + 6$

b) $\dfrac{9y - 6}{2y} + \dfrac{1}{6y^2}$

d) $\dfrac{5b}{15} - \dfrac{3}{2b}$

5. Simplify each expression.

a) $\dfrac{6}{x^2 - 4} + \dfrac{2}{x + 2}$

c) $\dfrac{3x}{3x + 2} + \dfrac{3x}{9x^2 - 4}$

b) $\dfrac{8x}{6x + 36} - \dfrac{x - 1}{x + 6}$

d) $\dfrac{x}{2x^2 - 4} - \dfrac{x^2}{2x}$

6. Simplify each expression.

a) $\dfrac{3 - x}{x + 3} - \dfrac{x - 2}{x - 3}$ b) $\dfrac{2x - 1}{5x - 3} - \dfrac{x}{4x + 5}$ c) $\dfrac{7 - 2x}{2x^2 - 3} + \dfrac{x - 1}{4x + 3}$

MULTIPLE CHOICE

Questions 7, 8, and 9 refer to the following pair of rational expressions.

$\dfrac{t + 1}{t^2 + 2t - 3}, \dfrac{t + 2}{t^2 + 4t - 5}$

7. Which values of t are non-permissible?

   A. $1, 3, 5$ **B.** $-1, -3, -5$ **C.** $-5, -3, 1$ **D.** $0, 1$

8. What is the lowest common denominator?

   A. $(t + 3)(t - 1)(t + 5)$ **B.** $(t + 1)(t + 2)$ **C.** $(t + 3)(t + 5)$ **D.** $(t + 3)(t + 1)(t + 5)$

9. What is the sum of these expressions?

   A. $\dfrac{1}{t + 5}$ **B.** $\dfrac{t + 1}{(t + 3)(t + 5)}$ **C.** $(t + 3)(t + 5)$ **D.** $\dfrac{1}{(t + 3)(t + 5)}$

WRITTEN RESPONSE

10. Rami explained how he subtracted two rational expressions.
What was Rami's error? Write the correct solution.

I determined the restrictions.

$$\dfrac{2x}{3x + 2} - \dfrac{2x + 1}{x + 1}, x \neq -1, x \neq -\dfrac{2}{3}$$

I subtracted the second numerator from the first numerator and subtracted
the second denominator from the first denominator. Then I simplified.

$$\dfrac{2x}{3x + 2} - \dfrac{2x + 1}{x + 1} = \dfrac{2x - 2x - 1}{3x + 2 - x - 1}$$

$$= \dfrac{-1}{2x + 1}$$

4.5 Solving Rational Equations

YOU WILL NEED
• calculator

Keep in Mind

▶ To solve a rational equation algebraically, multiply each term by the lowest common denominator (LCD) to eliminate fractions. Then solve the resulting linear or quadratic equation.

▶ If a root of a rational equation is a non-permissible value of any rational expression in the equation, it is extraneous and is not a valid solution.

▶ When solving a contextual problem, check for solutions that may be valid for the equation but inadmissible in the context of the problem.

Example 1

Together, Tashi and Rosie can mow the lawn in 60 min. On her own, Rosie can mow the lawn in 15 min less time than when Tashi works alone. How long does Tashi take to mow the lawn on her own?

Solution

Step 1. I set up an expression, with x representing the amount of time Tashi takes on her own. In one minute, Tashi cuts $\frac{1}{x}$, $x > 0$, of the lawn on her own, Rosie cuts $\frac{1}{x - 15}$, $x > 15$, on her own, and together they cut $\frac{1}{60}$ of it. So,

$$\frac{1}{x} + \frac{1}{x - 15} = \frac{1}{60}, x > 15$$

Step 2. I solved for x. First, I multiplied by the LCD to eliminate fractions.

$$60x(x - 15)\left(\frac{1}{x}\right) + 60x(x - 15)\left(\frac{1}{x - 15}\right) = 60x(x - 15)\left(\frac{1}{60}\right)$$

$$\frac{60x(x - 15)}{x} + \frac{60x(x - 15)}{(x - 15)} = \frac{60x(x - 15)}{60}$$

Step 3. I simplified and then solved the resulting quadratic equation.

$$60(x - 15) + 60x = x(x - 15)$$

$$60x - 900 + 60x = x^2 - 15x$$

$$0 = x^2 - 135x + 900$$

$$x = 7.033\ldots \text{ or } x = 127.966\ldots$$

Step 4. I checked for extraneous solutions.

Since $x > 15$, then $x = 7.033\ldots$ is an extraneous solution. $x = 127.966\ldots$ is a valid solution. On her own, Tashi would cut the grass in 128 min, or 2 h 8 min.

Example 2

Solve the following equation for x: $\dfrac{14}{x^2 - 2x} = \dfrac{7}{x - 2} - \dfrac{6}{x}$

Solution

Step 1. I determined the restrictions: $x \neq 0, 2$

Step 2. I multiplied each term by the LCD, $x(x - 2)$, to eliminate the fractions.

$$x(x - 2) \cdot \dfrac{14}{x(x - 2)} = x(x - 2) \cdot \dfrac{7}{(x - 2)} - \dfrac{6}{x} \cdot x(x - 2)$$

Step 3. I simplified and then solved the resulting linear equation.

$$14 = 7x - 6(x - 2)$$
$$14 = 7x - 6x + 12$$
$$2 = x$$

Step 4. I considered the validity of the solution.

From step 1, 2 is not a permissible solution, so $x = 2$ is an extraneous root, and this equation has no solution.

Practice

For each question, state the non-permissible values as restrictions.

1. Solve each rational equation, or write "no solution."

   a) $\dfrac{1}{y} + \dfrac{1}{y + 2} = \dfrac{1}{24}$

   c) $\dfrac{x + 5}{x - 2} = 2$

   b) $\dfrac{3x - 9}{6x - 18} = 1$

   d) $\dfrac{1}{x - 2} - \dfrac{2}{x^2 - 4} = \dfrac{1}{3}$

2. Define a variable and write a rational expression to describe each situation. Then determine the non-permissible values of the variable.

a) the time to drive 100 km when detours have reduced the speed by 20 km/h

b) the speed of a cheetah that ran 150 m in twice the time

c) the fraction of a task completed by Belinda in 1 min, if it takes her 6 min longer than Blake to complete the task

3. Solve each rational equation. Verify your solution.

a) $\dfrac{x + 7}{x - 2} = 4$

b) $\dfrac{x + 5}{x - 2} = 2x + 2$

TIP

To verify a solution, substitute it into the original equation. If the left side equals the right side, then the solution is valid.

4. Solve each rational equation. Verify your solution.

a) $\dfrac{6}{3x - 2x} + \dfrac{2}{2x + 4} = \dfrac{3x + 2}{5}$

c) $\dfrac{x + 2}{x - 3} - \dfrac{x + 3}{x} = \dfrac{3x + 2}{4x}$

b) $\dfrac{5}{3x - 4} - \dfrac{4}{x + 4} = \dfrac{4x + 3}{6}$

d) $\dfrac{x - 4}{x^2 - 4} + \dfrac{x + 1}{x - 1} = \dfrac{x}{10}$

5. Refer to the rational equation $\dfrac{5}{3x + 3} + \dfrac{x + 2}{2x + 2} = \dfrac{6x + 1}{7x + 1}$.

    a) The non-permissible values of x are _____.

    b) The solution is $x =$ _____.

6. Refer to the rational equation $\dfrac{9x + 4}{5x - 5} + \dfrac{6x}{3x + 3} = \dfrac{15x}{2x + 7}$.

    a) The non-permissible values of x are _____.

    b) The solution is $x =$ _____.

WRITTEN RESPONSE

7. When working together, Marcia and Jon can do their housework in 90 min. Working independently, it takes Marcia 10 min longer than Jon to do all of the housework. How long does it take Jon to do all of the housework on his own? Explain, and verify your solution.

Complete the following to summarize the important ideas from this chapter.

Q: When is a rational expression undefined?

A: A rational expression is undefined for values of the _____ that make the

_____ equal to _____. These are called _____ values.

NEED HELP?
• See Lesson 4.1

Q: When is a rational expression stated in simplified form?

A: • The _____ common _____ (_____) of the

numerator and denominator is _____.

• The _____ values are stated based on the denominators before the

expression is _____.

NEED HELP?
• See Lesson 4.2

Q: How is dividing one rational expression by another *like* multiplying two
rational expressions?

A: Both processes involve the following steps:

• _____ the _____ and _____, if possible.

• Identify all _____ values and write them as restrictions.

• _____ the numerators and multiply the _____. Write as a

_____ rational _____.

• _____ using _____ factors.

• Write the product, stating the _____ on the _____.

NEED HELP?
• See Lesson 4.3

Q: How can you determine the lowest common denominator of two expressions?

A: The _____ is the product of all the _____ factors and all the

unique _____ of the _____. It is not always the _____

of _____ the factors.

NEED HELP?
• See Lesson 4.4

Q: What is the difference between an extraneous root and an inadmissible solution?

A: • An extraneous root is a root of the equation that is a non-permissible value.

It _____ a valid solution of the equation.

• An inadmissible solution _____ a valid solution of the equation, but is

ruled out by the _____ of the problem.

NEED HELP?
• See Lesson 4.5

4   Chapter Test

MULTIPLE CHOICE

Questions 1 and 2 refer to the following rational expression.

$$\frac{x - 2}{(x + 3)(x + 4)}$$

1. Identify which one of the following rational expressions is equivalent to the above expression.

   A. $\dfrac{2(x - 2)}{(x + 3)(x + 4)}$ **C.** $\dfrac{(2x - 4)(x - 1)}{(x - 1)(2x + 8)(x + 3)}$

   B. $\dfrac{x^2 + x - 6}{(x^2 + 9)(x + 4)}$ **D.** $\dfrac{-x^2 + x - 6}{x^2 - 9}$

2. Determine all of the non-permissible values for the expression.

   A. $x = 0, x = -3, x = -4$ **C.** $x = 0, x = 2$

   B. $x = -3, x = -4$ **D.** $x = 2, x = -3, x = -4$

Questions 3, 4, and 5 refer to the following pair of rational expressions.

$$\frac{x + 1}{x^2 - 2x - 3}, \frac{x + 2}{x^2 - x - 2}$$

3. Which values of x are non-permissible?

   A. $1, 2, 3$ **B.** $0, -1$ **C.** none   **D.** $-1, 2, 3$

4. What is the lowest common denominator?

   A. $(x + 1)(x - 3)(x - 2)$ **C.** $(x - 2)(x - 3)$

   B. $(x + 1)(x - 2)$ **D.** $(x + 3)(x + 2)$

5. What is the sum of these expressions?

   A. $\dfrac{4}{(x - 2)(x - 3)}$ **C.** $\dfrac{x - 2}{(x + 1)(x - 3)}$

   B. $(x + 2)(x + 3)$ **D.** $\dfrac{2(x^2 - x - 4)}{(x + 1)(x - 2)(x - 3)}$

6. Identify the solution to this rational equation.

$$\frac{5x + 3}{3x + 1} + \frac{2x + 4}{4x} = \frac{2x - 1}{x - 1}$$

   A. $x = 3$ **C.** $x = 3, x = -1$

   B. $x = 2$ **D.** none of these

7. Write an equivalent rational expression for each expression.

a) $\dfrac{3x}{2x+1} = $ _____, $x \neq$ _____

b) $\dfrac{5y + 10y^2}{10y} = $ _____, $y \neq$ _____

8. Simplify each rational expression. State any non-permissible values of the variable.

a) $\dfrac{-42x}{24x^3} = $ _____   non-permissible values: _____

b) $\dfrac{x^2 + 10x + 24}{2x + 8} = $ _____   non-permissible values: _____

c) $\dfrac{x^2 - x - 20}{x - 5} = $ _____   non-permissible values: _____

d) $\dfrac{25x^2}{125x^3} = $ _____   non-permissible values: _____

9. a) In the expression $\dfrac{2x}{(x-2)} \cdot \dfrac{3x(x+3)}{(4x-3)}$, the non-permissible values of the

variable, if any, are _____.

b) In the expression $\dfrac{x}{7} \cdot \dfrac{x(x+7)}{215}$, the non-permissible values of the

variable, if any, are _____.

10. Simplify each rational expression. State any non-permissible values of the variable.

a) $\dfrac{3x - 2}{x(2x + 5)} \cdot \dfrac{x(2 - x)}{(x - 6)} = $ _____   non-permissible values: _____

b) $\dfrac{5x}{2x(x + 3)} \div \dfrac{x(3 - 2x)}{3x + 9} = $ _____   non-permissible values: _____

c) $\dfrac{15}{4 - x} - \dfrac{3x}{x(x - 4)} = $ _____   non-permissible values: _____

11. Refer to the following rational equation.

$$\frac{2x + 7}{2x + 1} + \frac{2x}{3x} = \frac{2x + 1}{2x + 1}$$

a) The non-permissible values of x are _____.

b) The solution is $x = $ _____.

12. Refer to the following rational equation.

$$\frac{3x + 2}{4x + 3} + \frac{3x - 3}{5x - 2} = \frac{3x + 3}{x + 16}$$

   a) The non-permissible values of x are _____.

   b) The solution is $x =$ _____.

WRITTEN RESPONSE

13. Simplify $\dfrac{4x}{6x + 5} - \dfrac{x + 4}{x + 2}$. Explain each step.

14. Rob and Steve can do their weekly chores in 120 min when they work together. On his own, Rob takes 20 min longer than Steve to do all of the chores. How long does Steve take to do all of the chores on his own? Explain, and verify your solution.

Getting Started

1. Match each term with the picture, description, or example that best illustrates it.

a) range _____

b) *y*-intercept _____

c) maximum point _____

d) slope _____

e) decreasing function _____

f) quadratic function, opening up _____

i)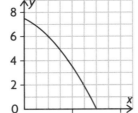

ii) $\{y \mid y \le 5, y \in \mathbb{R}\}$

iii)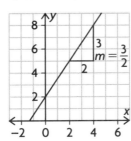

iv) $y = -3.57x^2 - 2.76x + 5.48$

v)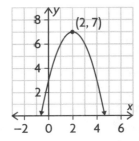

vi) the *y*-coordinate of the point where a function's graph crosses the *y*-axis

2. Write the equation of each linear function in slope-intercept form.

a)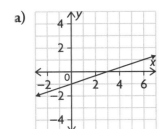

b) $x + 2y = 8$

c) line that includes points $(0, 4)$ and $(2, -2)$

d) line that includes points $(-1, -7)$ and $(3, 9)$

3. Determine the maximum or minimum value, the vertex, the axis of symmetry, the direction of opening, and the y-intercept of each quadratic function.

a)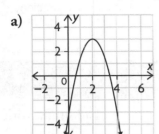

b) $y = 3(x + 1)^2 + 4$

4. For each function, do the following:

- State whether the graph is a line or a parabola.
- If the graph is a line, state whether it is increasing, decreasing, or constant.
- If the graph is a parabola, state the direction of opening and the maximum or minimum value.
- State the y-intercept of the graph.

a) $y = 0.4(x - 5)^2 - 3$

c) $y = -3(x - 4)(x + 2)$

b) $y = -1.6x + 5$

d) $y = -2$

5. State, with reasons, whether each table of values represents a linear function, a quadratic function, or neither.

a)

x	−1	0	1	2	3	4
y	6	1	−2	−3	−2	1

b)

x	−3	−2	−1	0	1	2
y	−1	0	3	4	2	0

c)

x	−2	−1	0	1	2	3
y	7	5	3	1	−1	−3

5.1 Exploring the Graphs of Polynomial Functions

YOU WILL NEED
• graphing technology

Keep in Mind

▶ A polynomial function in one variable contains only the operations of multiplication and addition, with real-number coefficients and whole-number exponents. The degree of a function in one variable is the greatest exponent. For example, $y = x^3 + 2x^2 - x + 4$ is a degree 3 polynomial function.

▶ The degree of a polynomial function indicates the shape of the function.

Function Type	constant	linear	quadratic	cubic
Degree, n	0	1	2	3
Sketch				
Number of x-intercepts	0 (except $y = 0$)	1	0, 1, or 2	1, 2, or 3
y-intercepts	1	1	1	1
Turning Points	0	0	1	0 or 2
End Behaviour	extends from Quadrant II to Quadrant I or from Quadrant III to Quadrant IV	extends from Quadrant III to Quadrant I or from Quadrant II to Quadrant IV	extends from Quadrant II to Quadrant I or from Quadrant III to Quadrant IV	extends from Quadrant III to Quadrant I or from Quadrant II to Quadrant IV
Domain	$\{x \mid x \in R\}$	$\{x \mid x \in R\}$	$\{x \mid x \in R\}$	$\{x \mid x \in R\}$
Range	$\{y \mid y = c, y \in R\}$	$\{y \mid y \in R\}$	$\{y \mid y \leq$ maximum, $y \in R\}$ or $\{y \mid y \geq$ minimum, $y \in R\}$	$\{y \mid y \in R\}$

Example

Determine which of graphs A and B could represent polynomial functions.

Solution

Step 1. I examined Graph A.

- It has two *x*-intercepts, one *y*-intercept, and one turning point.

- It extends from Quadrant II to Quadrant I.

- The domain is $\{x \mid x \in R\}$ and the range is $\{y \mid y \geq -3, y \in R\}$.

A graph that represents a quadratic function has all of these characteristics, so Graph A could represent a polynomial function.

Step 2. I examined Graph B.

Graph B appears to represent a polynomial function in these ways:

- It has one *y*-intercept.

- It extends from Quadrant II to Quadrant I.

- The domain is $\{x \mid x \in R\}$.

However, Graph B does not represent a polynomial function in these ways:

- It has no *x*-intercepts.

- Its range is $\{y \mid 2 \leq y \leq 4, y \in R\}$.

- It has many turning points.

This graph has some characteristics of a polynomial function, but not all of them, so it could not represent a polynomial function.

Practice

1. Determine which graphs represent polynomial functions, and of what types. Explain how you decided.

   a)

   b)

A.

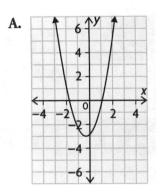

B.

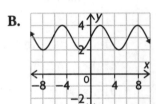

a)

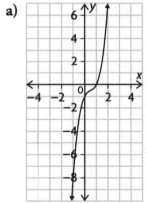

b)

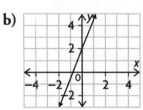

c)

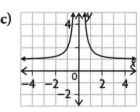

5.2 Characteristics of the Equations of Polynomial Functions

YOU WILL NEED

• graphing technology

Keep in Mind

▶ When a polynomial function is in standard form

  • The maximum number of x-intercepts the graph may have is equal to the degree of the function.

  • The maximum number of turning points the graph may have is equal to one less than the degree of the function.

  • The degree and leading coefficient indicate the end behaviour of the graph of the function.

  • The y-intercept of the graph is equal to the constant term of the function.

▶ Linear and cubic polynomial functions have similar end behaviour.

  • Negative leading coefficient: the graph extends from Quadrant II to Quadrant IV.

  • Positive leading coefficient: the graph extends from Quadrant III to Quadrant I.

▶ Quadratic polynomial functions have a different end behaviour.

  • Negative leading coefficient: the graph extends from Quadrant III to Quadrant IV.

  • Positive leading coefficient: the graph extends from Quadrant II to Quadrant I.

> **TIP**
>
> The standard form for a linear function is
> $f(x) = ax + b$
> where $a \neq 0$.
> The standard form for a quadratic function is
> $f(x) = ax^2 + bx + c$
> where $a \neq 0$.
> The standard form for a cubic function is
> $f(x) = ax^3 + bx^2 + cx + d$
> where $a \neq 0$.

Example 1

Determine the following characteristics of each function, using its equation.

a) $f(x) = 4x + 2$ **b)** $f(x) = -5x^2 + 2x - 1$

> **TIP**
>
> In your descriptions of characteristics of a function include
> • number of x-intercepts
> • y-intercept
> • end behaviour
> • domain
> • range
> • number of possible turning points

Solution

a) I considered each characteristic of the equation $f(x) = 4x + 2$.

  • The value of the greatest exponent is 1, so the degree is 1. Since the degree is 1, the function is linear, so its graph is a line, and the graph has one x-intercept.

  • The constant term is 2, so the y-intercept is 2.

  • The leading coefficient, 4, is positive, so the graph extends from Quadrant III to Quadrant I.

- There are no restrictions on x. The domain is $\{x \mid x \in R\}$.
- There are no restrictions on y. The range is $\{y \mid y \in R\}$.
- This function is linear, so it has no turning points.

b) I considered each characteristic of the equation $f(x) = -5x^2 + 2x - 1$.

- The value of the greatest exponent is 2, so the degree is 2. Since the degree is 2, the function is quadratic, so its graph is a parabola, and the graph may have 0, 1, or 2 x-intercepts.
- The constant term is -1, so the y-intercept is -1.
- The leading coefficient, -5, is negative, and the equation is quadratic, so the graph extends from Quadrant III to Quadrant IV.
- There are no restrictions on x. The domain is $\{x \mid x \in R\}$.
- The range is $\{y \mid y \leq \text{maximum}, y \in R\}$.
- This function is quadratic, so it has one turning point.

> **TIP**
> Quadratic functions always have one turning point. Cubic functions may have two turning points, or none.

Example 2

Match each graph to the correct polynomial function.

A.
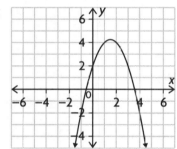

B.
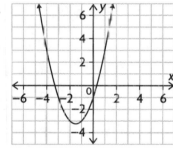

i) $f(x) = x^2 + 3x - 1$

ii) $g(x) = -x^2 + 3x + 2$

Solution

Step 1. I looked at the number of turning points in each graph.

Each graph has one turning point, so both $f(x)$ and $g(x)$ are quadratic functions.

Step 2. I looked at the end behaviour of each graph.

Graph A extends from Quadrant III to Quadrant IV, so the leading coefficient must be negative. Graph A matches with $g(x)$.

Graph B extends from Quadrant II to Quadrant I, so the leading coefficient must be positive. Graph B matches with $f(x)$.

Step 3. I verified my conclusion by looking at the y-intercepts.

The y-intercept of Graph A is 2. The constant term of $g(x)$ is 2, so again, the graph and equation match.

The y-intercept of Graph B is -1, matching the constant term of $f(x)$.

Graph A matches with $g(x)$, and Graph B matches with $f(x)$.

Practice

1. Match each graph with the correct polynomial function. Provide your reasoning.

A.

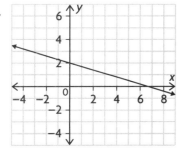

C.

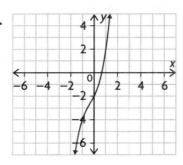

B.

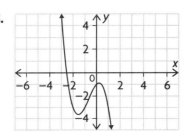

D.

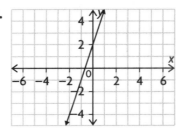

i) $f(x) = -x^3 - 2x^2 + x - 1$

iii) $h(x) = -0.3x + 2$

ii) $g(x) = 3x + 2$

iv) $j(x) = x^3 + x^2 + 2x - 2$

Graph A

number of x-intercepts: ___

y-intercept: ___

end behaviour: from Quadrant ___ to Quadrant ___, so the leading coefficient is _____

domain: _____   range: _____

number of turning points: ___

Graph A represents a _____ polynomial function. It matches with function ___.

Graph B

number of x-intercepts: ___

y-intercept: ___

end behaviour: from Quadrant ___ to Quadrant ___, so the leading coefficient is _____

domain: _____   range: _____

number of turning points: ___

Graph B represents a _____ polynomial function. It matches with function ___.

Graph C

number of x-intercepts: ___

y-intercept: ___

end behaviour: from Quadrant ___ to Quadrant ___, so the leading coefficient is _____

domain: _____   range: _____

number of turning points: ___

Graph C represents a _____ polynomial function. It matches with function ___.

Graph D

number of x-intercepts: ___

y-intercept: ___

end behaviour: from Quadrant ___ to Quadrant ___, so the leading coefficient is _____

domain: _____   range: _____

number of turning points: ___

Graph D represents a _____ polynomial function. It matches with function ___.

2. Write a polynomial function that satisfies each set of characteristics.

a) extending from Quadrant III to Quadrant IV, one turning point, y-intercept of 4

c) extending from Quadrant III to Quadrant I, y-intercept of -3

b) degree 1, decreasing, y-intercept of -2

d) two turning points, y-intercept of 5

NUMERICAL RESPONSE

3. State the characteristics of each polynomial function.

a) $f(x) = -3x^2 - 2x + 1$

- degree: ___
- leading coefficient: ___
- constant term: ___
- number of x-intercepts: _____
- y-intercept: ___
- extends from Quadrant ___ to Quadrant ___
- domain: _____
- range: _____
- number of turning points: ___

b) $h(x) = 4x^3 + 2x^2 - x + 34$

- degree: ___
- leading coefficient: ___
- constant term: ___
- number of x-intercepts: _____
- y-intercept: ___
- extends from Quadrant ___ to Quadrant ___
- domain: _____
- range: _____
- number of turning points: ___

WRITTEN RESPONSE

4. The life expectancy of Canadian males born from 1920 to 2008 can be modelled by the polynomial function $E(y) = 0.2339x - 390.8$, where E is the life expectancy in years and x is the year of birth.

a) Describe the characteristics of the graph of the polynomial function. Explain your answer.

b) Would you use this graph to estimate the life expectancy of a male born in the year 1000? Explain.

> **TIP**
> In your descriptions of characteristics of a function include
> - number of x-intercepts
> - y-intercept
> - end behaviour
> - domain
> - range
> - number of possible turning points

5.3 Modelling Data with Lines of Best Fit

YOU WILL NEED
• graphing technology

Keep in Mind

▸ A scatter plot is useful when looking for trends in a given set of data.

▸ If the points on a scatter plot seem to follow a linear trend, then there may be a linear relationship between the independent and dependent variables.

▸ If the points on a scatter plot follow a linear trend, technology can be used to determine and graph the equation of the line of best fit.

▸ A line of best fit can be used to predict values that are not recorded or plotted. To do so, read values from the line of best fit on a scatter plot, or use the equation of the line of best fit.

Example

The winning times for the men's 20 km biathlon in the Winter Olympics from 1964 to 2010 (except for 2002) are shown in the table.

Year	1964	1968	1972	1976	1980	1984
Winning Time (min)	80.4	73.8	75.9	74.2	68.3	71.9
Year	1988	1992	1994	1998	2006	2010
Winning Time (min)	56.6	57.6	57.4	56.2	54.3	48.4

a) Use technology to create a scatter plot, and use linear regression to determine the equation of the line of best fit.

b) Determine a possible winning time for the event in the 2002 Winter Olympics.

c) Compare your estimate with the actual winning time of 51.0 min.

Solution

Step 1. I entered the data into my graphing calculator.

A year	B time	C	D
1 1964.	80.4		
2 1968.	73.8		
3 1972.	75.9		
4 1976.	74.2		
5 1980.	68.3		

Step 2. I plotted the points, with "year" as the independent variable and "time" as the dependent variable.

The data looked roughly linear.

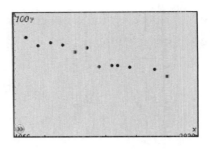

Step 3. I determined the equation for the line of best fit using linear regression.

a) The equation is

$f(x) = -0.682\ldots x + 1419.390\ldots$

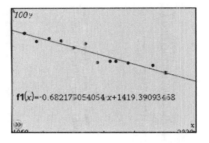

Step 4. I traced along the graph to determine a possible winning time in 2002.

b) According to the equation, the winning time would be about 53.7 min.

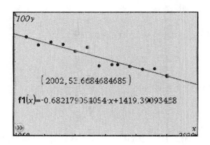

Step 5. I compared the estimated time with the actual time.

c) The estimate was about 4 min slower than the actual winning time of 51.0 min.

Practice

1. The winning times for the women's 100 m freestyle swim in the Summer Olympics for most years from 1984 to 2008 are shown.

   a) Use linear regression to determine the equation for the line of best fit for the data.

   b) Determine a possible winning time for the event in the 1996 Summer Olympics.

   c) Compare your estimate with the actual winning time of 54.50 s.

Year	Winning Time (s)
1984	55.92
1988	54.93
1992	54.64
2000	53.83
2004	53.84
2008	53.12

2. A city council needs to buy 15 000 L of liquid de-icer for the coming winter. One supplier provides the following quote:

TIP

Recall that 1 kL = 1000 L.

- 9 kL for $1.30/L

- 10 kL for $1.20/L

- 11 kL for $1.15/L

- 12 kL for $1.10/L

- 13 kL for $1.05/L

- 14 kL for $0.95/L

- 16 kL for $0.84/L

a) Use linear regression to determine the equation of the line of best fit for the data.

b) What price should the city expect to pay per litre?

c) What price will be paid in all?

3. The provincial government plans to buy 500 winter parkas with goose down for park rangers. One supplier offers these prices:

- 100 parkas for $395 each

- 150 parkas for $380 each

- 200 parkas for $350 each

- 250 parkas for $340 each

- 300 parkas for $320 each

- 350 parkas for $300 each

- 600 parkas for $205 each

a) Use linear regression to determine the equation of the line of best fit for the data.

b) What price should the government expect to pay for each of the 500 parkas?

c) How many parkas would the government need to order for each parka to cost less than $360?

4. Daniella, a real estate agent, helps businesses move to new offices. If an office does not have enough area, the employees will not be able to work productively. If there is too much area, the business will pay too much rent.

   One client is a business with 14 employees. Daniella has made the following table about other businesses in one building.

Number of Employees	4	6	10	12	20	35
Office Space (m²)	23.2	36.6	75.0	72.0	118.0	245.0

   There are two areas for rent in the building.

   Area P has 86 m². Area Q has 100 m².

   Which area should Daniella show to her client?

   A. Area P only   **B.** Area Q only   **C.** neither P nor Q   **D.** both P and Q

5. Darcy is planning to build a stable for 15 horses. He has found that other reputable stables in the neighbourhood have the following areas:

Number of Horses	3	5	6	11	17	21
Area (ft²)	480	750	930	1881	2600	3024

   Darcy has decided his stable will have a comparable amount of area. Use linear regression to determine how many square feet the stable should have. Explain what you did.

Modelling Data with a Curve of Best Fit

YOU WILL NEED
• graphing technology

Keep In Mind

▶ If a scatter plot seems to follow a curved trend, then

- There may be a quadratic or cubic relationship between the independent variable and the dependent variable.
- Graphing technology can be used to determine and graph the equation of the curve of best fit.

▶ Technology uses polynomial regression to determine the curve of best fit. Polynomial regression results in an equation of a curve that balances the points on both sides of the curve.

▶ A curve of best fit can be used to predict values that are not recorded or plotted. To do so, read values from the curve of best fit on a scatter plot, or use the equation of the curve of best fit.

Example

A pebble falls from a cliffside into the river 30 m below. This table gives the height of the pebble as it falls.

Time (s)	0	0.5	1.0	1.2	1.5	2.0
Height (m)	30.00	28.77	25.11	22.97	18.98	10.42

a) Use technology to create a scatter plot, and use quadratic regression to determine the equation of the curve of best fit.

b) Use your equation to determine the height of the pebble after 1.25 s.

c) When does the pebble hit the river, to the nearest hundredth of a second?

Solution

Step 1. I entered the data into my graphing calculator and created a scatter plot.

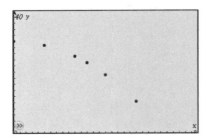

Step 2. I ran the quadratic regression on my
calculator, which gave me the curve of
best fit and its equation.

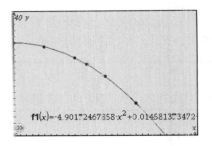

f1(x)=-4.901?2467858·x²+0.0145813?3472

a) The equation of the quadratic regression
function that models the data is

$$h = -4.901... \, t^2 + 0.014... \, t + 29.996....$$

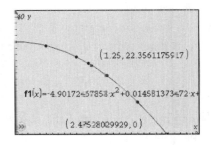

(1.25, 22.3561175917)

f1(x)=-4.90172457858·x²+0.014581373472·x+

(2.47528029929, 0)

Step 3. I used my calculator to determine the height of the pebble after 1.25 s.

b) The height of the pebble after 1.25 s is about 22.36 m.

Step 4. I used the Zero application to determine when the pebble had a height
of 0 m.

c) The pebble hits the river after about 2.48 s.

Practice

1. The following table shows Canada's population growth from 1871 to 2001.

Year	1871	1881	1891	1901	1911	1921	1931
Population (1000s)	3689	4325	4833	5371	7207	8788	10 377
Year	1941	1951	1961	1971	1981	1991	2001
Population (1000s)	11 507	13 648	18 238	21 568	24 820	28 031	31 021

Source: Statistics Canada.

a) Describe the trend in the data.

b) Use quadratic regression to determine the equation of the curve of best fit
for the data.

c) Use quadratic regression to estimate the population of Canada in 2006, to
the nearest thousand.

d) If the population of Canada continues to grow according to this trend,
what will the population be in 2020, to the nearest thousand?

2. Arnold hit a golf ball from the top of a hill. The height of the ball above the green is given in the table.

Time (s)	0.5	1	1.5	2.5	3.5	4
Height (m)	30.890	45.025	54.397	58.858	44.279	29.848

a) Describe the trend in the data.

b) Use quadratic regression to determine the equation of the curve of best fit for the data.

c) Use the equation to determine the height of the ball after 2.0 s.

d) When did the ball hit the ground, to the nearest tenth of a second?

3. A biochemist is studying the growth of recently discovered bacteria. She collects the data shown.

Day	1	2	3	4	5	6	7	8
Mass (g)	3.2	4.6	5.4	4.2	5.5	7.1	8	9.2

a) Describe the trend.

b) Use cubic regression to determine the equation of the curve of best fit for the data.

c) Estimate the mass of the bacteria on Day 11.

4. A pebble drops from a cliffside into a river 25 m below. This table gives the height of the pebble as it falls.

Time (s)	0	0.3	0.5	0.7	0.9	1.0
Height (m)	25.00	23.84	22.68	21.21	19.43	18.42

a) Plot the data on a scatter plot. Use quadratic regression to determine the equation of the curve of best fit for the data.

b) Determine the height of the pebble after 1.2 s.

5. A spherical balloon is being inflated. The table shows the volume of the balloon at different times.

Time (s)	0	1	2	3	3.5	4
Volume (cm³)	0	43.5	123.1	278.1	540.0	914.8

a) Use technology to plot the data as a scatter plot. Describe the trend that you see.

b) Use cubic regression to create a curve of best fit.

c) Determine the volume of the balloon after 2.5 s, to the nearest tenth of a cubic centimetre.

NUMERICAL RESPONSE

6. Cierra, an architect, is designing a suspension bridge. There will be a suspension cable on each side of the bridge, with support wire hanging down from the cable at different distances, as shown.

Distance from Centre of Bridge (m)	10	20	30	40	50	60
Length of Support Wire (m)	5.56	7.12	9.68	13.24	17.80	23.36

a) A quadratic regression function that models the data is

$f(x) = $ _____$x^2 + $ _____$x + $ _____.

b) The support wire that is 60 m from the centre of the bridge should be _____ m long, to the nearest centimetre.

7. Bob likes to solve jigsaw puzzles on the Internet. He recorded the times he took to solve puzzles with different numbers of pieces.

Number of Pieces in Puzzle	0	12	20	54	72	120
Time to Solve (s)	0	53	100	442	817	2293

a) Plot the data as a scatter plot. Describe the trend.

b) Use quadratic regression to determine the equation of the curve of best fit for the data.

c) How long would Bob take to solve a puzzle with 100 pieces, to the nearest second?

8. Jen likes to solve chess puzzles on the Internet. She recorded the times she took to solve different puzzles.

Difficulty of Puzzle	1 star	2 stars	3 stars	4 stars	5 stars	6 stars
Time to Solve (min)	11.5	17.0	26.5	40.0	57.5	79.0

a) Plot the data as a scatter plot. Describe the trend.

b) Use quadratic regression to determine the equation of the curve of best fit for the data.

c) How long would Jen take to solve a 3.5-star chess puzzle, to the nearest tenth of a minute?

Complete the following to summarize the important ideas from this chapter.

Q: How can a function's range help you determine if it could be polynomial?

A: Possible types of ranges for polynomial functions are _____,

$\{y \mid y \leq \text{maximum}, y \in \text{R}\}$, and _____. A range such as

$\{y \mid \text{minimum} \leq y \leq \text{maximum}, y \in \text{R}\}$ <u>also matches/does not match</u> a
polynomial function (circle one response).

NEED HELP?
• See Lesson 5.1

Q: How does the degree of a polynomial function relate to the number of
x-intercepts and turning points it could have?

A: • The _____ number of *x*-intercepts is equal to the _____
of the function.

• The _____ number of turning points is equal to _____
the degree of the function.

• A quadratic function always has one _____. A cubic function may

have _____ or two _____.

NEED HELP?
• See Lessons 5.1 and 5.2

Q: How do the degree and leading coefficient of a polynomial determine the end
behaviour of its graph?

A: • Linear and _____ functions with a negative _____

_____ extend from Quadrant ___ to Quadrant ___.

• _____ functions extend from Quadrant ___ to Quadrant ___ when

the _____ _____ is positive, and from Quadrant III to

Quadrant IV when it is _____.

• _____ and _____ functions with a _____
leading coefficient extend from Quadrant III to Quadrant I.

NEED HELP?
• See Lesson 5.2

Q: How can you use technology to create a model of data?

A1: To create a graphical model, create a _____.

A2: To create an algebraic model, use linear, _____, or cubic

_____ to determine the _____ of the line or _____

of _____.

NEED HELP?
• See Lessons 5.3 and 5.4

MULTIPLE CHOICE

1. Which graphs represent polynomial functions?

I. 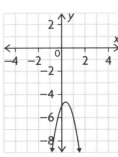   II.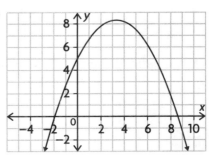

   A. I only   **B.** II only   **C.** both I and II   **D.** neither I nor II

2. Which graph represents the polynomial function $f(x) = -3x^2 + 2x - 5$?

A. 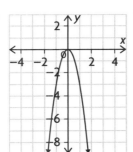   **B.** 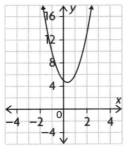   **C.**   **D.**

3. The winning times for the men's 50 km walk in various Summer Olympics from 1984 to 2008 are shown.

Year	1984	1988	1992	2000	2004	2008
Winning Time (min)	227.43	218.93	230.23	222.36	222.76	217.15

Predict the winning time for the event in the 1996 Summer Olympics.

   A. 220.0 min   **B.** 219.83 min   **C.** 217.44 min   **D.** 223.14 min

4. A spherical weather balloon is being inflated. The table shows the volume of the balloon at different times.

Time (s)	0	1	2	3	4
Volume (cm³)	0	95	120	365	1070

Use cubic regression to determine the volume of the balloon after 5 s.

   A. 1205 cm³   **B.** 2055 cm³   **C.** 2475 cm³   **D.** 1020 cm³

5. Consider the graph shown.

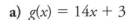

- The graph is a _____, _____ line.
- There are ___ *x*-intercepts and ___ *y*-intercept(s).
- The graph extends from Quadrant ___ to Quadrant ___.
- The domain is {*x* | _____}.
- The range is {*y* | _____}.
- There is (are) ___ turning point(s).
- This graph represents a _____, _____ function.

6. Enter the characteristics for each polynomial function.

a) $g(x) = 14x + 3$

- degree: ___
- leading coefficient: _____
- constant term: ___
- number of *x*-intercepts: ___
- *y*-intercept: _____
- extends from Quadrant ___ to Quadrant ___
- domain: _____
- range: _____
- number of turning points: ___

b) $j(x) = 9x^3 - 3x^2 + 2x - 1$

- degree: ___
- leading coefficient: _____
- constant term: ___
- number of *x*-intercepts: ___
- *y*-intercept: _____
- extends from Quadrant ___ to Quadrant ___
- domain: _____
- range: _____
- number of turning points: ___

7. Each year, the Mapleton health department tests about 15 000 water samples for drinking water and swimming pools. These tests are done with a chemical medium called differential coliform media (DCM). This table shows what one supplier charges for various quantities of DCM.

Number of Samples	2 500	5 000	12 500	14 000	16 000	20 000
Cost ($)	1 200	2 000	5 000	5 618	6 400	8 000

Use linear regression to complete this statement:

The Mapleton health department should expect to spend $_____ on DCM next year.

8. Etienne, an architect, is designing a suspension bridge. There will be a suspension cable on each side of the bridge, with support wire hanging down from the cable at different distances, as shown.

Distance from Centre of Bridge (m)	15	30	40	45	50	60
Length of Support Wire (m)	2.84	5.48	8.24	9.91	11.80	16.16

a) The quadratic regression function that models the data is

$f(x) =$ _____$x^2 +$ _____$x +$ _____.

b) The support wire that is 75 m from the centre of the bridge should be ___ m long, to the nearest centimetre.

WRITTEN RESPONSE

9. Determine whether each graph represents a polynomial function. Explain how you decided.

a)

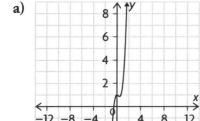
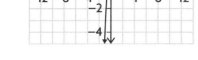

b)

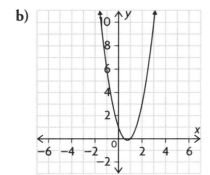

10. The manager of a large chain of outdoor stores is buying sealed meal packets for camping from a supplier. The supplier offers the prices shown. Based on previous sales, the manager expects to sell 6000 packets. Use linear regression to determine what price she should expect to pay in total. Explain your answer.

- 3000 packets for $8.75 each
- 3500 packets for $8.35 each
- 4000 packets for $7.95 each
- 4500 packets for $7.25 each
- 5000 packets for $6.50 each

11. A biochemist is studying the growth of recently discovered bacteria. She collects the data shown.

Day	1	2	3	4	5	6	7	8
Mass (g)	5.42	4.56	3.14	1.88	1.50	2.72	6.26	12.84

a) Describe the trend.

b) Use cubic regression to determine the equation of the curve of best fit for the data.

c) Estimate the mass of the bacteria on Day 11.

12. Kendall likes to solve Kakuro puzzles in the morning newspaper. The puzzles increase in difficulty from Monday to Sunday. The table shows how long Kendall takes to solve the puzzle each day. Use quadratic regression to determine how long Kendall would take to solve Friday's puzzle. Explain what you did.

Day of Week	Monday	Tuesday	Wednesday	Thursday	Saturday	Sunday
Time to Solve (min)	2	3	5	8	17	23

MULTIPLE CHOICE

1. Which of the following is an equivalent expression for $\dfrac{36x^3}{6x^4}$?

    A. $6x$, $x \neq 0$
    B. $\dfrac{18x}{3x^2}$, $x \neq 0$
    C. $\dfrac{6}{x}$, $x \neq 0$
    D. Both B and C.

2. Which are the correct non-permissible values for the expression $\dfrac{5x}{(x-4)(3x+2)}$?

    A. $x = 4$, $x = -\dfrac{2}{3}$
    B. $x = -4$, $x = \dfrac{2}{3}$
    C. $x = 4$, $x = -\dfrac{3}{2}$
    D. $x = -4$, $x = \dfrac{3}{2}$

3. Which is the correct simplified expression for $\left(\dfrac{27a^3}{3a^4}\right)\left(\dfrac{a^2}{18a^4}\right)$?

    A. $\dfrac{27a^5}{54a^8}$, $a \neq 0$
    B. $\dfrac{1}{2a^3}$, $a \neq 0$
    C. $\dfrac{1}{2a^2}$, $a \neq 0$
    D. $2a^3$, $a \neq 0$

4. Which of the following statements is false for this polynomial function?

    A. Domain: $\{x \mid x \in R\}$

    B. Range: $\{y \mid y \in R\}$

    C. End behaviour: Graph extends from Quadrant II to Quadrant IV

    D. x-intercepts: $x = -3$, $x = 0$, $x = 5$

5. Which of the following is not a polynomial function?

    A. $f(x) = 2x - 9$

    B. $g(x) = 4x^2 + 5x + 1$

    C. $m(x) = x^3 + 3x^2 - x + 3$

    D. $n(x) = 4^x$

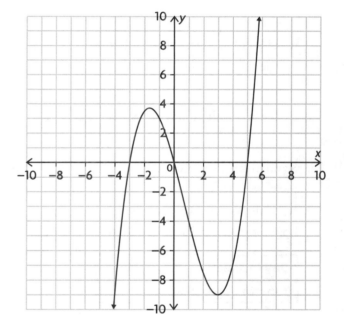

NUMERICAL RESPONSE

6. What is the solution to the rational equation $\dfrac{1}{a} + \dfrac{9}{4} = \dfrac{6}{a}$?

    $a = \underline{\hspace{1cm}}$, $a \neq \underline{\hspace{1cm}}$

7. State the y-intercept of $y = x^3 + 3x - 5$.

    $y = \underline{\hspace{1cm}}$

8. State the maximum possible number of turning points of the graph of
$f(x) = -x^3 + 3x^2 - x + 1$.

___

9. State the maximum possible number of x-intercepts of the graph of
$f(x) = -x^3 + 3x^2 - x - 1$.

___

WRITTEN RESPONSE

10. a) Write an equivalent rational expression for $\dfrac{2y^2 + 8y}{y + 4}$.

b) State the non-permissible values for the equivalent expressions.

c) Demonstrate that your expressions are equivalent by substituting a permissible value into both expressions.

11. Determine the non-permissible values for each rational expression, state these values as restrictions, and simplify.

a) $\dfrac{-24x^2}{4x^4}$

b) $\dfrac{3n - 6}{n^2 - 4}$

12. Simplify.

a) $\left(\dfrac{10x^3}{4}\right)\left(\dfrac{16x}{5x^2}\right)$

b) $30b^5 \div \dfrac{6}{b^3}$

c) $\dfrac{20}{(2y)^3} \div 4y^2$

13. Simplify.

a) $\dfrac{6a - 18}{a + 3} \div \dfrac{a - 3}{a + 3}$

b) $\left(\dfrac{25y^2 - 9}{5y - 3}\right)\left(\dfrac{10y^2 + 6y}{25y^2 + 30y + 9}\right)$

14. Simplify.

a) $\dfrac{3}{2x^2} - \dfrac{1}{5x^3}$

b) $\dfrac{2y}{y + 5} + \dfrac{y}{y - 2}$

15. State the restrictions, and then solve the rational equation. Verify your solution.

$\dfrac{12}{x + 5} + \dfrac{16}{x - 5} = -2$

16. It takes Ted 10 min longer to cut the grass than it does his older brother Cam. If they work together, they can cut the grass in 50 min. How long does it take for each person to cut the grass when working alone?

17. Determine the domain, range, intercepts, and end behaviour for the polynomial function shown.

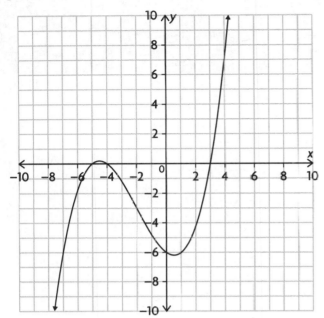

18. Determine the end behaviour, the possible number of turning points, the possible number of x-intercepts, the y-intercept, the domain, and the range of each function.

a) $v(x) = x^2 + 4x - 12$

b) $w(x) = -2x^2 + 4x + 1$

19. Jess and Brad own a business walking dogs and pet-sitting. Their monthly income for the last 10 months is shown in the table.

Month	1	2	3	4	5	6	7	8	9	10
Income ($)	60	84	80	110	105	125	140	130	135	160

a) Create a scatter plot of the data and determine the linear regression equation of the line of best fit.

b) Use your graph to estimate their income at the end of the 12th month.

c) Use your regression model to determine when they can expect their monthly income to exceed $200.

Getting Started

1. Match each term with the example that best illustrates it.

a) domain ____

b) range ____

c) decreasing function ____

d) continuous data ____

e) quadratic function ____

f) intercepts ____

i) $x = -1, x = 2, y = -2$ for $y = x^2 - x - 2$

ii) a person's body mass over time

iii) $\{x \mid x \in R\}$ for $y = x^2$

iv) for $y = -x^2 + 5$, when $x > 0$

v) $\{y \mid y \in R\}$ for $y = 3x + 2$

vi) $y = x(x - 4) + 7$

2. State the domain and range of each function.

a) $y = -2x + 3.5$

domain: _____

range: _____

b) $y = -\dfrac{1}{2}x^2 - 3$

domain: _____

range: _____

c) $y = 0.01x^3$

domain: _____

range: _____

d) $y = 5x(x - 2)$

domain: _____

range: _____

3. State whether each function in question 2 is increasing, decreasing, or both. If necessary, state where the function is increasing and where it is decreasing.

a)

b)

c)

d)

4. State the domain of each function, given the context.

a) the number of cookies needed for a student council meeting with n members

$$C(n) = 3n + 6$$

b) the height of a stone thrown from a 50 m cliff

$$h = 20t - 5t^2$$

5. Determine the range of each function in question 4, given the context.

a)

b)

6. Determine the x-intercepts and the y-intercept of each function.

a) $y = 3x^2 - 27$

x-intercept(s):

y-intercept:

b) $y = -0.25x + 0.75$

x-intercept(s):

y-intercept:

c) $y = 2x^2(x - 1)$

x-intercept(s):

y-intercept:

d) $y = \dfrac{1}{2}x^2 + 3$

x-intercept(s):

y-intercept:

7. a) Write the equation of a linear function that has intercepts at (4, 0) and (0, 3).

b) Justin says that the quadratic function $y = \dfrac{3}{16}(x - 4)^2$ has exactly the same intercepts, (4, 0) and (0, 3). Is he correct? Explain how you know.

6.1 Exploring the Characteristics of Exponential Functions

YOU WILL NEED
• graphing technology

Keep in Mind

▶ An exponential function has the form $f(x) = a(b)^x$, where x is the exponent and $a \neq 0$, $b > 0$, and $b \neq 1$.

▶ The graph of an exponential function can have two different shapes, as shown.

▶ All exponential functions of the form $f(x) = a(b)^x$, where $a > 0$, $b > 0$, and $b \neq 1$, have the following characteristics:

• number of x-intercepts: 0

• number of y-intercepts: 1

• end behaviour: The curve extends from Quadrant II to Quadrant I.

• domain: $\{x \mid x \in R\}$

• range: $\{y \mid y > 0, y \in R\}$

Shape I: An increasing function

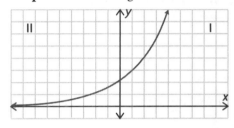

Shape II: A decreasing function

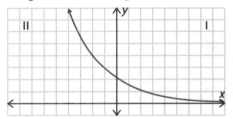

Example

a) Determine which of these two graphs represents an exponential function. If possible, identify the type of function.

b) For each function that is exponential, state

• the number of x-intercepts

• the y-intercept

• the end behaviour

• the domain

• the range

I.

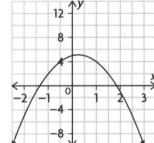

II.

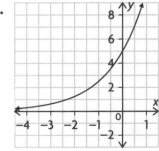

Solution

a) Step 1. I looked at each graph.

Graph I has two x-intercepts. It extends from Quadrant III to Quadrant IV. It appears to represent a quadratic function, not an exponential function.

Graph II has no x-intercepts. It extends from Quadrant II to Quadrant I. It increases. It appears to represent an increasing exponential function.

b) Step 2. I looked at the characteristics of Graph II.

- It does not touch the *x*-axis: there are 0 *x*-intercepts.

- It touches the *y*-axis at (0, 5): the *y*-intercept is 5.

- End behaviour: it extends from Quadrant II to Quadrant I.

- domain: $\{x \mid x \in R\}$

- range: $\{y \mid y > 0, y \in R\}$

Practice

1. Graph each exponential function, using technology. Determine the number of *x*-intercepts, the *y*-intercept, the end behaviour, the domain, and the range.

a) $y = 5(2)^x$

There are ___ *x*-intercepts.

The *y*-intercept is ___.

end behaviour: from Quadrant ___ to Quadrant ___.

domain: _____

range: _____

b) $y = 4\left(\dfrac{1}{4}\right)^x$

There are ___ *x*-intercepts.

The *y*-intercept is ___.

end behaviour: from Quadrant ___ to Quadrant ___.

domain: _____

range: _____

MULTIPLE CHOICE

2. Which graph represents a decreasing exponential function?

A.

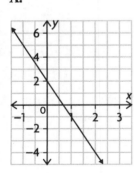

B.

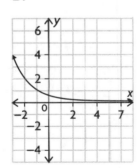

C.

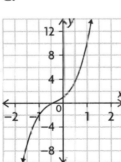

D.

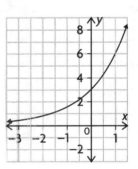

NUMERICAL RESPONSE

3. For the decreasing exponential function you identified in question 2,

a) There are ___ *x*-intercepts.

b) The *y*-intercept is ___.

c) The graph extends from Quadrant ___ to Quadrant ___.

d) The domain is _____.

e) The range is _____.

6.2 Relating the Characteristics of an Exponential Function to Its Equation

YOU WILL NEED
• graphing technology

Keep in Mind

▸ For an exponential function, there is a constant ratio between consecutive y-values when the x-values increase by the same amount.

▸ In an exponential function of the form $y = a(b)^x$, a is a non-zero multiplier and b is the base (where $b > 0$ and $b \neq 1$).

  • The value of a is the y-intercept of the graph of the function.

  • The value of b is the ratio of y-values whenever the x-value increases by 1.

▸ An exponential function is increasing if $a > 0$ and $b > 1$ and decreasing if $a > 0$ and $0 < b < 1$.

▸ Regardless of the value of b, all exponential functions $y = a(b)^x$ with $a > 0$

  • have no x-intercepts

  • extend from Quadrant II to Quadrant I

  • have a domain of $\{x \mid x \in R\}$ and a range of $\{y \mid y > 0, y \in R\}$

Example

For the function $y = 8\left(\dfrac{2}{3}\right)^x$, predict

• the number of x-intercepts

• the domain and the range

• the y-intercept

• whether this function is increasing or decreasing

• the end behaviour

Verify your predictions by graphing the function using technology.

Solution

Step 1. I recognized that this is an exponential equation of the form $y = a(b)^x$.

$$a = 8, \text{ so } a > 0 \qquad b = \frac{2}{3}, \text{ so } 0 < b < 1$$

Step 2. I used this information to predict the characteristics.

  • Since it is an exponential equation, it has no x-intercepts.

  • Since $a = 8$, the y-intercept must be 8.

  • The graph must extend from Quadrant II to Quadrant I.

  • The function must have a domain of $\{x \mid x \in R\}$ and a range of $\{y \mid y > 0, y \in R\}$.

  • Since $0 < b < 1$, this function is decreasing.

Step 3. I graphed the function to verify my predictions.

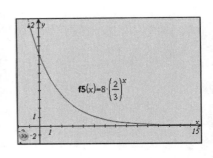

$$f5(x)=8 \cdot \left(\frac{2}{3}\right)^x$$

Practice

1. Determine if the data in each table represents an exponential function. Provide your reasoning.

a)

x	0	1	2	3	4	5
y	6	12	24	48	96	192

b)

x	0	1	2	3	4
y	2	4	16	256	65 536

c)

x	0	1	2	3	4	5
y	4096	1024	256	64	16	4

2. Determine whether an exponential function could be used to model the data. Explain how you know. If it is an exponential function, identify the y-intercept, and state whether the function is increasing or decreasing.

a)

x	0	1	2	3	4	5
y	3	6	12	24	48	96

b)

x	−5	−4	−3	−2	−1	0
y	10	12	14	16	18	20

3. Describe the characteristics of each exponential graph.

a)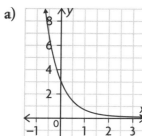

b)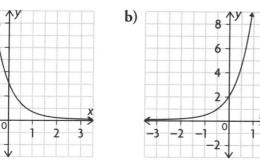

c)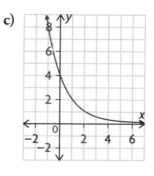

d)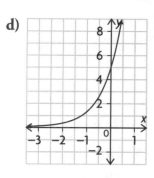

	Number of x-intercepts	y-intercept	End Behaviour	Domain	Range
a)			from Quadrant ____ to Quadrant ____		
b)			from Quadrant ____ to Quadrant ____		
c)			from Quadrant ____ to Quadrant ____		
d)			from Quadrant ____ to Quadrant ____		

4. Complete the table to predict the characteristics of each function. Verify your predictions by graphing each function using technology.

	Function	Number of x-intercepts	y-intercept	End Behaviour	Domain	Range
a)	$y = 2.5(5)^x$			from Quadrant ____ to Quadrant ____		
b)	$y = 14(0.4)^x$			from Quadrant ____ to Quadrant ____		
c)	$y = 3\left(\dfrac{1}{3}\right)^x$			from Quadrant ____ to Quadrant ____		
d)	$y = 3.1\left(\dfrac{1}{4}\right)^x$			from Quadrant ____ to Quadrant ____		
e)	$y = 20(2.1)^x$			from Quadrant ____ to Quadrant ____		
f)	$y = 10(0.5)^x$			from Quadrant ____ to Quadrant ____		

5. Use the base to determine whether each function is increasing or decreasing. Explain your answer briefly.

a) $y = \dfrac{1}{2}(7)^x$

b) $y = 2\left(\dfrac{3}{4}\right)^x$

6. Complete the table to predict the characteristics of each exponential function.

	Function	y-intercept	Base	Increasing or Decreasing
a)	$y = 5(2)^x$			
b)	$y = 6\left(\dfrac{1}{3}\right)^x$			
c)	$y = 5(6)^x$			
d)	$y = 25\left(\dfrac{1}{7}\right)^x$			
e)	$y = 20(1.8)^x$			
f)	$y = (0.4)^x$			

MULTIPLE CHOICE

7. Which graph represents the function $y = 7(2.5)^x$?

A. 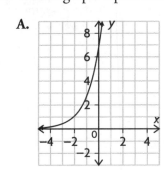 B. 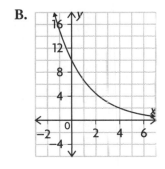 C. 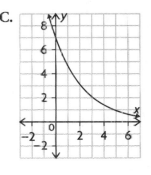 D.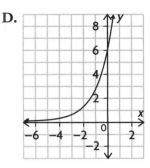

WRITTEN RESPONSE

8. Predict whether each function is increasing or decreasing, without graphing it. Explain how you know. Verify your predictions by graphing the functions.

a) $y = 4(3)^x$

b) $y = 10\left(\dfrac{2}{3}\right)^x$

6.3 Solving Exponential Equations

YOU WILL NEED

• graphing calculator

Keep in Mind

▸ Two exponential expressions with the same base are equal if their exponents are equal. For example, if $a^m = a^n$, then $m = n$, where $a > 0$, $a \neq 1$, and $m, n \in R$.

▸ You can solve an exponential equation algebraically or graphically.

▸ You can estimate the solution to an exponential equation by graphing or determine an exact solution algebraically, where possible.

Example 1

Estimate a solution to the following equation by graphing:

$$6^{x+3} = \sqrt{1296}$$

Then determine an exact solution algebraically.

Solution

Step 1. I entered the equation as a system of equations on a graphing calculator.

According to the calculator, the x-coordinate of the point of intersection is -1, so an estimated solution is -1.

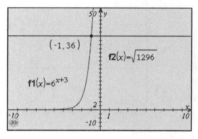

Step 2. I expressed the right side of the equation with the same base as the left side.

$$6^{x+3} = \sqrt{1296}$$
$$6^{x+3} = \sqrt{6^4}$$
$$6^{x+3} = (6^4)^{\frac{1}{2}}$$
$$6^{x+3} = 6^2$$

TIP

Begin by writing the equation in the form $a^m = a^n$ if possible.

Step 3. I solved for x. Since the bases are equal, the exponents must also be equal.

$$x + 3 = 2$$
$$x = -1$$

Step 4. I verified my answer by substitution.

LS	RS
6^{x+3}	$\sqrt{1296}$
$6^{(-1+3)}$	36
6^2	
36	
	LS = RS

The solution is $x = -1$.

Example 2

Radioactive elements decay into other elements in a predictable way over time. Suppose the percent of a radioactive element, $A(t)$, left in a sample is modelled by the half-life function

$$A(t) = A_0\left(\frac{1}{2}\right)^{\frac{t}{20}}$$

where t represents the time, in years, after the initial time, and A_0 represents the initial amount, 100% of the sample. Determine

a) when a sample of this element will decay to half its initial amount

b) what percent of the sample will remain after 5 years

c) when 20% of this sample will remain

Solution

a) **Step 1.** I entered the values in the equation and solved for t.

$$50 = 100\left(\frac{1}{2}\right)^{\frac{t}{20}}$$

$$\frac{50}{100} = \left(\frac{1}{2}\right)^{\frac{t}{20}}$$

$$\frac{1}{2} = \left(\frac{1}{2}\right)^{\frac{t}{20}}$$

$$\left(\frac{1}{2}\right)^1 = \left(\frac{1}{2}\right)^{\frac{t}{20}}$$

$$1 = \frac{t}{20}$$

$$20 = t$$

In 20 years, 50% of the sample will remain.

b) **Step 2.** I entered the values in the equation and solved for $A(t)$.

$$A(t) = 100\left(\frac{1}{2}\right)^{\frac{5}{20}}$$

$$A(t) = 100\left(\frac{1}{2}\right)^{0.25}$$

$$A(t) = 100(0.840...)$$

$$A(t) = 84.089...\%$$

About 84% of the sample will remain after 5 years.

c) **Step 3.** I could have solved for this the same way as in part a), but I decided to plot a system of equations on a graphing calculator instead.

According to the calculator, the point of intersection occurs when $x = 46.438...$, so the sample will decay to 20% of its original amount in 46.4 years.

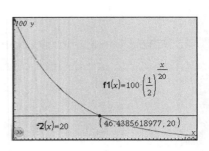

Practice

1. For each exponential function shown, estimate the x-values at $y = 4$ and $y = 10$. Round the values to two decimal places.

   a)
   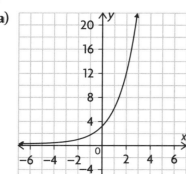

   b)
   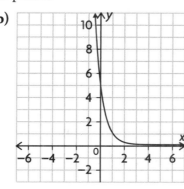

2. Solve each equation by expressing both sides with the same base. Verify your answer by substitution.

   a) $6^x = 36$ substitute:

   b) $5^{x+1} = \sqrt{125}$ substitute:

3. Solve each equation by expressing both sides as powers with the same base. Verify each solution.

   a) $4^{-x} = 64$ substitute:

   c) $2^{x+3} = 64$ substitute:

   b) $5^n = \dfrac{1}{625}$ substitute:

   d) $2^{2x} = \dfrac{1}{128}$ substitute:

4. Solve each exponential equation using graphing technology. Round your answer to one decimal place.

   a) $7^{2x} = \left(\dfrac{1}{7}\right)^{x+2}$

   b) $8^{1-x} = 4^{x+2}$

5. Bellamy is working with two exponential equations.

- The first is an increasing function: $y = 5^x$

- The second is a decreasing function: $y = \left(\dfrac{1}{3}\right)^{x-2}$

What are the coordinates of the point that is common to both functions? Round your answer to the nearest tenth.

NUMERICAL RESPONSE

6. The element cesium-137 is radioactive. Radioactive elements decay into other elements in a predictable way over time. The percent of cesium-137, $A(t)$, left in a sample can be modelled by the half-life function

$$A(t) = A_0\left(\frac{1}{2}\right)^{\frac{t}{30}}$$

where t represents the time, in years, after the initial time, and A_0 represents the initial amount, 100% of the cesium.

a) A sample of cesium-137 will decay to half its initial amount in ___ years.

b) After 10 years, _____% of a sample of cesium-137 will remain. Round your answer to one decimal place.

c) A sample of cesium-137 will decay to 10% of its original amount in _____ years, rounded to one decimal place.

WRITTEN RESPONSE

7. The population of a specific type of bacteria growing in a Petri dish is modelled by the function $P(t) = 700(5)^{\frac{t}{6}}$, where $P(t)$ represents the number of bacteria and t represents the time, in hours, after the initial count.

a) Determine the value of t when $P(t) = 87\,500$ by rewriting both sides of the equation with the same base. Verify your solution.

b) What does your answer from part a) mean in this context? Explain.

8. A car was bought for $36 000 in January 2012. The book value, $V(t)$, in dollars, of the vehicle can be modelled by the exponential function

$$V(t) = 36\,000(0.90)^t$$

where t represent the time, in years, since the purchase date.

a) What will the vehicle be worth 5 years after the purchase date? Round to the nearest dollar.

b) How long after the purchase date will the vehicle be worth $18 000? Explain what you did.

c) Is it possible to determine the year that your answer from part b) corresponds to? Explain.

6.4 Modelling Data Using Exponential Functions

YOU WILL NEED
- graphing technology

Keep in Mind

▸ An exponential function of the form $f(x) = a(b)^x$, with $a > 0$, $b > 0$, and $b \neq 1$, models growth when $b > 1$.
The y-values increase from left to right along the x-axis.

▸ An exponential function models decay when $a > 0$ and $0 < b < 1$.
The y-values decrease from left to right along the x-axis.

▸ The exponential regression model is $f(x) = a(b)^x$, where a represents the initial value in the model, and b represents the growth factor if $b > 1$ or the decay factor if $0 < b < 1$.

▸ To predict values, you can read them from the curve of best fit on a scatter plot or use the equation of the exponential regression function.

Example

The population of Manitoba is given for the years from 1951 to 2011.

Year	1951	1961	1971	1981	1991	2001	2011
Population (1000s)	776.5	921.7	988.9	1035.5	1109.6	1151.4	1250.6

a) Construct a scatter plot to display the data.

b) Use exponential regression to define a function that models the data.

c) Assume the same growth rate as in part b). Estimate the population in 2020, to the nearest ten thousand. Explain.

d) Assume the same growth rate as in part b). Estimate when the population will reach 1 500 000. Explain.

Solution

a) **Step 1.** I entered the data and created the scatter plot.

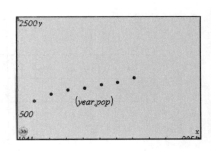

Copyright © 2012 by Nelson Education Ltd.

b) **Step 2.** I used exponential regression to determine a function that models the data.

The regression function is $f(x) = 0.008\ldots(1.007\ldots)^x$.

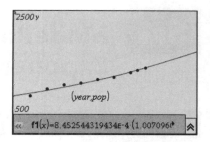

c) **Step 3.** I used the graph to determine the y-coordinate when the x-coordinate is 2020.

The population will be about 1 350 000 in 2020.

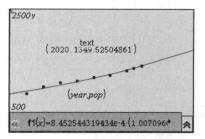

d) **Step 4.** I entered the equation $f(x) = 1500$ and located the intersection point with the regression function.

I needed to change the window settings to see the intersection point.
The population will be 1 500 000 in 2035.

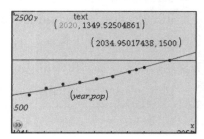

Practice

1. Determine whether each data set involves exponential growth, exponential decay, or neither. Explain how you know. Then, for each data set that does involve exponential growth or decay:

- Graph the data set.
- Determine the equation of the exponential regression function.
- Graph the regression function on the same screen as the data set.

a)

x	0	1	2	3	4	5
y	2.0000	5.0000	12.5000	31.2500	78.1250	195.3125

b)

x	0	1	2	3	4	5
y	0.0	2.1	4.2	6.3	8.4	10.5

c)

x	0	1	2	3	4	5
y	7047	2349	783	261	87	29

2. The population of Alberta is given for the years from 2007 to 2011.

Year	2007	2008	2009	2010	2011
Population (1000s)	3512.7	3591.8	3671.7	3720.9	3779.4

a) Construct a scatter plot to display the data.

b) Use exponential regression to define a function that models the data.

c) Assume the same growth rate as in part b). Estimate the population of Alberta in 2020, to the nearest ten thousand.

d) Assume the same growth rate as in part b). Estimate when the population will reach 4 200 000.

3. The consumer price index (CPI) is an index of how prices change over time. Consider the Canadian CPI data shown here.

Year	1990	1994	1996	2000	2004	2007
CPI	78.3	85.7	88.9	95.4	104.7	111.4

a) Use regression to determine an exponential equation that models the data.

b) Use your equation to estimate the CPI in 1998.

c) How close was your estimate to the actual value of 91.3?

NUMERICAL RESPONSE

4. The number of Internet hosts in Canada is given for certain years.

a) An exponential regression equation that models the number of Internet hosts is $f(x) = $ _____.

b) In the year 2007, there would have been about _____ Internet hosts in Canada, to the nearest thousand.

c) Assuming the trend continues, the number of hosts should reach 10 000 000 near the end of the year _____.

Year	Number of Internet Hosts (1000s)
2003	3210
2005	3525
2006	3934
2008	5119
2010	7770

5. Jamia has determined that a proposed well site in Alberta would produce 100 barrels of oil per week for 5 years. At that point, production would begin to drop, according to the function $P(t) = 100\left(\dfrac{5}{6}\right)^{\frac{t}{12}}$, where P represents the weekly amount of oil produced in barrels and t represents the number of weeks after production begins to drop.

a) Determine the expected production of this well, to the nearest barrel per week, 24 weeks after production begins to drop. Show your work.

b) The well will require mechanical assistance to bring up the oil once production drops to 30 barrels a week. During which week will production reach this level?

c) Jamia reports that the well will no longer be profitable once production drops to 5 barrels per week. During which week should the company cap the well?

YOU WILL NEED
- graphing calculator or spreadsheet

Keep in Mind

▶ Compound interest is charged on most loans and paid on some investments. To calculate compound interest, add any accumulated interest to the amount invested or borrowed (the principal) and multiply the result by the interest rate.

▶ To model compound interest, use $A(n) = P(1 + i)^n$, where

- A represents the value of the investment/loan at a given time (the future value)
- P represents the principal
- i represents the interest rate per compounding period, as a decimal
- n represents the number of compounding periods

▶ To determine the interest rate per compounding period, divide the annual rate by the number of times interest is paid.

Compounding Period	Number of Times Interest Is Paid	Interest Rate per Compounding Period, i	For Example: 4.8%/Year
daily	365 times per year	$i = \dfrac{\text{annual rate}}{365}$	$\dfrac{0.048}{365} = 0.00013\ldots$
weekly	52 times per year	$i = \dfrac{\text{annual rate}}{52}$	$\dfrac{0.048}{52} = 0.00092\ldots$
bi-weekly	24 times per year	$i = \dfrac{\text{annual rate}}{24}$	$\dfrac{0.048}{24} = 0.002$
monthly	12 times per year	$i = \dfrac{\text{annual rate}}{12}$	$\dfrac{0.048}{12} = 0.004$
quarterly	4 times per year	$i = \dfrac{\text{annual rate}}{4}$	$\dfrac{0.048}{4} = 0.012$
semi-annually	2 times per year	$i = \dfrac{\text{annual rate}}{2}$	$\dfrac{0.048}{2} = 0.024$
annually	1 time per year	$i = \dfrac{\text{annual rate}}{1}$	$\dfrac{0.048}{1} = 0.048$

Example

Sheldon invested \$3500 in an account that pays 4.8% interest, compounded monthly. This table gives the value of his investment at the end of the first 5 months.

a) Use exponential regression to determine the compound interest function that models this situation.

b) How long, in months, will it take Sheldon's investment to grow to \$3800?

Time (months)	Value of Investment ($)
0	3500.00
1	3514.00
2	3528.056
3	3542.168224
4	3556.3368969
5	3570.56224448

Solution

Step 1. I plotted the scatter plot of time versus value. Then I used exponential regression to determine the function.

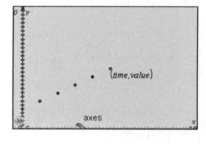

Step 2. I performed the exponential regression.

    a) The compound interest formula is $A = 3500(1.004)^n$.

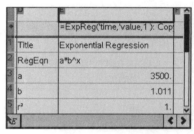

Step 3. I determined when the investment would grow to \$3800.

The point of intersection for the graphs

$$f(x) = 3500(1.004)^x \text{ and } f(x) = 3800$$

is (20.600..., 3800).

    b) Sheldon's investment will grow to \$3800 after 20.6 months; that is, in the 21st month.

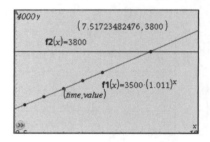

Practice

1. Francis invested money in two different accounts that pay interest compounded annually. His investments can be modelled by the following growth functions, where x represents the number of years:

   I. $y = 2000(1.06)^x$ **II.** $y = 3500(1.025)^x$

   a) What principal did Francis invest in each account?

   b) State the annual interest rate for each investment.

   c) Determine the value of each investment at the end of 5 years.

   d) How long, in years, did it take for each account to contain $4000?

> **TIP**
> When stating the interest rate, also state the compounding period.

2. Feather invested $4000 in a bank account that pays compound interest annually. Her bank gave her yearly figures for her investment over the next few years, as shown in the table.

Time (years)	0	1	2	3	4
Value of Investment ($)	4000	4023.33	4046.80	4070.41	4094.15

   a) Use these values to create an exponential regression function that models the investment.

   b) What is the future value of the investment after 5 years?

3. The price of a particular style of sweater is shown over the course of several years. Use exponential regression to estimate the price of the sweater in Year 5.

Time (years)	0	1	2	3	4	6
Cost of Sweater ($)	65.00	68.25	70.50	73.75	76.25	80.00

4. Barnabas has just graduated from college. The interest-free period of his student loan has come to an end. Barnabas must now pay $400 per month at an interest rate of 4.8%, compounded monthly.

a) The bank manager gave Barnabas this equation to determine how long it would take to pay off his loan.

$$(1.004)^{-n} = 0.75$$

Determine the number of months Barnabas will take to pay off the loan.

b) What is the total amount that Barnabas will end up paying the bank? Explain.

5. Emily took out a loan to buy an oven. She does not have to make any payments until the 5th year. The table shows how much she will owe at the end of each of the next 4 years.

End of Year	1	2	3	4
Amount Owed ($)	3075.00	3151.88	3230.67	3311.44

a) Use exponential regression to determine the annual rate of interest that Emily is paying on her loan.

b) Determine the sale price of the oven. How do you know?

c) How much will Emily owe for the oven at the end of the 5th year?

6. Kevin purchased an antique Roman coin for $32 in 2006. He has been tracking the value of the coin every year since he bought it.

Years since Purchase, t	0	1	2	3	4	5
Value ($), $A(t)$	32.00	38.56	48.00	53.76	67.25	80.64

a) Which regression equation best models the value of the coin over time?

   A. $A(t) = 9.5t + 29.4$ C. $A(t) = 0.9t^2 + 5t + 32.4$

   B. $A(t) = 32(1.2)^t$ D. $A(t) = 1.2(32)^t$

b) Assume the same growth rate as in part a). What will the coin most likely be worth 10 years after it was purchased?

   A. $120   B. $150   C. $200   D. $320

WRITTEN RESPONSE

7. Arkita recently opened a restaurant. Her accountant told her that, for tax purposes, the depreciation rate of her restaurant equipment will be 15%, starting after the 2nd year.

a) At the end of Year 2, the value of the equipment is $40 000. Determine its value over the next 6 years. Explain your method.

Time (end of year)	2	3	4	5	6	7
Value of Equipment ($)	40 000					

b) Use your values from part a) to create a scatter plot; then perform an exponential regression to determine a function that models this situation.

c) How much will Arkita's equipment be worth 10 years after the purchase date? Explain.

Complete the following to summarize the important ideas from this chapter.

Q: What are the characteristics of an exponential function?

NEED HELP?
• See Lesson 6.1

A: An exponential function of the form $f(x) =$ _____, where $a >$ ___, ___ > 0,

and $b \neq$ ___,

• has ___ x-intercept(s) and ___ y-intercept(s)

• extends from Quadrant ___ to Quadrant ___

• has domain _____ and range _____

Q: For the exponential function $y = a(b)^x$, what is the significance of the values of a and b?

NEED HELP?
• See Lesson 6.2

A: • The value of a is the _____ of the _____ of the function.

• The value of ___ in the exponential function determines whether the

function increases or _____. The function increases when b _____.

The function _____ when _____.

Q: How can you solve an exponential equation?

NEED HELP?
• See Lesson 6.3

A1: _____: Write both _____ of the equation as _____ of the same

base (if possible). If $a^m = a^n$ with $a > 0$, a _____, and $m, n \in$ R, then _____.

A2: _____: Enter the equation as a system of equations on a

_____, and then determine the point(s) of

_____. The ___-coordinate of this point is the _____

of the equation.

Q: How can you use an exponential function as a model for data?

NEED HELP?
• See Lesson 6.4

A: • If a _____ plot of the data appears to follow an _____ curve,

you can use exponential _____ to determine the _____
function that models the data.

• You can make predictions by reading values from the curve of

_____ or by using the equation of the _____ regression
function.

6 Chapter Test

1. Which graph represents an increasing exponential function?

A.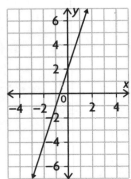

B.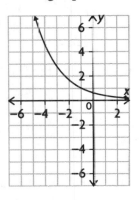

C.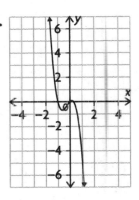

D.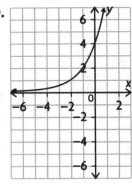

2. Which graph represents the function $y = 6(3.5)^x$?

A.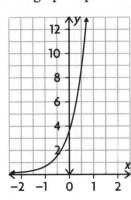

B.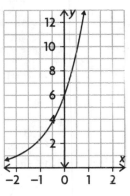

C.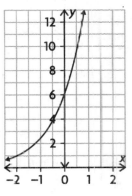

D.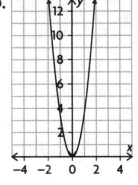

3. Which graph shows the solution to the equation $5^{2x+1} = \left(\dfrac{1}{5}\right)^{x+2}$?

A.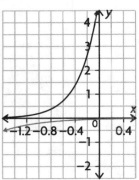

B.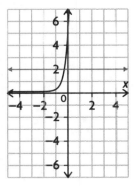

C.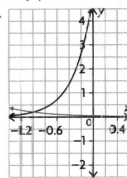

D.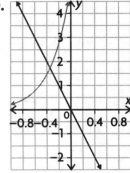

4. A biologist has been studying the effects of acid rain on the population of fish in a lake. The observations are shown in the table.

Time (years), *x*	0	1	2	3	4	5
Fish Population (estimated), *f(x)*	2700	2300	1950	1660	1400	1200

a) By what percent is the fish population declining every year?

   A. 100%   **B.** 15%   **C.** 400%   **D.** 10%

b) Which exponential regression function models the decline in the fish population?

   A. $f(x) = 2700(1.15)^x$ **C.** $f(x) = 2700(0.15)^x$

   B. $f(x) = 2700(0.85)^x$ **D.** $f(x) = 1200(3.2)^x$

5. Arlene bought a rare stamp for $47 in 2006. She has been tracking the value of the stamp every year since she bought it.

Years since Purchase, *t*	0	1	2	3	4	5
Stamp Value ($), *A(t)*	47.00	61.57	79.43	106.43	138.36	179.87

a) Which regression equation best models the value of the stamp over time?

   A. $A(t) = 47t + 2$ **C.** $A(t) = 47(1.3)^t$

   B. $A(t) = 2.1t + 47$ **D.** $A(t) = 1.3(47)^t$

b) Assume the same growth rate as in part a). What will the stamp be worth 10 years after it was purchased?

   A. $120   **B.** $210   **C.** $470   **D.** $695

NUMERICAL RESPONSE

6. Examine the graph of the exponential function.

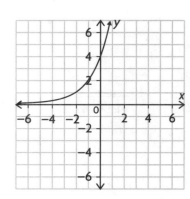

a) There are ____ *x*-intercepts.

b) The *y*-intercept is ____.

c) The graph extends from Quadrant ____ to Quadrant ____.

d) The domain is _____.

e) The range is _____.

7. Complete the table to predict the characteristics of each exponential function.

	Function	y-intercept	Base	Increasing or Decreasing
a)	$y = 7(3)^x$			
b)	$y = 4\left(\dfrac{1}{3}\right)^x$			
c)	$y = 6(2)^x$			

8. The element strontium-90 is radioactive. The percent of strontium-90, $A(t)$, left in a sample can be modelled by the half-life function

$$A(t) = A_0\left(\frac{1}{2}\right)^{\frac{t}{29}}$$

where t represents the time, in years, after the initial time, and A_0 represents the initial amount, 100% of the strontium.

a) A sample of strontium-90 will decay to half its initial amount in ___ years.

b) After 20 years, _____% of a sample of strontium-90 will remain. Round your answer to one decimal place.

c) A sample of strontium-90 will decay to 20% of its original amount in _____ years, rounded to one decimal place.

9. The height of a sunflower was recorded every 7 days as it grew.

Day Number, d	7	14	21	28	35	42
Height (cm), f(d)	14.3	16.4	18.8	21.8	25.1	28.9

a) An exponential regression equation that models the growth of the sunflower is $f(d) =$ _____.

b) On Day 12, the height of the sunflower will be about _____ cm, rounded to the nearest tenth of a centimetre.

10. Canada's exports, in billions of dollars, are shown from 2002 to 2008.

Year, t	2002	2003	2004	2005	2007	2008
Exports (billions of dollars), E(t)	261	261	279	316	405	459

a) An exponential regression equation for Canada's exports over this period is _____.

b) An estimated value for Canada's exports in 2006 is $___ billion. This value is $___ billion less than the actual value of $365 billion.

c) An estimated value for Canada's exports in 2009 is $___ billion. This value is $___ billion more than the actual value of $323 billion.

11. Does either graph represent an exponential function? Explain how you know.

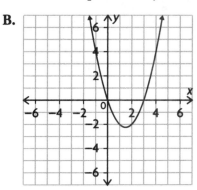

A.

B.

12. Predict whether each function is increasing or decreasing, without graphing it. Explain how you know. Verify your predictions by graphing the functions.

a) $y = 6(2)^x$ **b)** $y = 5(0.9)^x$

13. The Place for Stuff is having a sale. The price of all stock will be reduced by 15% at the start of each week until all the stock is sold. The exponential function that models the price of a sofa from the start of the sale is $C(t) = 2000(0.85)^t$, where $C(t)$ represents the cost of the sofa at the end of the week and t represents the time in weeks since the sale began.

a) After which week did the sofa cost less than half its initial price? Explain.

b) Dimitri bought the sofa for $1288.25. In which week did Dimitri buy the sofa?

14. The population of British Columbia is given from 2007 to 2011.

Year	2007	2008	2009	2010	2011
Population (1000s)	4309.6	4384.0	4459.9	4529.7	4573.3

a) Construct a scatter plot to display the data.

b) Use exponential regression to define a function that models the data.

c) Assuming the same growth rate as in part b), estimate the population of British Columbia in 2020. Describe your process.

d) Assuming the same growth rate as in part b), when would you expect the population to reach 4 700 000? Describe your process.

15. Carla invested $12 000 in a guaranteed investment certificate that pays 4% interest, compounded annually, over the next 5 years.

Years since Investment	0	1	2	3	4	5
Value of Investment ($)	12 000	12 480	12 979	13 498	14 038	14 600

a) Use exponential regression to determine the equation of a function that models the growth of Carla's investment over x years.

b) Determine the value of Carla's investment after 8 years, assuming that the interest rate remains the same over the entire time.

Chapter 7

Logarithmic Functions

Getting Started

1. Match each term with the example that best illustrates it.

   a) increasing function ___   **i)** $y = -6$ and $x = 2$ for $y = 3x - 6$

   b) exponential function ___   **ii)** $y = 3(x - 2)^2 + 5$, when $x > 2$

   c) discrete data ___   **iii)**   the number of cars passing an intersection in 1 min

   d) range ___   **iv)** $y = 5(0.2)^x$

   e) intercepts ___   **v)** $\{y \mid y \geq -7.5, y \in \text{R}\}$ for $y = 0.5x^2 - 7.5$

2. State the domain of each function, given the context.

   a) the volume of a spherical balloon, V, being inflated over time, t
   $$V = 5.5t^3$$

   b) the value of an investment, A, earning compound interest over n compounding periods
   $$A = 5000(1.005)^n$$

3. Determine the range of each function in question 2, given the context.

   a)   b)

4. Use an algebraic method to determine the x-intercept(s) and y-intercept of each function.

   a) $y = 4x + 9$ b) $y = 3x^3 - 24$ c) $y = -x(x - 2)$

5. Verify your answers to question 4, using graphing technology.

6. State the domain and range of each function.

a) $y = 3(2)^x$

domain: _____

range: _____

b) $y = \dfrac{1}{3}\left(\dfrac{1}{2}\right)^x$

domain: _____

range: _____

7. State whether each function in question 6 is increasing or decreasing or both. If necessary, state where the function is increasing and where it is decreasing.

a)

b)

TIP

You can use graphing technology to help you determine where a function is increasing or decreasing.

8. Solve each exponential equation by an algebraic method. Verify your answers using graphing technology.

a) $81 = 3^x$

c) $3^{x-1} = (\sqrt{27})^{2x}$

b) $9^x = \dfrac{1}{27}$

d) $8^{3-x} = 2^{2x-1}$

9. The element carbon-14 is radioactive. Radioactive elements decay into other elements in a predictable way over time. The amount, $A(t)$, of carbon-14 left in a sample can be modelled by the half-life function

$$A(t) = A_0\left(\frac{1}{2}\right)^{\frac{t}{5730}}$$

where t represents the time, in years, after the initial time, and A_0 represents the initial amount of carbon-14.

a) A sample of carbon-14 will decay to half its initial amount in _____ years.

b) After 7000 years, _____% of a sample of carbon-14 will remain, to the nearest tenth of a percent.

c) A sample of carbon-14 will decay to 15% of its original amount in _____ years, to the nearest 100 years.

7.1 Characteristics of Logarithmic Functions with Base 10 and Base e

YOU WILL NEED
• graphing technology

Keep in Mind

▶ A logarithmic function has the form $f(x) = a \log_b x$, where $a \neq 0$, $b > 0$, and $b \neq 1$.

▶ All logarithmic functions of the form $f(x) = a \log x$ and $f(x) = a \ln x$ have these characteristics:

- *x*-intercept: 1

- number of *y*-intercepts: 0

- end behaviour: The curve extends from Quadrant IV to Quadrant I or from Quadrant I to Quadrant IV.

- domain: $\{x \mid x > 0, x \in \mathbb{R}\}$; range: $\{y \mid y \in \mathbb{R}\}$

▶ A logarithmic function of the form $f(x) = a \log x$ or $f(x) = a \ln x$ is increasing if $a > 0$ and decreasing if $a < 0$.

Case I: An increasing logarithmic function, $a > 0$

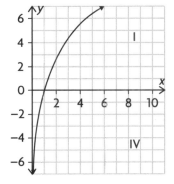

Case II: A decreasing logarithmic function, $a < 0$

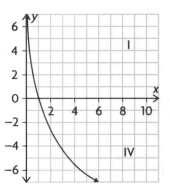

Example

Predict the *x*-intercept, the number of *y*-intercepts, the end behaviour, the domain, and the range of the function

$$y = 14 \log x$$

Use the equation to make your prediction. Verify your prediction using graphing technology.

> **TIP**
>
> $a \log_{10} x$ is usually written $a \log x$.
>
> $a \log_e x$ is usually written $a \ln x$.

Solution

Step 1. I recognized this as a logarithmic function of the form $y = a \log_b x$.

$$y = 14 \log x$$

$a = 14$. Since b is not written, $b = 10$.

Step 2. I used this information to predict the characteristics.

x-intercept: 1; number of *y*-intercepts: 0; domain: $\{x \mid x > 0, x \in \mathbb{R}\}$; range: $\{y \mid y \in \mathbb{R}\}$

Step 3. I considered the function's end behaviour.

Since $a = 14$, $a > 0$ and the function is increasing. Therefore, it extends from Quadrant IV to Quadrant I.

Step 4. I graphed the function to verify my predictions.

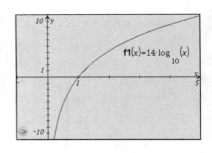

Practice

1. Describe the characteristics of each logarithmic graph.

a)

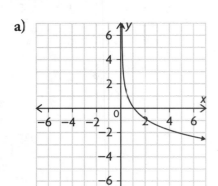

b)

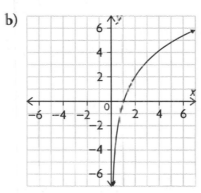

	x-intercept	Number of y-intercepts	End Behaviour	Domain	Range
a)			from Quadrant ___ to Quadrant ___		
b)			from Quadrant ___ to Quadrant ___		

2. Complete the table to predict the characteristics of each function. Verify your predictions using graphing technology.

	Function	x-intercept	Number of y-intercepts	End Behaviour	Domain	Range	Increasing or Decreasing
a)	$y = -4 \log x$			from Quadrant ___ to Quadrant ___			
b)	$y = 13 \ln x$			from Quadrant ___ to Quadrant ___			
c)	$y = 20 \log x$			from Quadrant ___ to Quadrant ___			
d)	$y = -10 \ln x$			from Quadrant ___ to Quadrant ___			

3. Match each function with its corresponding graph. Explain.

   i) $y = 3.6 \log x$ **ii)** $y = -2 \log x$ **iii)** $y = 5^x$

a)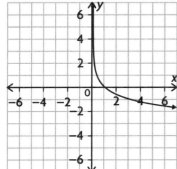

b)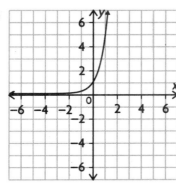

c)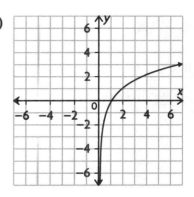

4. Decide whether each graph represents a logarithmic function or not. Give five reasons for your answer in each case.

a)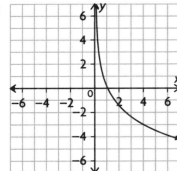

b)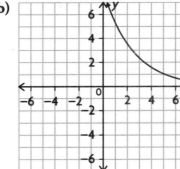

MULTIPLE CHOICE

5. Which graph corresponds to the following equation?

$$y = 23 \log x$$

A.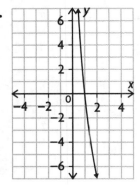

B.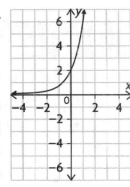

C.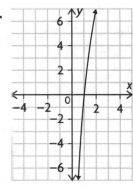

6. Which equation corresponds to this graph?

A. $y = -10 \log x$ **C.** $y = 10 \log x$

B. $y = 10(2)^x$ **D.** $y = 10^x$

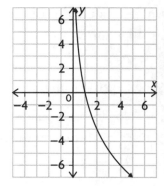

WRITTEN RESPONSE

7. Strontium-90 decays naturally over time. The approximate time for strontium-90 to decay is given by the function

$$t = -96.336 \log \left(\frac{P}{100} \right)$$

where t represents the time in years and P represents the percent of strontium-90 that remains.

a) Describe the intercepts, the domain and range, whether the function is increasing or decreasing, and the value at $P = 100$. What does the P-intercept represent in this case?

b) A sample of strontium-90 is taken from a reactor. Estimate the time after which 50% of it will remain. Explain what you did.

7.2 Evaluating Logarithmic Expressions

YOU WILL NEED
• graphing technology

Keep in Mind

▸ The logarithmic function $y = \log_b x$ is equivalent to the exponential function $x = b^y$.

▸ A logarithm is an exponent. The expression $\log_b x$ means "the exponent that must be applied to base b to give the value of x."

▸ The common logarithmic function, $y = \log x$, is equivalent to the exponential function $x = 10^y$.

▸ The natural logarithmic function, $y = \ln x$, is equivalent to the exponential function $x = e^y$.

▸ The logarithm of a negative number does not exist, because you cannot write a negative number as a power with a positive base.

▸ A logarithmic scale can be used to compare values that differ greatly, such as the magnitude of earthquakes, the acidity of solutions, and the loudness of sound.

Example 1

Evaluate the logarithmic expression

$$\log_2 32$$

Solution

Step 1. I set the logarithmic expression equal to y.

$$\log_2 32 = y$$

Step 2. I rewrote the equation in exponential form.

$$2^y = 32$$

Step 3. I rewrote the equation as powers with the same base.

$$2^y = 2^5$$

Step 4. I knew that since the bases were equal, the exponents were also equal.

$$y = 5$$

$$\log_2 32 = 5$$

TIP

To evaluate a logarithmic expression:

• Set the expression equal to y, and write the equivalent exponential form.

• Determine the exponent to which the base must be raised to get the required number.

• You can use special function keys on a scientific or graphing calculator when the base of the logarithm is 10 or e.

Example 2

Solve the following exponential equation:

$$10^x = 16\ 384$$

Solution

Step 1. I wrote the equation in logarithmic form.

$$y = \log_{10} 16\ 384$$

Step 2. I used my calculator to evaluate.

The solution is $x = 4.214...$, so $10^{4.214...} = 16\ 384$.

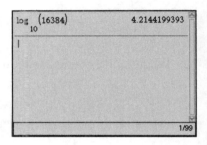

Example 3

The logarithmic pH scale is defined by the equation $p(x) = -\log x$, where the concentration of hydrogen atoms in a solution, x, is measured in moles per litre (mol/L). Use this equation and the pH scale to determine how many times as acidic lemon juice is as soft drinking water.

| | Acidity increases in this direction → | | | | | | | |
Solution	distilled water	saliva	soft drinking water	tomato juice	grapefruit juice	lemon juice	acid in stomach lining	car battery acid
pH Level	7	6	5	4	3	2	1	0

Solution

Step 1. I determined the equation for each solution.

for lemon juice:

$$p(x) = -\log x_{\text{lemon juice}}$$
$$2 = -\log x_{\text{lemon juice}}$$
$$-2 = \log x_{\text{lemon juice}}$$

for soft drinking water:

$$p(x) = -\log x_{\text{soft water}}$$
$$5 = -\log x_{\text{soft water}}$$
$$-5 = \log x_{\text{soft water}}$$

Step 2. I wrote each equation in exponential form.

$$x_{\text{lemon juice}} = 10^{-2} \qquad x_{\text{soft water}} = 10^{-5}$$

Step 3. I used a ratio to determine the relative acidity.

$$\frac{x_{\text{lemon juice}}}{x_{\text{soft water}}} = \frac{10^{-2}}{10^{-5}}$$

$$\frac{x_{\text{lemon juice}}}{x_{\text{soft water}}} = 10^{(-2-(-5))}, \text{ or } 10^3$$

Lemon juice is 10^3 or 1000 times as acidic as soft drinking water

Practice

1. Write each logarithmic function in exponential form.

   a) $y = \log_6 x$　　　　　　　　　**b)** $y = \log_{12} x$

2. Explain why $\log_b b = 1$.

3. Write each exponential equation in logarithmic form.

   a) $x = 3^y$　　　　　　　　　　**c)** $x = 5^y$

   b) $\dfrac{1}{16} = 4^y$　　　　　　　　**d)** $1024 = 2^y$

4. Evaluate each logarithmic expression to the nearest hundredth, using technology.

   a) $\log 15 = $ _____　　　　**c)** $\ln 15 = $ _____

   b) $\log 36 = $ _____　　　　**d)** $\ln 36 = $ _____

5. Evaluate each logarithmic expression without using technology. Show your steps.

   a) $\log_7 49$　　　　**b)** $\log_4 256$　　　　**c)** $\log_5 625$

6. Estimate the value of y in each equation. Check your estimate by writing the equation in logarithmic form and evaluating with a calculator.

   a) $300 = 10^y$　　　**b)** $12 = e^y$　　　**c)** $6 = 10^y$

7. Evaluate each logarithmic expression without using technology. Show your work.

   a) $\log_4 64$　　　**b)** $\log_3 243$　　　**c)** $\log_5\left(\dfrac{1}{625}\right)$

8. Insert ">", "<", or "=" between the expressions in each pair.

a) $\log_{\frac{1}{2}} 5$ ___ $\log_{\frac{1}{2}} 7$

b) $\log_3 5$ ___ $\log_5 3$

c) $\log_{\frac{1}{4}} 4$ ___ $\log_{\frac{1}{5}} 5$

d) $\log\left(\dfrac{1}{16}\right)$ ___ $\log 4^{-2}$

NUMERICAL RESPONSE

Refer to the pH scale in Example 3 on page 433 in your textbook to answer questions 9 and 10.

9. a) The acid used in car batteries is 10___ or _____ times as acidic as saliva.

b) The acid in stomach lining is 10___ or _____ times as acidic as grapefruit juice.

c) Tea has a pH level of 5.5. Cola has a pH level of 2.5. Cola is 10___ or _____ times as acidic as tea.

d) Coffee may have a pH level of 5.1. Cola is 10___ or about _____ times as acidic as coffee.

WRITTEN RESPONSE

10. Water from a tap has a pH of 6.6. How many times as acidic is this tap water as distilled water? Round to the nearest tenth. Show your work.

Keep in Mind

▶ The laws of logarithms are directly related to the exponent laws, since logarithms are exponents.

▶ The laws of logarithms can be used to simplify logarithmic expressions if all the terms have the same base.

▶ The laws of logarithms can be expressed as follows, where b, m, and $n > 0$ and $b \neq 1$.

• **Product Law of Logarithms:** $\log_b mn = \log_b m + \log_b n$

• **Quotient Law of Logarithms:** $\log_b\left(\dfrac{m}{n}\right) = \log_b m - \log_b n$

• **Power Law of Logarithms:** $\log_b m^n = n \log_b m$

Example 1

Simplify and then evaluate each logarithmic expression.

a) $\log_2 5 + \log_2 25.6$ **b)** $\log_6 144 - \log_6 4$ **c)** $\log_5 25^2$

Solution

Step 1. I checked the bases of each logarithmic expression.

The terms in each expression had the same base, so the expression could be simplified.

Step 2. I used the Product Law of Logarithms to simplify the expression with addition.

$$\begin{aligned}
\textbf{a)} \quad \log_2 5 + \log_2 25.6 &= \log_2 (5 \cdot 25.6) \\
&= \log_2 128 \\
&= \log_2 2^7 \\
&= 7
\end{aligned}$$

Step 3. I used the Quotient Law of Logarithms to simplify the expression with subtraction.

$$\begin{aligned}
\textbf{b)} \quad \log_6 144 - \log_6 4 &= \log_6\left(\frac{144}{4}\right) \\
&= \log_6 36 \\
&= \log_6 6^2 \\
&= 2
\end{aligned}$$

Step 4. I used the Power Law of Logarithms to simplify the expression with the exponent.

$$\begin{aligned}
\textbf{c)} \quad \log_5 25^2 &= 2 \log_5 25 \\
&= 2 \log_5 5^2 \\
&= 2 \cdot 2 \\
&= 4
\end{aligned}$$

Example 2

Write the following expression as a single logarithm, and then evaluate.

$$\log_7 112 - 2\log_7 4$$

Solution

Step 1. I checked that the bases of the logarithms were the same.

Step 2. I used the Power Law of Logarithms to rewrite the second expression.

$$\log_7 112 - 2\log_7 4 = \log_7 112 - \log_7 4^2$$
$$= \log_7 112 - \log_7 16$$

Step 3. I used the Quotient Law of Logarithms to simplify the expression.

$$= \log_7 \left(\frac{112}{16}\right)$$
$$= \log_7 7$$
$$= 1$$

Practice

1. Write each of the following as a sum of logarithms.

   a) $\log_4 (5 \cdot 6)$

   b) $\log_a (cd)$

2. Write each expression as the logarithm of a product or quotient, where possible. If it is not possible, explain why.

   a) $\log_2 5 + \log_2 4$

   b) $\log_3 5 - \log_2 5$

3. Write each of the following as a difference of logarithms, where possible. If it is not possible, explain why.

   a) $\log_4\left(\dfrac{42}{31}\right)$

   b) $\log_5\left(\dfrac{d}{c}\right)$

4. Write each expression as the logarithm of a quotient.

   a) $\log_3 14 - \log_3 13$

   b) $\log_4 25 - \log_4 4$

5. Write each expression as a single logarithm, and then evaluate.

a) $\log_6 4 + \log_6 9$

c) $\log 4 + \log 0.0025$

b) $\log_3 45 - \log_3 15$

d) $\log_2 32 - \log_2 2$

6. Write each expression as a single logarithm, and then evaluate. Round your answer to two decimal places, where necessary.

a) $\log_2 128 - \log_2 4$

c) $\ln 20 - \ln 3.5$

b) $\log 4 + 2 \log 3$

d) $\log_2 4 - \dfrac{1}{2} \log_2 4$

7. Josephine says she can write $\log_3 49$ as the sum of two logarithms because $49 = 7 \cdot 7$. Is she correct? Explain.

8. Write each logarithm as a sum and as a difference of two logarithms.

a) $\log_2 64$

d) $\log_3 49$

b) $\log_5 169$

e) $\log_4 144$

c) $\log_4 216$

f) $\log_6 2401$

9. Write each logarithm in question 8 as the product of an integer and a logarithm.

a) _____

d) _____

b) _____

e) _____

c) _____

f) _____

10. Simplify and then evaluate each logarithmic expression. Round your answer to two decimal places, where necessary.

a) $\log 50 - \log 8$

b) $\log_2 32^4$

MULTIPLE CHOICE

11. Which of the following choices has a value of 2? Choose the best response.

A. $2 \log_5 5$

B. $\log_5 5^2$

C. $\log_5 125 - \log_5 5$

D. all of the above

12. Which of the following choices has a value of 3? Choose the best response.

A. $\log_6 6^3$

B. $\log_6 6 + \log_6 6$

C. $\log_6 36 - \log_6 6$

D. none of the above

WRITTEN RESPONSE

13. Aaron said that these three expressions are equivalent.
Do you agree or disagree? Explain, without using technology.

$\log_x 14 - \log_x 1 \qquad \log_x 14 + \log_x 1 \qquad \log_x 14$

7.4 Solving Exponential Equations Using Logarithms

YOU WILL NEED
• graphing technology

Keep in Mind

▸ If two expressions are equal, then the logarithms of those expressions are also equal: if $M = N$, then $\log_{10} M = \log_{10} N$, where $M > 0$, $N > 0$.

▸ You can use one of these three methods to solve an exponential equation:

- If possible, write both sides of the equation with the same base, set the exponents equal to each other, and solve for the unknown.
- Take the logarithm of each side and solve for the unknown.
- Use graphing technology, using the systems of equations strategies you have employed for other kinds of equations.

▸ Some calculators will only calculate logarithms with base 10. Even so, you can evaluate any logarithm with base b using the change of base formula: $\qquad \log_b x = \dfrac{\log x}{\log b}$

Example 1

Solve the following exponential equation:

$$4^{x+2} = 31$$

Round to three decimal places.

Solution

Step 1. Since 31 is difficult to write as a power of 4, I took the logarithm of both sides.

$$4^{x+2} = 31$$

$$\log 4^{x+2} = \log 31$$

Step 2. I rewrote the expression on the left using the Power Law of Logarithms.

$$(x + 2) \log 4 = \log 31$$

Step 3. I isolated the expression with x.

$$\frac{(x + 2) \log 4}{\log 4} = \frac{\log 31}{\log 4}$$

$$x + 2 = \frac{\log 31}{\log 4}$$

$$x = \frac{\log 31}{\log 4} - 2$$

Step 4. I evaluated for x, using a calculator.

To three decimal places, $x = 0.477$.

Example 2

Solve the following exponential equation. Round to two decimal places.
$$5^{x+2} = 7^{x-1}$$

Solution

Step 1. Since the two sides of the equation cannot be written with the same base, took the logarithm of both sides.

$$5^{x+2} = 7^{x-1}$$
$$\log 5^{x+2} = \log 7^{x-1}$$

Step 2. I rewrote each side using the Power Law of Logarithms.

$$(x+2) \log 5 = (x-1) \log 7$$
$$x \log 5 + 2 \log 5 = x \log 7 - \log 7$$

Step 3. I isolated the expressions with x.

$$2 \log 5 + \log 7 = x \log 7 - x \log 5$$
$$2 \log 5 + \log 7 = x (\log 7 - \log 5)$$
$$\frac{2 \log 5 + \log 7}{\log 7 - \log 5} = x$$

Step 4. I evaluated for x, using a calculator.

To two decimal places, $x = 15.35$.

Practice

1. Estimate the value of x in each equation to one decimal place. Then solve the equation. Show your work. Round your answer to three decimal places.

   a) $10 = 4^x$ **b)** $4.2^x = 20$

2. Estimate the value of x in each equation to one decimal place. Then solve the equation. Show your work. Round your answer to three decimal places.

   a) $40 = 5(4^x)$ **b)** $60 = 100\left(\frac{1}{4}\right)^x$

3. Estimate the value of each logarithm, and then evaluate to three decimal places, using the change of base formula.

a) $\log_{\frac{1}{2}} 12$

b) $\log_8 2$

c) $\log_6 40$

4. Write each expression as a base 10 logarithm. Evaluate to three decimal places.

a) $\log_4 40$

c) $\log_{\frac{1}{6}} 1000$

b) $\log_2 \dfrac{3}{8}$

d) $\log_{0.2} 400$

5. Solve each equation, and round your answer to two decimal places.

a) $6^{x+1} = 22$

b) $\left(\dfrac{2}{3}\right)^{-x} = 12$

> **TIP**
> log 0 is undefined.

6. Freya has $3400 in an investment that earns 5% interest, compounded annually. Determine the number of years it will take for her balance to surpass $5000. Use the compound interest formula $A = P(1 + i)^n$, where A represents the future value, P represents the present value, i represents the interest rate per compounding period, and n represents the number of compounding periods. Show your calculations.

7. Solve each equation, and round your answer to two decimal places.

   a) $6^{x-1} = 3^{x+1}$

   b) $10^{x-2} = 7^{x-1}$

8. The healing of a wound with an initial area of 60 cm^2 can be modelled by the function $A(t) = 60(10^{-0.023t})$, where $A(t)$ represents the area of the wound, in square centimetres, after t days of healing. In how many days will 50% of the wound be healed? Show your calculations.

MULTIPLE CHOICE

9. Which is closest to the value of x in the following exponential equation?

$$5^{x-1} = 4^{x+2}$$

   A. 0.05   **B.** 2.1   **C.** 4.2   **D.** 19.6

10. Which is closest to the value of x in the following exponential equation?

$$7^{x-2} = 3^{x+2}$$

   A. 7.2   **B.** 2.7   **C.** 2.9   **D.** 1.0

NUMERICAL RESPONSE

11. Kim has invested $7000 at 7.6% interest, compounded quarterly. The investment will be worth at least $10 000 after ___ quarters, or ___ years and ___ months.

12. $5000 is invested at 3.5% interest, compounded annually. The investment will have doubled in value after ___ years.

13. Jolene currently has $3900 in credit card debt. The interest rate on her credit card is 19.5%, compounded daily. If she makes no payments against the balance, her debt will have doubled after _____ days, or about _____ years.

7.5 Modelling Data Using Logarithmic Functions

YOU WILL NEED
• graphing technology

Keep in Mind

▶ A logarithmic function may be a good model for a set of data if a scatter plot of the data forms an increasing or decreasing curve in Quadrant I and/or Quadrant IV.

▶ The general form of the logarithmic regression model is
$y = (constant) + (multiplier) \cdot \ln x$.

▶ Most graphing calculators and spreadsheets provide the equation of the logarithmic regression function in the form $y = a + b \ln x$.

▶ A logarithmic curve of best fit can be used to predict values that are not recorded or plotted. Predictions can be made by reading values from the curve of best fit on a scatter plot or by using the equation of the logarithmic regression function.

Example

The population of Canada is given in the table, in 10-year intervals.
Use logarithmic regression to interpolate to determine in which year the population surpassed 20 million people.

Population (1000s), P	34 278	31 021	28 031	24 820	21 568	18 238	13 648	11 507
Years since 1870, t	141	131	121	111	101	91	81	71
Population (1000s), P	10 377	8 788	7 207	5 371	4 833	4 325	3 689	
Years since 1870, t	61	51	41	31	21	11	1	

Solution

Step 1. I entered the data in my graphing calculator and created a scatter plot with population on the *x*-axis and years on the *y*-axis.

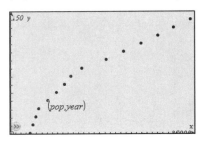

The scatter plot appeared to be logarithmic.

Copyright © 2012 by Nelson Education Ltd.

Step 2. I used my calculator to determine a logarithmic regression function to represent the data.

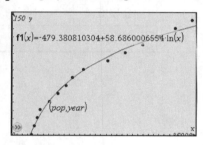

Step 3. I graphed the regression function on the same axes.

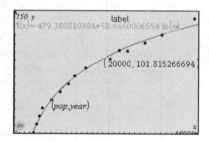

Step 4. I determined the point at which the population was 20 000 000.

The *y*-coordinate is 101.815....

According to this model, the population of Canada surpassed 20 million people 102 years after 1870, or in 1972.

Practice

1. Determine the equation of the logarithmic regression function that models the given data, and describe these characteristics of its graph:

   - the location of any intercepts
   - the end behaviour
   - the domain and range
   - whether the function is increasing or decreasing

x	y
2	16.6
4	33.1
6	42.8
8	49.7
10	55.0
12	59.4
14	63.0
16	66.2
18	69.0
20	71.6

2. a) Use the data to create a scatter plot to show how time, t, is related to the population, P, of Yukon.

b) Determine the equation of the logarithmic regression function that models the data, and describe these characteristics of the graph:

- the location of any intercepts
- the end behaviour
- the domain and range
- whether the function is increasing or decreasing

Population of Yukon	Years since 1940
35 175	71
28 674	61
27 797	51
23 140	41
18 390	31
14 628	21
9 096	11
4 914	1

c) Interpolate to determine the year in which Yukon's population exceeded 25 000.

3. a) Use the data to create a scatter plot to show how time, t, is related to the population, P, of Nunavut.

b) Determine the equation of the logarithmic regression function that models the data, and describe these characteristics of the graph:

- the location of any intercepts
- the end behaviour
- the domain and range
- whether the function is increasing or decreasing

Population of Nunavut	Years since 1996
33 330	15
32 194	13
31 272	11
30 328	9
29 320	7
28 134	5
26 820	3
25 884	1

c) Extrapolate the year in which Nunavut's population will exceed 40 000.

4. Fraser earned $6000 in his part-time job at the library. He invested it in a GIC that earns 3.5% interest, compounded annually. He would like his investment to accumulate so he can travel to Europe. The table shows Fraser's balance, to the nearest dollar, over the first 5 years.

Amount, A ($)	6000	6210	6427	6652	6885	7126
Time, t (years)	0	1	2	3	4	5

At this rate, the investment will grow to $10 000 in ___ years.

At this rate, the investment will grow to double its original amount in ___ years.

WRITTEN RESPONSE

5. Jamia earned $4000 in her job after school. She invested it in a GIC that earns 4.2% interest, compounded annually. The table shows Jamia's balance, to the nearest dollar, over the first 5 years. Use logarithmic regression to determine when the investment will grow to $6000. Explain what you did.

Amount, A ($)	4000	4168	4343	4525	4716	4914
Time, t (years)	0	1	2	3	4	5

Complete the following to summarize the important ideas from this chapter.

Q: What are the characteristics of a logarithmic function?

A: A logarithmic function of the form $f(x) =$ ___ $\log x$ or $f(x) =$ _____, where $a \neq$ ___,

- has ___ x-intercept(s) and ___ y-intercept(s)

- extends from Quadrant ___ to Quadrant ___ if a ___, or from Quadrant I to Quadrant ___ if _____

- has domain _____ and range _____

NEED HELP?
- See Lesson 7.1

Q: To which function is a logarithmic function equivalent?

A: • The logarithmic function $y = \log_b x$ is equivalent to the _____ function _____.

NEED HELP?
- See Lesson 7.2

Q: What are the laws of logarithms, and when can they be used?

A1: • Product Law of Logarithms: _____ $= \log_b m + \log_b n$

- Power Law of Logarithms: $\log_b\left(\dfrac{m}{n}\right) =$ _____

- _____ Law of Logarithms: _____

A2: The laws of logarithms can be used when all the terms have the same _____.

NEED HELP?
- See Lesson 7.3

Q: How can you solve an exponential equation?

A: • You can use one of these three methods:

- If possible, write both sides of the equation with the same _____, set the _____ equal to each other, and solve for the unknown.

- Take the _____ of each side and solve for the unknown.

- Use graphing technology, using systems of equations strategies.

• You can evaluate any logarithm with base b using the _____

formula $\log_b x = \dfrac{\boxed{}}{\boxed{}}$.

NEED HELP?
- See Lesson 7.4

Q: How can you use a curve of best fit to predict new values with a logarithmic model?

A: • Use logarithmic _____ to determine the equation of the curve of _____.

NEED HELP?
- See Lesson 7.5

MULTIPLE CHOICE

1. Which graph corresponds to the following equation?

$$y = -14 \log x$$

A.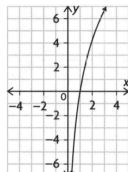

B.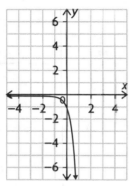

C.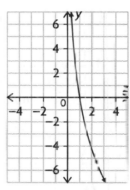

D.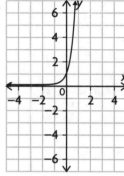

2. What is the value of $\log_6 1296$? Answer without using technology.

   A. 6   B. 4   C. 35   D. 3.89

3. Which of the following choices has a value of 4?
   Choose the best response.

   A. $\log_4 144 - \log_6 6$ C. $4 \log_5 5$

   B. $\log_4 4^2$ D. $4 \log_5 5 - 2 \log_4 2$

4. Which is closest to the value of x in the following exponential equation?

   $$3^{x+2} = 7^{x-1}$$

   A. 6.9   B. 3.9   C. 4.3   D. 5

5. $25 000 is invested at 3.8% interest, compounded annually. The table shows the value of the investment at the end of each year for 5 years.

Amount, A ($)	25 000	25 950	26 936	27 960	29 022	30 125
Time, t (years)	0	1	2	3	4	5

   After how many years will the investment double its original value?

   A. 2 years   B. 6 years   C. 18 years   D. 19 years

6. Complete the table to predict the characteristics of each function.
Verify your predictions using graphing technology.

	Function	x-intercept	Number of y-intercepts	End Behaviour	Domain	Range	Increasing or Decreasing
a)	$y = -6 \log x$			from Quadrant ___ to Quadrant ___			
b)	$y = 12 \ln x$			from Quadrant ___ to Quadrant ___			

Answer questions 7 and 8 without using technology.

7. a) $\log_8 512 =$ ___   **b)** $\log_{11} 121 =$ ___   **c)** $\log_9 729 =$ ___

8. a) $\log_3 486 - \log_3 6 =$ ___   **b)** $\log_2 160 - \log_2 5 =$ ___

9. Round each answer to one decimal place.

a) The value of x in the equation $44 = 10^x$ is _____.

b) The value of x in the equation $e^x = 25$ is _____.

10. $15\,000 is invested at 5.5% interest, compounded annually. The table shows the value of the investment at the end of each year for 5 years.

Amount, A ($)	15 000	15 825	16 695	17 614	18 582	19 604
Time, t (years)	0	1	2	3	4	5

The investment will double its original value after ___ years.

WRITTEN RESPONSE

11. The element strontium-90 decays naturally over time. The time for strontium-90 to decay is given by $t = -96.336 \log P$, where t represents the time in years and P represents the percentage of strontium-90, as a decimal, that remains. A sample of strontium-90 is taken from a reactor. Estimate the time at which 40% of it will remain. Explain what you did.

12. Write the logarithm $\log_4 121$ in each form. Explain what you did.

   a) as the sum of two logarithms

   b) as the difference of two logarithms

   c) as the product of a whole number and a logarithm

13. A telephone dial tone has a sound level of 80 dB. A motorcycle engine has a sound level of 100 dB. How many times louder is the motorcycle engine than the telephone dial? Explain.

> **TIP**
> The loudness of sound is measured in decibels (dB). The decibel scale is logarithmic, like the pH scale. A measure of 11 dB is 10 times louder than a measure of 1 dB.

14. Solve for x, to two decimal places. Show your calculations.

$$3^{x+2} = 2^{x+5}$$

15. $9000 is invested at 9.5% interest, compounded annually. The table shows the value of the investment at the end of each year for 5 years. When will the investment double its original value? Explain what you did.

Amount, A ($)	9000	9855	10 791	11 816	12 939	14 168
Time, t (years)	0	1	2	3	4	5

Getting Started

1. Match each term with the picture or example that best illustrates its meaning.

a) scatter plot ____

b) range ____

c) sine ratio ____

d) cosine ∠BCA ____

e) arc AB ____

f) central angle ____

i) $\dfrac{10}{12}$

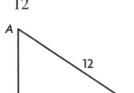

ii)

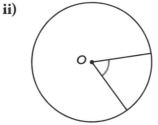

iii)

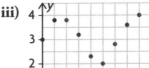

iv)

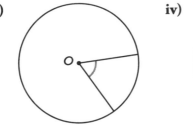

v) $\{y \mid -1 \le y \le 2, y \in \mathbb{R}\}$

vi) $\dfrac{\text{opposite}}{\text{hypotenuse}}$

2. Determine each value, to the nearest thousandth.

a) sin 78° = _____

b) sin 54° = _____

c) cos 78° = _____

d) cos 54° = _____

3. The number of bacteria in a culture was recorded over a period of 6 h. The results are given in the table.

x (h)	0	1	2	3	4	5	6
y (millions)	1.27	1.35	1.46	1.58	1.70	1.84	1.99

a) Use technology to determine the equation of the exponential regression function that models the number of bacteria, where *y* represents the number of bacteria, in millions, and *x* represents the time, in hours.

$$y = \underline{\hspace{2cm}}(\underline{\hspace{2cm}})^x$$

b) Interpolate to estimate the number of bacteria after 2.5 h.

4. Determine the range of each function.

a)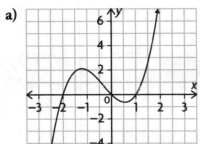

b)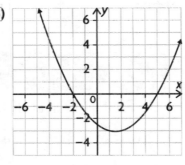

c)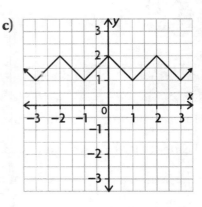

5. a) Complete the table. Round to the nearest hundredth.

x	0°	10°	25°	40°	55°	70°	85°	90°
sin x								
cos x								

b) What do you notice about the value of sin x as the value of x increases?

c) What do you notice about the value of cos x as the value of x increases?

6. Determine the length of each arc as described. Round to the nearest tenth.

a) one-half of a circle with radius 3.0 units

b) one-third of a circle with radius 6.7 units

c) 20% of a circle with radius 4.2 units

8.1 Radian Measure

YOU WILL NEED
• ruler
• protractor

Keep in Mind

▸ Radian measure is an alternative way to express the size of an angle.

▸ Using radians allows you to express the measure of an angle as a real number without units.

▸ The central angle formed by one complete revolution in a circle is 360°, or 2π in radian measure.

▸ Use benchmarks to estimate the degree measure of an angle given in radians. In radian measure,

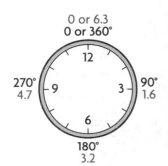

• 1 is equivalent to about 60°;

• π is equivalent to 180°; and

• 2π is equivalent to 360°.

▸ Use decimal approximations as benchmarks to visualize the approximate size of an angle measured in radians.

$$\theta = 57.3° \text{ or } 1 \text{ in radian measure}$$

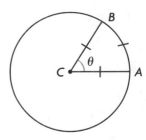

Example 1

a) Estimate the value of 120° in radian measure.

b) Estimate the value of 220° in radian measure.

Solution

a) I decided on a benchmark to use to estimate 120°.

60° is slightly more than 1 in radian measure.

120° is twice 60°, so 120° is about 2 in radian measure.

b) I decided to use a combination of benchmarks to estimate 225°.

$$225° = 180° + 45°$$

• 180° is about 3.2 in radian measure.

• 45° is one-quarter of 180°. I can estimate 45° as $\dfrac{3.2}{4}$, or 0.8.

So, 225° = 180° + 45° is about 3.2 + 0.8 = 4.0 in radian measure.

Example 2

Determine which angle is larger, 4π or 11.

Solution

I decided to use benchmarks and visualization.

2π is equivalent to 1 complete revolution, so 4π must be equivalent to 2 complete revolutions. This is like the minute hand on a clock starting at 12 and going around twice.

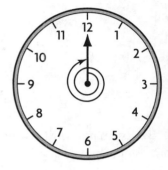

One revolution is about 6.3 in radian measure, so two revolutions s about double that, or 12.6 in radian measure.

Therefore, 4π is greater than 11.

My answer seems reasonable. π is about 3.2 in radian measure, and 4(3.2) is 12.8, which is greater than 11.

Practice

1. Sketch an angle with each degree measure, and then estimate the measure in radians.

   a) 25°   b) 235°

2. Estimate the value of each radian measure in degrees. Estimate to the nearest degree.

   a) 1.4   b) 2.8   c) 3.7   d) 6.1

3. Estimate the measure of each central angle in degrees. Check your estimate with a protractor.

   a) 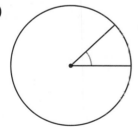   b) 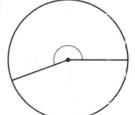   c)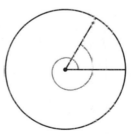

4. Sketch an angle with each given measure, and then estimate, to the nearest tenth, the equivalent measure in radians.

a) 400°   **b)** 750°

5. Estimate, to the nearest tenth, the measure of each central angle in radians. Check your estimate by measuring the angle with a protractor and then expressing the degree measure in radian measure.

a) 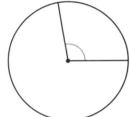   **b)** 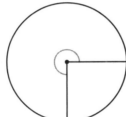   **c)**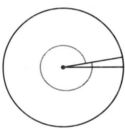

MULTIPLE CHOICE

Questions 6 and 7 refer to the following diagrams.

I. 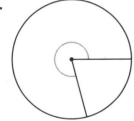   **II.** 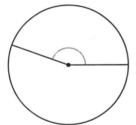   **III.** 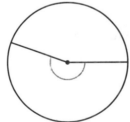   **IV.**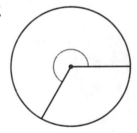

6. Which diagram shows an angle of 160°?

    A. I   **B.** II   **C.** III   **D.** IV

7. Which diagram shows an angle of 5 in radian measure?

    A. I   **B.** II   **C.** III   **D.** IV

8. Estimate, to the nearest degree, the measure of the central angle shown. Then express the value of the angle in radian measure. Explain what you did.

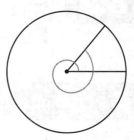

9. Patty starts at the bottom of a Ferris wheel with a radius of 10 m. The Ferris wheel rotates so Patty is now at the top. Arlene is on a merry-go-round with a radius of 5 m. The merry-go-round moves two-thirds of the way around its axle. Who travels farther? How much farther, to the nearest metre? Explain.

8.2 Exploring Graphs of Periodic Functions

YOU WILL NEED
• ruler
• graphing technology

Keep in Mind

▶ The functions $y = \sin x$ and $y = \cos x$ are periodic.

▶ The graphs of these two periodic functions have the following common characteristics:

• multiple x-intercepts

• one y-intercept

• a domain of $\{x \mid x \in R\}$

• a range of $\{y \mid -1 \leq y \leq 1, y \in R\}$

• an amplitude of 1

• a period of 360°, or 2π

• a midline defined by the equation $y = 0$. This midline is the horizontal line halfway between the maximum and minimum values. The two graphs oscillate about this line.

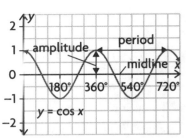

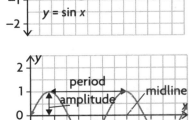

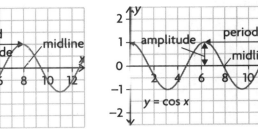

▶ The graphs of $y = \sin x$ and $y = \cos x$ are congruent curves. That is, if all the points on a cosine curve are translated to the right by 90°, or $\dfrac{\pi}{2}$, the result is a sine curve.

▶ The cycle of a graph is one complete unit in the repeating pattern of the graph.

▶ The period of a graph is the length of one cycle.

Example

Emily says that this graph is a graph of $y = \sin x$. Is she correct? Explain.

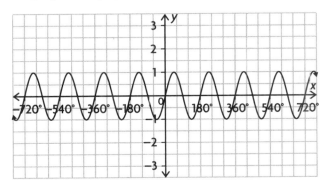

Solution

Step 1. I compared the graph's characteristics to those of $y = \sin x$.

The Graph of $y = \sin x$	Emily's Graph
• has multiple x-intercepts	Yes; the graph crosses the x-axis more than once.
• has one y-intercept	Yes; it crosses the y-axis just once.
• has a domain of $\{x \mid x \in R\}$	Yes; the graph can continue along the x-axis in either direction.
• has a range of $\{y \mid -1 \leq y \leq 1, y \in R\}$	Yes; the graph oscilates between -1 and 1.
• has an amplitude of 1	Yes; the amplitude is 1.
• has a period of 360°, or 2π	No; the period of this graph is 180°.

Step 2. I considered the results.

Emily's graph is not a graph of $y = \sin x$ because the periods are not the same.

Practice

1. Is each graph a graph of $y = \sin x$, $y = \cos x$, or neither? Briefly explain your answer.

a)

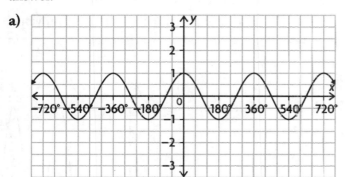

c)

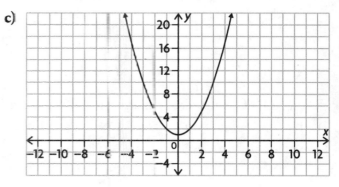

b)

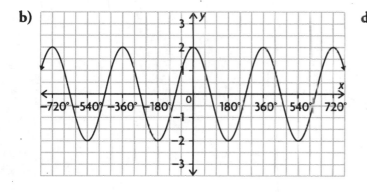

d)

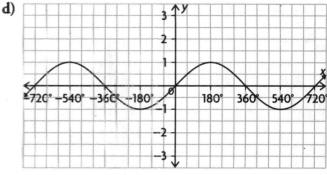

8.3 The Graphs of Sinusoidal Functions

Keep in Mind

▶ Sinusoidal functions can be used as models to solve problems that involve repeating or periodic behaviour, such as circular or oscillating motion at a constant speed.

▶ Periodic graphs with the same shape and characteristics as the graph of a sine function are called sinusoidal graphs.

▶ You can determine the characteristics of a sinusoidal function from its graph.

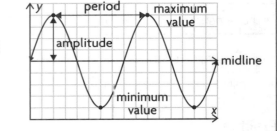

- The period is the horizontal distance between consecutive maximum values or consecutive minimum values. It is also twice the horizontal distance between a maximum value and the next minimum value.

- The equation of the midline is the average of the maximum and minimum values:
$$y = \frac{\text{maximum value} + \text{minimum value}}{2}$$

- The amplitude is the positive vertical distance between the midline and either a maximum or a minimum value. It is also half the vertical distance between a maximum value and a minimum value.

Example

The graph of a sinusoidal function is shown. Describe this graph by determining its range, the equation of its midline, its amplitude, and its period.

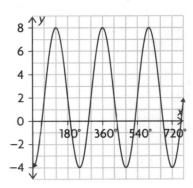

Solution

Step 1. I determined the range using the maximum and minimum values.

The minimum value is −4. The maximum value is 8.

The range of the graph is $\{y \mid -4 \le y \le 8, y \in R\}$.

Step 2. I used the same values to determine the equation of the midline.

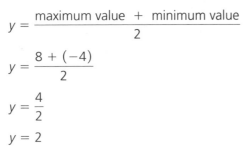

$$y = \frac{\text{maximum value} + \text{minimum value}}{2}$$

$$y = \frac{8 + (-4)}{2}$$

$$y = \frac{4}{2}$$

$$y = 2$$

Step 3. I determined the amplitude.

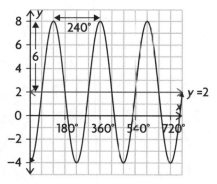

$$\text{Amplitude} = 8 - 2$$

$$\text{Amplitude} = 6$$

The amplitude is 6.

Step 4. I determined the period.

The first maximum value is at 120°. The second maximum value is at 360°.
The period is the distance, or difference, between the two values.

$$\text{Period} = 360° - 120°$$

$$\text{Period} = 240°$$

The graph goes through one complete cycle every 240°.

Step 5. To verify my solution, I considered the graph.

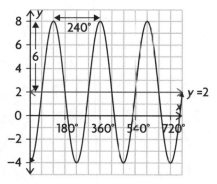

> **TIP**
>
> To determine the amplitude of a sinusoidal graph, calculate the distance from a maximum to the midline.

The values I calculated all checked out with the graph.

Practice

1. Determine the range and amplitude of each graph.

a)

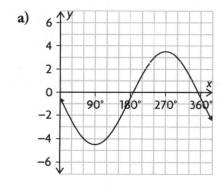

b)

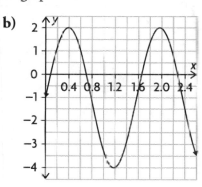

2. Determine the equation of the midline and the amplitude of each graph.

a)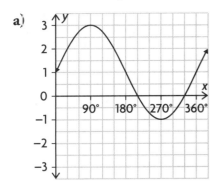

b)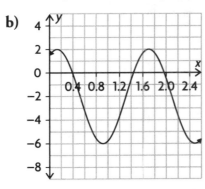

3. Determine the period of each graph. Show your calculations.

a)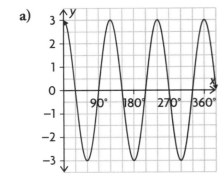

b)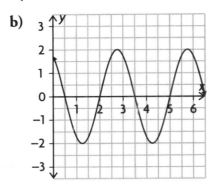

4. Determine the range, equation of the midline, amplitude, and period of each graph. Show your calculations.

a)

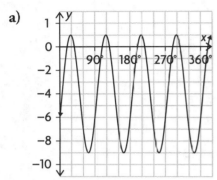

b)

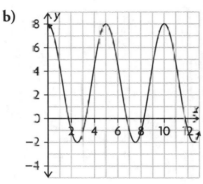

5. Determine the characteristics of this graph. Show your calculations.

domain: _____   period:

range: _____

equation of the midline:

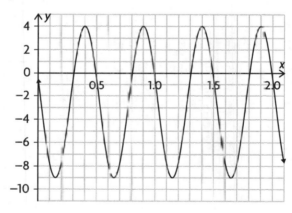

amplitude:

6. Sketch a possible graph of a sinusoidal function with each set of characteristics. Draw and label the midline.

a) *y*-intercept: 3

domain:
$\{x \mid 0° \le x \le 720°, x \in R\}$

range:
$\{y \mid 3 \le y \le 8, y \in R\}$

period: $360°$

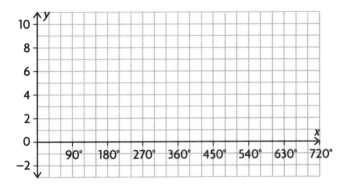

b) *y*-intercept: 2

domain:
$\{x \mid 0° \le x \le 720°, x \in R\}$

maximum value: 5

minimum value: −1

period: $720°$

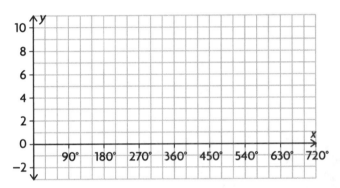

c) *y*-intercept: 0

domain:
$\{x \mid 0 \le x \le 12, x \in R\}$

maximum value: 4

minimum value: −4

period: 3

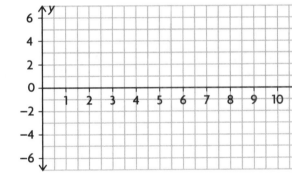

d) *y*-intercept: 4

domain:
$\{x \mid 0 \le x \le 12, x \in R\}$

range: $\{y \mid 2 \le y \le 6, y \in R\}$

period: 6

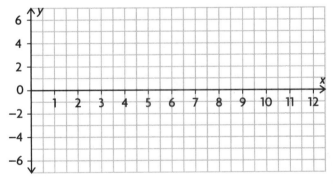

MULTIPLE CHOICE

7. Which one of these graphs has all of the following characteristics?

- a range of $\{y \mid -1 \leq y \leq 3, y \in R\}$
- an amplitude of 2
- a maximum value of 3
- a midline equation of $y = 1$
- a minimum value of -1
- a period of $120°$

A.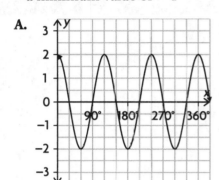

C.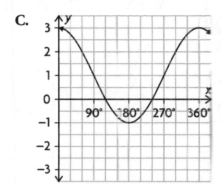

B.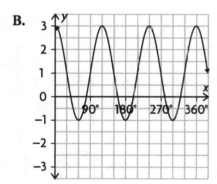

D.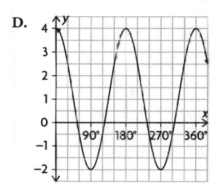

WRITTEN RESPONSE

8. Suppose two sinusoidal graphs, A and B, have different maximum and minimum values. Is each of the following statements true or false? (Support your claim with an example, where possible.)

- A and B can have the same midline equation.

- A and B can have the same amplitude.

- A and B can have the same midline equation and the same amplitude.

The Equations of Sinusoidal Functions

YOU WILL NEED
• graphing technology

Keep in Mind

▸ A sinusoidal function of the form

$$y = a \sin b(x - c) + d \text{ or } y = a \cos b(x - c) + d$$

has the following characteristics:

• The value of a is the amplitude: $a = \dfrac{\text{maximum value} - \text{minimum value}}{2}$

• The value of b is the number of cycles in $360°$, or 2π.

  The period is $\dfrac{360°}{b}$, or $\dfrac{2\pi}{b}$.

• The value of c indicates the horizontal translation that has been applied to the graph of $y = \sin x$ or $y = \cos x$. The graph is shifted to the right if c is positive and to the left if c is negative.

• The equation of the midline is $y = d$, where $d = \dfrac{\text{maximum value} + \text{minimum value}}{2}$.

• The maximum value is $d + a$, and the minimum value is $d - a$.

▸ The graph shown represents a sine curve. In the graph of a cosine curve, c is the distance from the vertical axis to the first maximum point.

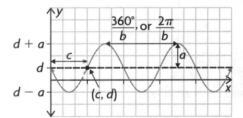

▸ Any sinusoidal function can be expressed as either a cosine function or a sine function.

▸ Adding whole periods to or subtracting whole periods from the horizontal translation, c, yields other points on the graph.

Example

Consider the function $y = 3 \cos 2(x - 45°) + 2$, where x is measured in degrees.

Describe the graph of the function by stating the amplitude, equation of the midline, range, period, and horizontal translation of $y = \cos x$.

Verify your description by drawing a graph of this function using graphing technology.

Solution

Step 1. I determined a, b, c, and d.

$$y = a \cos b(x - c) + d$$
$$y = 3 \cos 2(x - 45°) + 2$$
$$a = 3, b = 2, c = 45°, d = 2$$

Step 2. I determined the amplitude and the equation of the midline.

The amplitude is a, which is 3.

The equation of the midline is $y = d$, or $y = 2$.

Step 3. I used these values to determine the range.

Minimum value $= d - a$ Maximum value $= d + a$

Minimum value $= 2 - 3$ Maximum value $= 2 + 3$

Minimum value $= -1$ Maximum value $= 5$

The range is $\{y \mid -1 \le y \le 5, y \in R\}$.

Step 4. I determined the period.

Since $b = 2$, the graph completes 2 cycles in 360°.

$$\text{Period} = \frac{360°}{b}$$

$$\text{Period} = \frac{360°}{2}, \text{ or } 180°$$

Step 5. I considered whether the graph of $y = \cos x$ had been translated horizontally.

Since $c = 45°$, the graph has been translated horizontally, 45° to the right. Since $y = \cos x$ has a maximum at $x = 0$, I knew that this function must have its maximum value, 5, at $x = 45°$.

From the graph, the y-intercept is at $y = 2$.

Step 6. I graphed the function using technology.

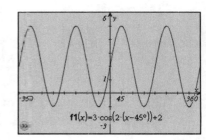

I used a domain of $\{x \mid -360° \le x \le 360°\}$ and a scale for x with an interval of 45°, which is one-quarter of the period.

- The amplitude is 3.
- The equation of the midline is $y = 2$.
- The range is $\{y \mid -1 \le y \le 5, y \in R\}$.
- The period is 180°.
- The cosine graph has been translated horizontally, 45° to the right, so the y-intercept is 2.

Practice

1. Arrange these functions in order from least amplitude to greatest amplitude. Provide your reasoning.

   a) $y = 4 \cos 4x$ b) $y = 5 \sin 3x$ c) $y = 2 \sin x + 6$

2. Arrange these functions in order from least range to greatest range. Provide your reasoning.

   a) $y = 8 \sin 6x$ b) $y = 9 \sin 3x - 1$ c) $y = 6 \sin x + 2$

3. Arrange these functions in order from least period to greatest period. Provide your reasoning.

   a) $y = 5 \cos 4(x - 2) + 3$ b) $y = 6 \sin 2(x - 5)$ c) $y = 3 \cos 0.5x + 4$

4. Describe the horizontal translation, if there is one, of each function.

   a) $y = \cos 2(x + 45°) + 2$ c) $y = 3 \cos 5(x - 90°) + 3$

   b) $y = 2 \sin 0.1(x - 180°) + 5$ d) $y = 2 \cos 5x + 3$

5. Determine the equation of the midline of each function. Provide your reasoning.

   a) $y = 5 \cos 4(x - 22.5°) + 2$

   b) $y = 7 \sin 3(x + 30°) - 6$

6. Determine the amplitude and the range of each function. Provide your reasoning.

a) $y = 7 \cos 2(x - 4)$

b) $y = 15 \sin 0.25(x - 15) + 2$

7. Determine the direction, and the distance in degrees or radians, by which $y = \sin x$ or $y = \cos x$ would be translated horizontally to create the graph of each function.

a) $y = 3.5 \sin 2(x - 30°) + 5$

c) $y = 4 \sin 6.5(x - 4.5) - 1$

b) $y = 10 \cos (x + 90°) - 3$

d) $y = 6 \cos (x + 4) + 3$

MULTIPLE CHOICE

8. Which equation describes this graph best?

A. $y = 4 \sin 3(x - 30°) + 1$

B. $y = 3 \sin 3(x - 30°) + 1$

C. $y = 4 \sin 2(x + 30°) + 2$

D. $y = 2 \sin 0.5(x - 180°) + 4$

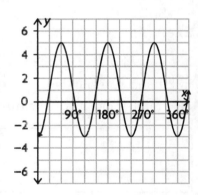

WRITTEN RESPONSE

9. Consider $y = 3 \sin 6(x - 45°) - 1$.

a) Describe the graph of the function, including the amplitude, the equation of the midline, the range, the period, and the horizontal translation from $y = \cos x$. Provide your reasoning.

b) Confirm your description using technology.

8.5 Modelling Data with Sinusoidal Functions

YOU WILL NEED
- graphing technology

Keep in Mind

▶ If the data points on a scatter plot seem to follow a regular, periodic pattern of increasing and decreasing curves, then there may be a sinusoidal relationship between the independent and dependent variables.

▶ If the points on a scatter plot show a sinusoidal trend, then graphing technology can be used to determine the equation of the sinusoidal regression function that models the data.

▶ Unrecorded or unplotted values can be predicted by reading values from a graph or by using the equation of the sinusoidal regression function.

▶ When the data in a set repeat in a regular, periodic pattern, interpolation or extrapolation can be used to make predictions.

Example

The table shows the maximum altitude, in degrees, at which the Moon appeared in Edmonton from January 1 to February 29 in 2012. Use sinusoidal regression to determine the maximum altitude of the Moon on February 6 and on March 1.

Date/Day	Jan. 1, Day 1	Jan. 4, Day 4	Jan. 7, Day 7	Jan. 10, Day 10	Jan. 13, Day 13	Jan. 16, Day 16	Jan. 19, Day 19
Altitude (°)	47.3	56.5	57.0	51.4	36.8	48.1	13.1
Date/Day	Jan. 22, Day 22	Jan. 25, Day 25	Jan. 28, Day 28	Jan. 31, Day 31	Feb. 3, Day 34	Feb. 6, Day 37	Feb. 9, Day 40
Altitude (°)	17.9	31.2	45.4	55.4	57.5		39.0
Date/Day	Feb. 12, Day 43	Feb. 15, Day 46	Feb. 18, Day 49	Feb. 21, Day 52	Feb. 24, Day 55	Feb. 27, Day 58	Mar. 1, Day 61
Altitude (°)	22.8	13.6	16.8	29.1	43.4	54.2	

Solution

Step 1. I entered the data in my graphing calculator and created a scatter plot.

The data has a regular, periodic pattern of increasing and decreasing curves. The data is sinusoidal.

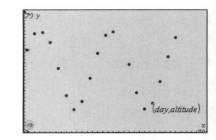

Step 2. I determined the equation of the function that models the data using the sinusoidal regression feature on my calculator.

$$y = 22.244...\sin(0.229...x + 0.213...) + 36.811...$$

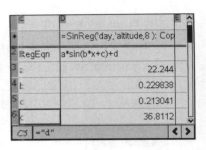

Step 3. I graphed the equation on the same grid as my scatter plot

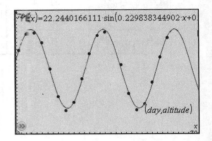

Step 4. I used the graph to determine the altitude on February 6, or Day 37.

On February 6, the Moon's altitude was at an angle of about 51.3°.

Step 5. I used the graph to determine the altitude on March 1, or Day 61.

On March 1, the Moon's altitude was at an angle of about 60.0°.

Practice

1. The table below shows what percent of the Moon was illuminated in Edmonton during January and February of 2012. Use sinusoidal regression to determine what percent of the Moon was illuminated on January 15 and March 4.

Date/Day	Jan. 1, Day 1	Jan. 5, Day 5	Jan. 10, Day 10	Jan. 15, Day 15	Jan. 20, Day 20	Jan. 25, Day 25	Jan. 30, Day 30
Illumination (%)	57.8	90.5	98.7		8.2	7.5	49.0
Date/Day	Feb. 4, Day 35	Feb. 9, Day 40	Feb. 14, Day 45	Feb. 19, Day 50	Feb. 24, Day 55	Feb. 29, Day 60	Mar. 4, Day 65
Illumination (%)	91.8	97.1	51.9	5.3	8.7	50.2	

2. The table below shows the maximum altitude, in degrees, at which the Moon appeared in Vancouver during March and April of 2012. Determine the maximum altitude at which the Moon appeared on March 20 and on May 4.

Date/Day	Mar. 1, Day 1	Mar. 5, Day 5	Mar. 10, Day 10	Mar. 15, Day 15	Mar. 20, Day 20	Mar. 25, Day 25	Mar. 30, Day 30
Altitude (°)	61.9	50.9	29.2	18.5		57.4	59.5
Date/Day	Apr. 4, Day 35	Apr. 9, Day 40	Apr. 14, Day 45	Apr. 19, Day 50	Apr. 24, Day 55	Apr. 29, Day 60	May 4, Day 65
Altitude (°)	37.5	19.5	26.5	49.0	61.6	50.3	

3. The table below shows what percent of the Moon was illuminated in Vancouver during March and April of 2012. Use sinusoidal regression to determine what percent of the Moon was illuminated on April 14 and on May 4.

Date/Day	Mar. 1, Day 1	Mar. 5, Day 5	Mar. 10, Day 10	Mar. 15, Day 15	Mar. 20, Day 20	Mar. 25, Day 25	Mar. 30, Day 30
Illumination (%)	60.4	93.9	94.2	44.0	3.4	9.9	53.0
Date/Day	Apr. 4, Day 35	Apr. 9, Day 40	Apr. 14, Day 45	Apr. 19, Day 50	Apr. 24, Day 55	Apr. 29, Day 60	May 4, Day 65
Illumination (%)	96.4	89.9		2.2	11.5	57.6	

MULTIPLE CHOICE

Questions 4 and 5 refer to the table below, which shows the maximum altitude, in degrees, at which the Moon appeared in Regina during June and July of 2012.

Date/Day	Jun. 1, Day 1	Jun. 5, Day 5	Jun. 10, Day 10	Jun. 15, Day 15	Jun. 20, Day 20	Jun. 25, Day 25	Jun. 30, Day 30
Altitude (°)	21.6	17.2	35.4	56.0	58.1	37.9	17.6
Date/Day	Jul. 5, Day 35	Jul. 10, Day 40	Jun. 15, Day 45	Jul. 20, Day 50	Jul. 25, Day 55	Jul. 30, Day 60	Aug. 4, Day 65
Altitude (°)		47.3	60.2	49.2	24.9	19.0	

4. Which choice is the best estimate for the altitude of the Moon in Regina on July 5? Use sinusoidal regression.

A. 63.2°   B. 24.0°   C. 0°   D. 35.2°

5. Which choice is the best estimate for the altitude of the Moon in Regina on August 4? Use sinusoidal regression.

A. 41.2°   B. 24.0°   C. 10°   D. 35.2°

WRITTEN RESPONSE

6. The average monthly temperatures for Flin Flon, Manitoba, and Lethbridge, Alberta, are given in the table. Use sinusoidal regression to predict the difference between the average temperatures for the two communities on April 1. Explain what you did.

Average Monthly Temperature (°C)			
Month	Month Number	Flin Flon	Lethbridge
January	1	−20.4	−7.8
February	2	−15.3	−4.6
March	3	−8.1	−0.2
April	4	1.8	6.0
May	5	9.8	11.3
June	6	15.7	15.5
July	7	18.5	18.0
August	8	17.2	17.7
September	9	10.1	12.6
October	10	3.0	7.0
November	11	−8.0	−1.5
December	12	−17.5	−6.1

8 | Test Prep

Complete the following to summarize the important ideas from this chapter.

Q: How is radian measure related to degree measure?

A: In radian measure, ___ is equivalent to about 60° and π is equivalent to _____. A complete revolution, or 360°, is ___ in radian measure.

NEED HELP?
• See Lesson 8.1

Q: What are some characteristics of the graphs of $y = \sin x$ and $y = \cos x$?

A: • Both graphs are periodic, with _____ 360° or ___ in radian measure.

• Both graphs have domain _____ and range _____.

• Both graphs have _____ 1 and _____ $y = 0$.

NEED HELP?
• See Lesson 8.2

Q: How can the characteristics of sinusoidal functions be determined?

A: Sinusoidal functions have graphs the same shape as the _____ of a _____ function. For any sinusoidal function:

• The period is the _____ distance between consecutive _____ values or _____ minimum values.

• The midline has equation $y = \dfrac{\boxed{}}{\boxed{}}$.

• The _____ is the positive _____ distance between the _____ and either a _____ or a _____ value.

NEED HELP?
• See Lesson 8.3

Q: What are the general forms of equations of sinusoidal functions?

A: $y = $ ___ $\sin$ _____ $+$ ___ and $y = $ ___ $\cos$ _____ $+$ ___, where

• a is the _____

• b is the number of _____ in 360°, or ___, so the _____ is $\dfrac{360°}{b}$, or $\dfrac{2\pi}{b}$

• c gives the _____ translation of the graph of $y = \sin x$ or $y = \cos x$

• $y = $ ___ is the equation of the midline

NEED HELP?
• See Lesson 8.4

Q: How can you create a model for data if a scatter plot of the data shows a regular pattern of increasing and decreasing curves?

A: Use _____ to determine the equation of the _____ of _____.

NEED HELP?
• See Lesson 8.5

MULTIPLE CHOICE

1. Estimate the value of 1.2 in degree measure.

   A. 75°   **B.** 1.2°   **C.** 30°   **D.** 70°

2. Estimate the value of 420° in radian measure.

   A. 20   **B.** 3.7   **C.** 7.3   **D.** 10

3. Which reason explains how you know that this graph is not the graph of $y = \sin x$ or $y = \cos x$?

   A. It has just one x-intercept.

   B. The amplitude is 0.5.

   C. The period is 270°.

   D. The equation of the midline is $y = 1$.

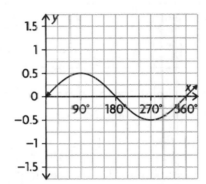

4. Which one of these graphs has all of the following features?

   • a range of $\{y \mid -2 \le y \le 6, x \in R\}$

   • a maximum value of 6 and a minimum value of -2

   • an amplitude of 4

   • a midline equation of $y = 2$

   • a period of 120°

A.
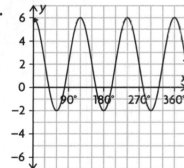

C.
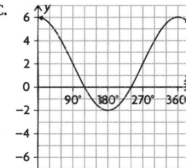

B.
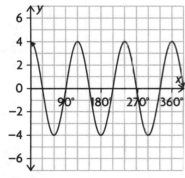

D.
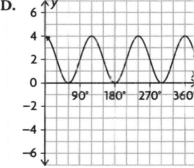

5. Which equation describes this graph best?

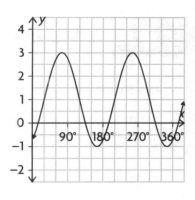

A. $y = 2 \sin 2(x + 30°) + 1$

B. $y = 2 \sin 2(x - 30°) + 1$

C. $y = 4 \sin 3(x - 30°) + 2$

D. $y = 3 \cos 0.5(x + 180°) + 3$

The table shows the monthly average high temperatures for Lethbridge, Alberta, in degrees Celsius. Use the table to answer questions 6 and 7.

Month	Jan.	Feb.	Mar.	Apr.	May	Jun.	Jul.	Aug.	Sep.	Oct.	Nov.	Dec.
Average High (°C)	−1.8	1.5	6.0		18.2	22.3	25.5	25.4	20.1	14	4.3	

6. Which choice is the best estimate for the average high temperature in Lethbridge in April? Use sinusoidal regression.

A. 4°   **B.** 10°   **C.** 0°   **D.** 13°

7. Which choice is the best estimate for the average high temperature in Lethbridge in December? Use sinusoidal regression.

A. 4.3°   **B.** −1°   **C.** 2.6°   **D.** 26°

NUMERICAL RESPONSE

8. a) To the nearest tenth, 75° is about ___ in radian measure.

   b) To the nearest tenth, 480° is about ___ in radian measure.

   c) The value of 2.6 in degree measure is about _____°.

   d) The value of 4.1 in degree measure is about _____°.

9. Consider this graph.

   The amplitude of this graph is ___ and the period is ___, so it is not a graph of $y = \sin x$ or $y = \cos x$.

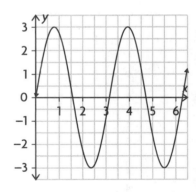

10. Consider the graph shown.

   The range is _____.

   The equation of the midline is _____.

   The amplitude is ___.

   The period is ___.

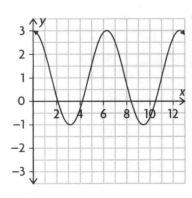

11. Describe the graph of this function:

$$y = 4 \sin 2(x - 45°) + 2$$

There is a horizontal translation of ___° to the _____.

The amplitude is ___.

The equation of the midline is _____.

The range is _____.

The period is ___°.

12. The table below shows the percent of the Moon illuminated from June 1 to July 27 of 2012 in Regina. Enter estimates for what percent of the Moon was illuminated on June 3 and on July 25. Use sinusoidal regression.

Date/Day	Jun. 1, Day 1	Jun. 3, Day 3	Jun. 5, Day 5	Jun. 7, Day 7	Jun. 9, Day 9	Jun. 11, Day 11	Jun. 13, Day 13
Illumination (%)	92.4%		98.9%	88.1%	69.8%	49.2%	29.7%
Date/Day	Jun. 15, Day 15	Jun. 17, Day 17	Jun. 19, Day 19	Jun. 21, Day 21	Jun. 23, Day 23	Jun. 25, Day 25	Jun. 27, Day 27
Illumination (%)	13.7%	3.3%	0.1%	5.0%	18.0%	37.5%	60.5%
Date/Day	Jun. 29, Day 29	Jul. 1, Day 31	Jul. 3, Day 33	Jul. 5, Day 35	Jul. 7, Day 37	Jul. 9, Day 39	Jul. 11, Day 41
Illumination (%)	82.1%	96.5%	99.6%	96.5%	83.8%	65.5%	45.6%
Date/Day	Jul. 13, Day 43	Jul. 15, Day 45	Jul. 17, Day 47	Jul. 19, Day 49	Jul. 21, Day 51	Jul. 23, Day 53	Jul. 25, Day 55
Illumination (%)	26.9%	11.7%	2.2%	0.6%	8.1%	24.1%	

WRITTEN RESPONSE

13. Estimate the measure of the circle's central angle in degrees. Then express the value of the angle in radian measure. Explain what you did.

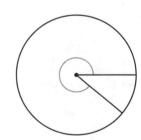

14. Is this a graph of $y = \sin x$ or $y = \cos x$? Explain.

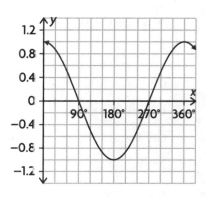

15. Determine the amplitude, equation of the midline, range, and period of this graph. Show your calculations.

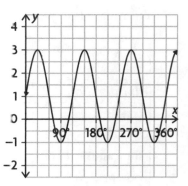

16. Consider $y = 2 \sin 4(x - 45°) + 1$, where x is measured in degrees.

a) Describe the graph of the function, including the amplitude, equation of the midline, range, period, and horizontal translation from $y = \cos x$. Provide your reasoning.

b) Confirm your description using graphing technology.

17. The average monthly temperatures for Flin Flon, Manitoba, and Lethbridge, Alberta, are given in the table. Use sinusoidal regression to predict the difference between the average temperatures for the two communities on April 1. Explain what you did.

Average Low Monthly Temperature (°C)		
Month	Flin Flon	Lethbridge
January	−24.5	−15.9
February	−20.1	−11.9
March	−13.6	−6.4
April	−3.8	−0.1
May	4.1	5.5
June	10.3	9.9
July	13.2	12.0
August	12.1	11.4
September	5.9	5.6
October	−0.4	−0.1
November	−11.0	−8.0
December	−21.2	−13.6

MULTIPLE CHOICE

1. Which of the following statements is false for the exponential function $y = 2(5)^x$?

   A. domain: $\{x \mid x \in R\}$

   B. range: $\{y \mid y \in R\}$

   C. y-intercept: $y = 2$

   D. end behaviour: graph extends from Quadrant II to Quadrant I

2. Which of the following statements is true for the logarithmic function $y = 5 \log x$?

   A. domain: $\{x \mid x > 0, x \in R\}$ C. x-intercept: $x = 1$

   B. range: $\{y \mid y \in R\}$ D. All of the above.

3. Which is the correct solution to the exponential equation $3^{4x-1} = \dfrac{1}{243}$?

   A. $x = 1$ C. $x = -1$

   B. $x = 0.5$ D. $x = -0.5$

4. Which of the following statements is false?

   A. $\log_2 64 = 6$ C. $\dfrac{\log_{10} 1}{100} = 2$

   B. $\log_5 1 = 0$ D. $\log_2 \sqrt{2} = \dfrac{1}{2}$

5. Which is the correct period of the sinusoidal function $f(x) = 2 \sin 4x$?

   A. $360°$ B. $180°$ C. $90°$ D. $720°$

6. Which is the correct range of the sinusoidal function $f(x) = 3 \cos x + 4$?

   A. $\{y \mid y \in R\}$

   B. $\{y \mid 1 \le y \le 7, y \in R\}$

   C. $\{y \mid 0 \le y \le 4, y \in R\}$

   D. $\{y \mid 3 \le y \le 4, y \in R\}$

NUMERICAL RESPONSE

7. State the y-intercept of $y = 4\left(\dfrac{1}{2}\right)^x$.

   $y = \underline{}$

8. State the value of $\log_3 135 - \log_3 5$.

___

9. State the value of $3 \log_8 4$.

___

10. A 500 g sample of radioactive krypton-88 has a half-life of 2.8 h. The mass of krypton, in grams, that remains after t hours can be modelled by

$$M(t) = 500\left(\frac{1}{2}\right)^{\frac{t}{2.8}}.$$

Determine the length of time needed for a 500 g sample to decay to 100 g, rounded to the nearest tenth of an hour.

_____

11. Determine each value of y. Round to two decimal places.

a) $y = \ln 45$ **b)** $y = -\log 50$

___ ___

12. Write the equation of the midline of the sinusoidal function $y = 5 \sin x - 6$.

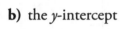 $y = $ ___

WRITTEN RESPONSE

13. For the exponential function shown, state

    a) the number of x-intercepts

    b) the y-intercept

    c) the end behaviour

    d) the domain

    e) the range

    f) whether the function is increasing or decreasing

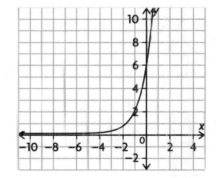

14. Predict the characteristics of each exponential function. Record your predictions in the table. Verify your predictions by graphing with technology.

a) $y = 4(5)^x$

b) $y = 2\left(\dfrac{1}{5}\right)^x$

	Number of x-Intercepts	y-Intercept	End Behaviour	Domain	Range	Increasing or Decreasing
a)						
b)						

15. A rare coin bought in 2000 appreciates in value according to the function $y = 550(1.08)^x$, where y represents the value of the coin and x represents the number of years since 2000.

   a) Determine the domain and the range of the function in this context.

   b) Determine the y-intercept of the function in this context. What does the y-intercept represent?

   c) Graph the function. Use the graph to estimate

   i) the value of the coin in 2025

   ii) when the coin will have a value greater than $1000

16. Solve each of the following.

   a) $6^{5-x} = 216$

   c) $3^{3x} = \dfrac{1}{27}$

   b) $4^{x+4} = 32^{2x}$

   d) $\sqrt{5} = 5^{2x-1}$

17. Solve each of the following. Round your answers to two decimal places.

a) $4^{3x} = 120$

b) $5^{2x + 1} = 10^{x - 1}$

18. An investor tracks the value of an initial investment of $1500 over several years.

Year, t	0	1	2	3	4	5
Value of Investment ($), $f(t)$	1500.00	1590.00	1685.40	1786.50	1893.70	2007.30

a) Create a scatter plot for the data and determine the exponential regression function that models the data.

b) Explain how the parameters in the equation are related to the context.

c) Determine when the investment doubles in value.

19. Predict the characteristics of each logarithmic function by stating

- the x-intercept

- the number of y-intercepts

- the end behaviour

- the domain

- the range

- whether the function is increasing or decreasing

Verify your predictions by graphing each function.

a) $y = 12 \log x$

b) $y = -2 \ln x$

20. Write each of the following as a single logarithm. Evaluate each logarithm to two decimal places.

a) $3 \log_6 4 + \log_6 5$

b) $\log_8 16 - 2 \log_8 1$

21. Mindy grows tomatoes in a greenhouse. She has planted and tracked the growth of a new variety of tomato.

Age of Plant (weeks)	1	2	3	4	5	6	7	8	9	10	11
Average Height (cm)	1	10	20	35	55	70	75	80	85	90	92

a) Create a scatter plot for the data using technology and determine the equation of a logarithmic regression function that models the plants' growth.

b) Determine the average height of a plant of this variety when it is 15 weeks old. Round to one decimal place.

c) Determine the age of a plant of this variety when it is 60 cm tall. Round to one decimal place.

22. Determine the range, the period, the amplitude, and the equation of the midline of the sinusoidal function shown in this graph.

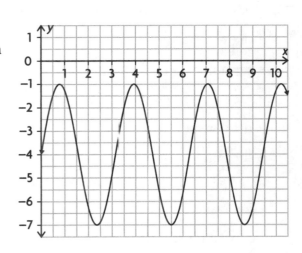

23. For the sinusoidal function

$$y = 4 \sin 3(x - 20°) + 5$$

state the amplitude, the period, the equation of the midline, the domain, the range, and the horizontal translation.

24. The average daily temperature for each month in Regina is shown in the following table.

a) Create a scatter plot for the data and state the equation of the sinusoidal regression function that models the relationship between the month of the year and average daily temperature.

b) Determine the average daily temperature in Regina in the middle of October. Round to one decimal place.

c) Estimate when the average daily temperature in Regina will be greater than 15° C.

Month Number	Average High Temperature (° C)
1 (Jan.)	−16.2
2	−11.9
3	−5.0
4	4.5
5	11.7
6	16.4
7	18.8
8	18.0
9	11.7
10	4.8
11	−5.5
12 (Dec.)	−13.2

MULTIPLE CHOICE

1. Consider two sets, A and B, where the formula $n(A \cup B) = n(A) + n(B)$ applies. Which statement best describes the relationship between sets A and B?

    A. $A \subset B$

    B. $B \subset A$

    C. $A \cap B = \{\}$

    D. $A = B$

2. In how many ways can Joan and her six friends line up for ice cream if Joan goes first, since it is her birthday?

    A. 120

    B. 720

    C. 5040

    D. None of the above.

3. The weather forecast is that there is an 80% chance of precipitation tomorrow. What are the odds in favour of precipitation occurring tomorrow?

    A. $4:1$ **B.** $1:4$ **C.** $4:5$ **D.** $5:4$

4. Which are the non-permissible values for the rational expression $\dfrac{2x}{x^2 - 11x + 30}$?

    A. $x = 0$ and $x = 5$

    B. $x = 0$ and $x = 6$

    C. $x = 5$ and $x = 6$

    D. $x = -5$ and $x = -6$

5. Which statement correctly describes the end behaviour of the polynomial function $f(x) = -2x^3 + 4x^2 - 5x + 3$?

    A. extends from Quadrant II to Quadrant IV

    B. extends from Quadrant I to Quadrant III

    C. extends from Quadrant III to Quadrant IV

    D. extends from Quadrant I to Quadrant II

6. Which statement correctly describes the intercepts of $f(x) = 4(3)^x$?

    A. $x = 3$ and $y = 4$

    B. $x = 4$ and $y = 3$

    C. no x-intercept and $y = 4$

    D. $x = 3$ and no y-intercept

7. Which of the following is not a law of logarithms?

    A. $\log_a m + \log_a n = \log_a (mn)$

    B. $\log_a m - \log_a n = \log_a \left(\dfrac{m}{n} \right)$

    C. $(\log_a m)(\log_a n) = \log_a m + \log_a n$

    D. $n \log_a m = \log_a m^n$

8. Which statement correctly describes the characteristics of the graphs of $y = \sin x$ and $y = \cos x$?

    A. Both graphs have an amplitude of 1.

    B. Both graphs have a period of $360°$.

    C. Both graphs have $y = 0$ as the equation of the midline.

    D. All of the above.

NUMERICAL RESPONSE

9. There are 45 guests at Mountain Lake Lodge. Of these guests, 35 plan to go fishing and 22 plan to go hiking. There are 8 guests who do not plan to fish or hike.

    a) Determine how many guests plan to fish and hike. ___

    b) Determine how many guests plan only to fish. ___

    c) Determine how many guests plan only to hike. ___

10. A builder offers 10 different house models on 3 lot sizes in 2 different subdivisions in the same community. How many different choices does the home buyer have with this builder in this community? Assume every house model fit on every lot size. _____

11. In the card game crazy eights, players are dealt 8 cards from a standard deck of cards. What is the probability that a hand consists of 4 kings, 2 queens, and 2 jacks? _____

12. What are the minimum and maximum number of x-intercepts the graph of a cubic function may have?

minimum = ___   maximum = ___

13. What is the solution to the exponential equation $4^{5x + 2} = 16$?

$x =$ ___

14. What is the value of $\log_2 288 - \log_2 9$?   ___

15. What is the x-intercept of $f(x) = 8 \log x$?

$x =$ ___

16. What is the measure in degrees of an angle measuring π in radian measure?

___

WRITTEN RESPONSE

17. Consider these sets:

$U = \{x \mid x \le 50, x \in W\}$

$A = \{x \mid 5x \le 50, x \in W\}$

$B = \{x \mid 10 \le x \le 20, x \in W\}$

a) Is $B \subset A$? Explain.

b) List $A \cup B$.

c) Determine $n(B)$.

d) Determine $n(A \cap B)$.

18. A survey of 100 students had these results:

70 of the students take the bus to school.

55 of the students walk to school.

55 drive a car to school.

30 sometimes take the bus to school and sometimes walk.

35 sometimes walk to school and sometimes drive a car.

38 sometimes take the bus to school and sometimes drive a car.

How many students surveyed sometimes take the bus, sometimes walk, and sometimes drive a car to school?

19. Simplify.

$$\frac{(n + 6)(n + 5)!}{(n + 4)!}$$

20. Six parents and five students volunteered to be on a school fund-raising committee. How many different four-person committees are possible if the committee must consist of

a) 2 parents and 2 students?

b) at least 1 student?

c) more parents than students?

21. How many different arrangements can be made using all the letters in the word SASKATOON?

22. Solve $_nP_4 = 12(_nC_2)$.

23. Amy and Jeff take turns rolling two dice. If the sum is less than 7 on her roll, Amy wins a point. If the sum is greater than 7 on his roll, Jeff wins a point. If the sum is 7, neither wins a point on their roll but they do roll again. The first player to 7 points wins. Is this a fair game? Explain.

24. Identify each pair of events as mutually exclusive, dependent, or independent.

a) rolling a six on a die and drawing the five of hearts from a standard deck of cards

b) drawing a heart or drawing the ace of clubs from a standard deck of cards

c) drawing two red cards in succession from a standard deck of cards without replacement

25. Tammy and Sara are evenly matched tennis players. However, each time Tammy losses a game, her probability of winning the next game is decreased by $\frac{1}{3}$. But when she wins, her probability of winning the next game increases by $\frac{1}{4}$. If they play two games, determine the probability that Sara will win both games.

26. Simplify.

$$\frac{x^2 + 2x - 15}{x^2 + 2x - 8} \div \frac{4x + 20}{x^2 - 2x}$$

27. Simplify.

$$\frac{2}{x + 2} + \frac{5}{x^2 - 4}$$

28. Solve.

$$\frac{3}{x + 5} = \frac{2}{4x}$$

29. Determine the domain, range, intercepts, and end behaviour for the polynomial function shown at right.

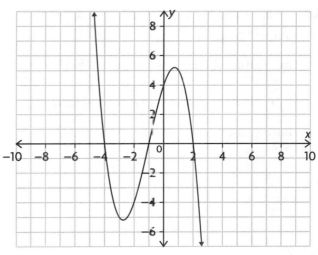

30. Determine the end behaviour, the possible number of turning points, the possible number of *x*-intercepts, the *y*-intercept, the domain, and the range of each function.

a) $f(x) = -5x + 3$

b) $u(x) = x^3 + 5x^2 + 2x - 8$

31. Sketch two possible graphs of polynomial functions that satisfy these conditions:

- cubic
- two *x*-intercepts
- negative leading coefficient

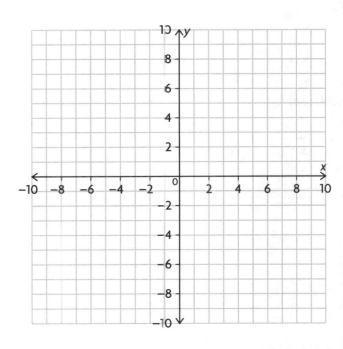

32. Kim flips a lacrosse ball into the air. The data show the height of the ball at different times during its flight.

Time (s)	0	0.25	0.50	0.75	1.00	1.25	1.50	1.75	2.00
Height (m)	0	2.19	3.78	4.74	5.10	4.84	3.98	2.49	0.40

a) Create a scatter plot of the data and determine the equation of the quadratic regression function that models the data.

b) Use your graph to estimate the times when the ball is at a height of 4.0 m.

c) Use your regression equation to determine the height of the ball at 0.8 s. Round to the nearest tenth of a metre.

33. For the exponential function shown, determine

a) the number of x-intercepts

b) the y-intercept

c) the end behaviour

d) the domain

e) the range

f) whether the function is increasing or decreasing

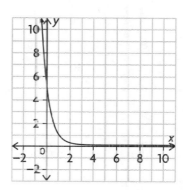

34. Solve $5^{x+1} = 3^{4x}$.

35. Actinium-225 has a half-life of 10.0 days.

The mass of actinium-225, in grams, that remains after t hours can be modelled by the function

$$M(t) = 250\left(\frac{1}{2}\right)^{\frac{t}{10}}$$

Determine the time needed for 250 g of actinium-225 to decay to 50 g. Round to the nearest tenth of a day.

36. Evaluate.

a) $\log_5 \sqrt{125}$

b) $\dfrac{\log_3 1}{9}$

37. Write each of the following as a single logarithm. Evaluate each logarithm to two decimal places.

a) $6 \log_3 5 + \log_3 8$

b) $\log_5 30 - \log_5 10$

38. Determine the range, period, amplitude, and equation of the midline of the sinusoidal function represented by this graph.

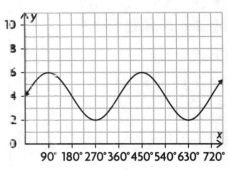

39. For the following sinusoidal function, state the amplitude, the period, the equation of the midline, the domain, the range, and the horizontal translation.

$$y = -2 \cos 2(x + 2) - 3$$

40. The average monthly rainfall in Calgary, Alberta, is shown in the table.

a) Determine the equation of the sinusoidal regression function that models the relationship between the month of the year and the average monthly rainfall.

b) Estimate when the average monthly rainfall in Calgary will below 40 mm.

Month Number	Average Monthly Rainfall (mm)
1 (Jan.)	0.2
2	0.1
3	1.7
4	11.5
5	51.4
6	79.8
7	67.9
8	58.7
9	41.7
10	6.2
11	1.2
12 (Dec.)	0.3

Source: http://www.calgaryarea.com/calgary_weather.htm.

Answers

Chapter 1

Getting Started, page 2

1. **b)** I; i)   **c)** Q; ii)   **d)** R; v)   **e)** N; iv)

2.

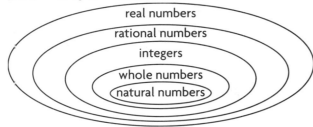

3. **a)** Q, R   **b)** Q, R   **c)** I, Q, R   **d)** N, W, I, Q, R   **e)** R   **f)** R

4. **a)** false; e.g., $\sqrt{0.25} = 0.5 > 0.25$
   b) false; e.g., a rhombus with side lengths 3 cm and angle measures 60°
      and 120°
   c) true

5. **a)** The evidence supports the conjecture.
   b) The evidence supports the conjecture.
   c) The evidence disproves the conjecture.
   d) The evidence supports the conjecture.

6. **a)** exterior $\angle C = 147°$ **b)** Pascal's car is fitted with snow tires.

Lesson 1.1, page 4

1. **a)**

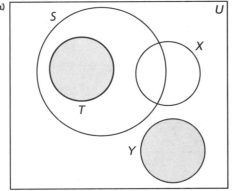

   b) Set Y is disjoint from sets S, T, and X. Set T is disjoint from set X.
   c) **i)**   false; $T \subset S$; e.g., Set T is completely inside set S, so T is a subset
         of S.
      ii) true; e.g., All sets are subsets of the universal set, U, so Y is a
         subset of U.
      iii) true; e.g., Every set is a subset of itself, so S is a subset of S.
      iv) false; $Y' = \{$numbers from 1 to 50 except 17 and 34$\}$
      v)   true; e.g., The universal set, U, does not contain any natural
         numbers greater than 50, so in this case, this is the empty set.

2. **a)**

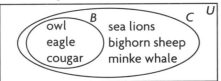

   b) yes, $B \subset C$; e.g., because all the elements of B are also elements of C

3. **a)**

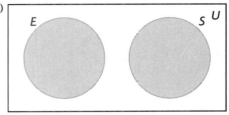

   b) Sets E and S are disjoint.

4. e.g., $U = \{$machines in home$\}$, $C = \{$machines for doing laundry$\}$,
   $K = \{$machines in the kitchen$\}$

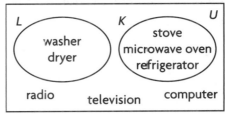

5. **a)** $S = \{A, E, F, 1, 4, 7\}$; $C = \{C, 3, 6, 8, 9, 0\}$
   b) False; e.g., Some characters, such as 2, are formed with curves and
      straight lines, so S' includes characters that are not in C.

6. A.   **7.** C.

8. e.g., I could have organized the material by format, but instead I chose
   to organize it by subject and genre. $U = \{$all material in library$\}$;
   $F = \{$fictional material$\}$; $N = \{$non-fiction material$\}$; $S = \{$social studies$\}$

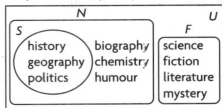

Lesson 1.2, page 8

1. **a)** 5   **b)** 12
   c)

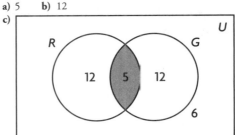

2. 41 guests; 23 guests; 10 guests

3.

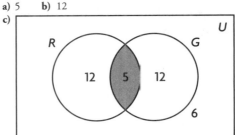

Lesson 1.3, page 10

1. a) {A, B, C, D, E, F, G, H, I, O, U, Y} b) 12 c) {Y} d) 1
2. a) $A \cup B = \{-5, -3, -1, 1, 2, 3, 4, 5, 6\}$, $n(A \cup B) = 9$,
   $A \cap B = \{1, 3, 5\}$, $n(A \cap B) = 3$
   b)

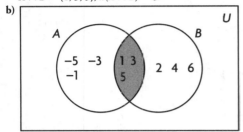

3. 21 people
4. both: 14; audiobooks only: 25; printed books only: 17
5. 146 people
6. 402 passengers
7. 30 people
8. 48 people
9. A.
10. e.g., Yes, he should. If 10 people liked neither, then $100 - 10 = 90$ people liked one or the other or both. Then $90 - 69 = 21$ liked only with pulp and $90 - 63 = 27$ liked only without pulp. So, $90 - 21 - 27 = 42$ people liked both. In this Venn diagram, P = {people who like pulp} and Q = {people who like without pulp}.

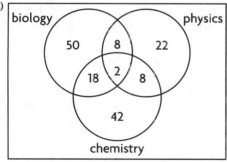

Lesson 1.4, page 14

1. e.g., $x = 5$, $y = 11$, $z = 8$
2. a) 70 b) 54 c) 111 d) 15
3. e.g., "tree-trekking," "holiday," "forests," "British Columbia." By combining two or more of these terms, Barney can search for the intersection of web pages related to these terms. For example, "tree-trekking" and "British Columbia" are more likely to give him useful information than either of these terms on its own.
4. e.g., Let W represent wing buyers and P represent pizza buyers. Let U represent all 500 people surveyed; $n(W \cap P)/n(U) = 0.26$, or 26%
5. 1 student
6. 6 members
7. 8 members
8. a)

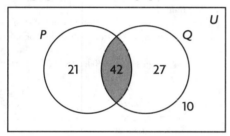

   b) 5 students

Chapter 1 Test Prep, page 18

Q1: • By listing the elements; for example, {7, 14, 21,...}
• By describing the set; for example, the set of all positive multiples of 7
• By using set notation; for example, $\{7x \mid x > 0, x \in I\}$
• By using a Venn diagram
• The complement of a set A can be written as A'. It contains all the elements in the universal set that are not in the set A.

Q2: • Each region represents a different set or combination of sets.
• Each element in a universal set appears once.
• An element that occurs in more than one set goes in the region where the sets containing the element overlap.

Q3: • For a set and its complement, $n(A) + n(A') = n(U)$.
• For two disjoint sets, $n(A \cup B) = n(A) + n(B)$ and $n(A \cap B) = 0$
• For two non-disjoint sets, the Principle of Inclusion and Exclusion states $n(A \cup B) = n(A) + n(B) - n(A \cap B)$
  or $n(A \cup B) = n(A \setminus B) + n(B \setminus A) + n(A \cap B)$
• For three non-disjoint sets, the Principle of Inclusion and Exclusion states
$n(A \cup B \cup C) = n(A) + n(B) + n(C) - n(A \cap B) - n(A \cap C) - n(B \cap C) + n(A \cap B \cap C)$

Chapter 1 Test, page 19

1. A. 2. C. 3. B. 4. C. 5. A.
6. 22 passengers; 13 passengers; 17 passengers
7. 277
8. 125 students; 136 students; 58 students
9. 7 members
10. 14 people
11. a) 425 people b) 136 people c) 127 people
12. a) 37 students b) 42 students c) 29 students
13. 12 customers

Chapter 2

Getting Started, page 22

1. a) ii) b) iv) c) iii) d) i)
2. a) e.g.,

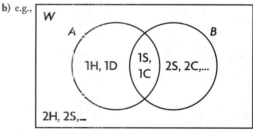

   b) e.g.,

3. a) 16 b) 39
4. a) 467 visitors b) 215 visitors
5. a) J♥, Q♥, K♥, J♦, Q♦, K♦
   b) 12, 13, 14, 21, 23, 24, 31, 32, 34, 41, 42, 43
   c) 1, 2, 3, 4, 5, 6, 8, 9, 10, 12, 15, 16, 18, 20, 24, 25, 30, 36

6. a) }, {□}, {◇}, {○},{□, ◇}, {□, ○}, {◇, ○},{□, ◇, ○}
  b) }, {25}
  c) }, {A}, {B}, {C}, {D}, {A, B}, {A, C}, {A, D}, {B, C}, {B, D}, {C, D}, {A, B, C}, {A, B, D},{A, C, D}, {B, C, D}, {A, B, C, D}

7. a) e.g.,

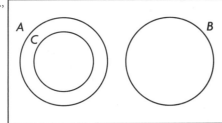

  b) *A* and *C* are not disjoint.

8. a) $A' = \{2, 3, 4, 6, 7, 9, 10, 11, 12, 14, 15\}$; e.g., B' is the set of odd numbers in S; $A \cup B = \{1, 2, 4, 5, 6, 8, 10, 12, 13, 14, 16\}$; $A \cap B = \{8, 16\}$
  b) $A' \cup B' = \{1, 2, 3, 4, 5, 6, 7, 9, 10, 11, 12, 13, 14, 15\}$; $A' \cap B' = \{3, 7, 9, 11, 15\}$

  c)

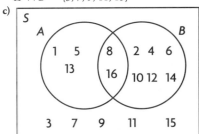

Lesson 2.1, page 24

1. a)

	Black	Milk	Cream
Sugar			
No sugar			6 ways

  b) e.g., There are 3 ways to decide on black, milk, or cream, AND 2 ways to decide on sugar or no sugar. So there are $3 \cdot 2 = 6$ ways Bryce can take his coffee.

2. a) e.g.,

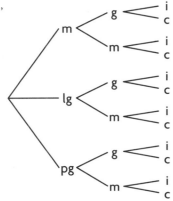

  b) e.g., There are 3 ways to choose the colour, AND 2 ways to choose the finish, AND 2 ways to choose the trim. So there are $3 \cdot 2 \cdot 2 = 12$ choices altogether.

3. a) yes; e.g., choosing the options are separate tasks related by AND.
  b) no; e.g., the options are related by OR.
  c) yes; e.g., the choices are separate tasks related by AND.
  d) no; e.g., what you roll on one die affects what you must roll on the other.

4. a) 16 choices **b)** 32 ways **c)** 18 choices **d)** 5 ways

5. a) 800 combinations **b)** 720 combinations

6. a) 30 ways **b)** 20 ways

7. 23 choices; e.g., The choices are mutually exclusive.

8. B.

9. a) 96 salads **b)** 24 salads

Lesson 2.2, page 28

1. a) 40 320 **b)** 5040

2. a) 120 **b)** 5040 **c)** 120 **d)** 420

3. a) $n + 1$ **b)** $n + 12$ **c)** $n!$ **d)** $\dfrac{1}{n^2 + n}$

4. $\dfrac{n!}{(n - 2)(n - 3)!} = \dfrac{n(n - 1)(n - 2)\dots(3)(2)(1)}{(n - 2)(n - 3)(n - 4)(n - 5)\dots(3)(2)(1)}$, or $n(n - 1)$

  So $n(n - 1) = 20$
  $n^2 - n = 20$
  $n^2 - n - 20 = 0$
  $(n - 5)(n + 4) = 0$
  $n - 5 = 0$ or $n + 4 = 0$
  $n = 5$ or $n = -4$

Lesson 2.3, page 30

1. a) 60 **b)** 210

2. a) 120 **b)** 360 **c)** 840

3. a) $_8P_8 = 40\ 320$ **b)** $_8P_5 = 6720$ **c)** $_8P_3 = 336$ **d)** $_8P_1 = 8$

4. a) 20 ways **b)** 60 ways

5. a) 2 **b)** 1 **c)** −2

6. a) 720 exchanges **b)** 999 exchanges

7. a) 2730 ways **b)** 3375 ways

8. a) e.g., No; the value of the expression equals $\dfrac{1}{n + 1}$ or at most $\dfrac{1}{2}$, which is not a whole number.
  b) e.g., No; the expression would have to represent the number of permutations of a set of objects chosen from a smaller set of objects, which is impossible.

9. a) e.g., Case 1: 5 letters and 3 digits; Case 2: 6 letters and 2 digits; Case 3: 7 letters and 1 digit
  b) 7200 passwords

10. a) $n = 5; n \geq 1$ **b)** $r = 3; 0 \leq r \leq 5$

11. $_9P_6$; e.g., Both permutations are products of 3 consecutive natural numbers, but each number is greater for $_9P_6$.

Lesson 2.4, page 34

1. a) 35 **b)** 210 **c)** 1120 **d)** 5040

2. a) 1260 arrangements **b)** 280 arrangements **c)** 980 arrangements

3. 15 120 rearrangements

4. a)

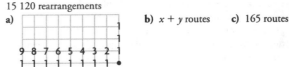

  b) $x + y$ routes **c)** 165 routes

5. a) 140 routes **b)** 95 routes

6. a) 17 153 136 ways **b)** 6 ways

7. a) e.g.,

Number of Objects, n	3	4	5	6	7	8
Number of Arrangements	1	4	20	120	840	6720

  e.g., The number of arrangements is multiplied by 4, then by 5, then by 6, etc.

  b) e.g.,

Number of Objects, n	6	7	8	9
Number of Arrangements	20	140	1120	10 080

  e.g., The number of arrangements is multiplied by 7, then by 8, then by 9, etc.

8. C. **9.** D.

10. a) 120 **b)** 120 **c)** 912

11. e.g., How many different arrangements are there of the letters A, A, A, B, B, C, and D?

Lesson 2.5, page 38

1. a) 60 permutations   b) 6 ways   c) 10 combinations
2. a) 120 permutations   b) 1 combination
   c) e.g., The order does not matter, so the set of all 5 symbols is the only combination possible.
3. a)
abc	acb	bac	bca	cab	cba
abd	adb	bad	bda	dab	dba
acd	adc	cad	cda	dac	dca
bcd	bdc	cbd	cdb	dbc	dcb

   24 permutations
   b) abc   abd   acd   bcd; 4 combinations
   c) 6; e.g., For each combination there are 6 ways to arrange the letters, contributing 6 to the total number of permutations.
4. 495 ways
5. a) e.g., $\dfrac{7!}{(7-4)!}$
   b) 4!
   c) e.g., $\dfrac{7!}{4!(7-4)!}$

Lesson 2.6, page 40

1. a)
○,□,◇	○,◇,□	□,○,◇	□,◇,○	◇,○,□	◇,□,○
○,□,△	○,△,□	□,○,△	□,△,○	△,○,□	△,□,○
○,◇,△	○,△,◇	◇,○,△	◇,△,○	△,○,◇	△,◇,○
□,◇,△	□,△,◇	◇,□,△	◇,△,□	△,□,◇	△,◇,□

   b) ○,□,◇   ○,□,△   ○,◇,△   □,◇,△
   c) e.g., The number of permutations is 6 times the number of combinations, because each combination can be arranged in 6 different ways.

2. a) $\underline{10}$
   b) $\dfrac{\boxed{7!}}{\boxed{3!}\cdot\boxed{4!}}$, or $\underline{35}$
   c) $\dfrac{\boxed{10!}}{\boxed{5!}\cdot\boxed{5!}}$, or $\underline{252}$
   d) $\dfrac{\boxed{13!}}{\boxed{1!}\cdot\boxed{12!}}$, or $\underline{13}$

3. a) 1716 ways   b) 210 ways
4. a) 210 ways   b) 840 ways   c) 1050 ways
5. a) $\dfrac{n!}{(n-r)!(n-(n-r))!}$
   b) e.g., $\dfrac{n!}{(n-r)!\cdot(n-(n-r))!} = \dfrac{n!}{(n-r)!\cdot(n-n+r)!}$
   $\dfrac{n!}{(n-r)!\cdot(n-(n-r))!} = \dfrac{n!}{(n-r)!\cdot r!}$
   $\dfrac{n!}{(n-r)!\cdot(n-(n-r))!} = \dfrac{n!}{r!\cdot(n-r)!}$
   $\dbinom{n}{n-r} = \dbinom{n}{r}$

6. 10 192 combinations
7. a) $_5C_3$ b) $_4C_2, _4C_3$ c) $_5C_3 = _4C_2 + _4C_3$
   $10 = 6 + 4$ d)
   ```
               1
             1   1
           1   2   1
         1   3   3   1
       1  4  [6] [4]  1
     1  5  10 [10]  5  1
   ```
8. a) $n = 7; n \geq 2$ b) $n = 11; n \geq 2$ c) $r = 2$ or $6; 0 \leq r \leq 8$
9. B.
10. a) 34 650 ways   b) 369 600 ways

Lesson 2.7, page 44

1. a) permutations; e.g., It is important who gets which position, so the order matters.
   b) combinations; e.g., The order in which the flavours are chosen does not matter.
   c) permutations; e.g., Even though the + symbols are identical and the × symbols are identical, the order in which they are selected changes the sequence.
2. a) 100 000 possibilities   b) 30 240 possibilities
3. a) permutations; e.g., In this case, the order of the cards matters for the sequence.
   b) 14 515 200 sequences
4. a) combinations; e.g., Once the passengers for each vehicle are determined, the order in which they are seated does not matter.
   b) Fundamental Counting Principle; e.g., Seating the squad in the vehicles is a collection of tasks that can be linked by the word AND.
   c) 1 441 440 ways
5. 1800 collages
6. 546 000 collections
7. 17 rolls
8. 120 ways
9. a) 840 arrangements   b) 480 arrangements
10. a) e.g., direct reasoning, as there are fewer cases than with indirect reasoning
    b) 1 299 480 hands

Chapter 2 Test Prep, page 48

Q1:
- AND often indicates two or more separate tasks. If one task can be performed in a ways and another can be performed in b ways, then by the <u>Fundamental Counting Principle</u>, both tasks can be performed in $a \cdot b$ ways.
- OR often indicates tasks or sets that may or may not be <u>mutually exclusive</u>.

Q2:
- The number of permutations of n <u>different</u> objects is $\underline{n!}$.
- The number of permutations of r objects chosen from n different objects is
$$_nP_r = \dfrac{\boxed{n!}}{\boxed{(n-r)!}}$$

Q3:
- For a set of n objects of which a are <u>identical</u>, another b are <u>identical</u>, another c are identical, and so on, the number of permutations is given by
$$\dfrac{\boxed{n!}}{\boxed{a!}\cdot\boxed{b!}\cdot\boxed{c!}\ldots}$$

Q4:
- Use combinations in situations where order <u>*does not*</u> matter.
- The number of combinations of r objects chosen from n different objects is
$$_nC_r = \left(\dfrac{\boxed{n}}{\boxed{r}}\right) = \dfrac{\boxed{n!}}{\boxed{r!(n-r)!}}$$

Chapter 2 Test, page 49

1. C.   2. A.   3. B.   4. C.   5. B.   6. D.
7. a) 10 000 codes   b) 5040 codes
8. a) 10 possibilities   b) 16 possibilities
9. a) 720 ways   b) 35 ways
10. 30 240 arrangements
11. 5 269 017 601 sequences
12. 30 240 groups
13. a) $\underline{21}$ triangles   b) $\underline{2\ 097\ 152}$ patterns

14. **a)**

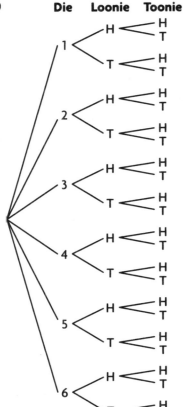

Die Loonie Toonie

24 outcomes

b) e.g., total number of outcomes

= outcomes for die · outcomes for loonie · outcomes for toonie

= 6 · 2 · 2, or 24

c) 20 outcomes

d) e.g., number of outcomes

= outcomes with multiple of 3 + outcomes with at least one tail

− outcomes with multiple of 3 and at least one tail

= 8 + 18 − 6, or 20

15. **a)** e.g., grid 2, because there are two ways to go across the join between the two parts of the grid

b) grid 1: 400 routes; grid 2: 600 routes

16. 1 237 792 hands

Chapter 3

Getting Started, page 52

1. **a)** intersection

b) combination

c) sample space

d) experimental

e) Fundamental Counting Principle

f) permutation

g) theoretical

2.

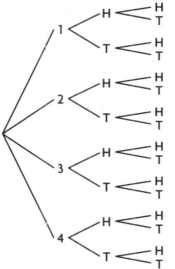

Die Roll Coin 1 Coin 2

3. **a)** 720   **b)** 21   **c)** 336   **d)** 604 800   **e)** 10   **f)** 113

4. **a)**

	1	2	3	4	5	6
1	0	1	2	3	4	5
2	1	0	1	2	3	4
3	2	1	0	1	2	3
4	3	2	1	0	1	2
5	4	3	2	1	0	1
6	5	4	3	2	1	0

b) $\frac{2}{9}$ **c)** $\frac{1}{36}$ **d)** $\frac{1}{18}$

5. **a)**

b)

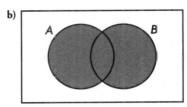

c)

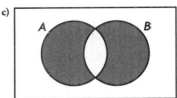

6. 90 090 ways

7. 9 979 200 ways

Lesson 3.1, page 54

1. e.g., adding one bracelet of some colour other than blue

2. **a)** fair, since both have a $\frac{3}{16}$ chance of winning

b) not fair, since Sabrina has only a $\frac{1}{4}$ chance of winning

3. A.

Lesson 3.2, page 56

1. a) 37.5%   b) 80%   c) 58.3%   d) 99.0%
2. a) 63.6%   b) 47.4%   c) 12.0%   d) 33.3%
3. a) 13:7   b) 1:1   c) 9:1   d) 3:17
4. a) 3:1, 1:3   b) 5:3, 3:5   c) 5:1, 1:5
5. a) 75%   b) 62.5%   c) 83.3%
6. experimental
7. a) 3:4   b) 57.1%
8. a) 25%   b) 3:1
9. a) 53.6%   b) 15:13   c) 28.6%   d) 2:5
10. a) 3:4   b) 4:3
11. 1:199
12. a) 54.5%   b) 5:6   c) 2:9
13. a) 7:13   b) 1:9
14. C.   15. B.   16. A.
17. no, 6 : 14 or 3 : 7
18. e.g., Based on past performance, the probability that Lei will do a pike perfectly, and earn a score of 5, is $\frac{4}{6}$ or 66.7%. The probability that she will do a backward tuck perfectly, and earn a score of 7, is $\frac{3}{5}$ or 60%.

    These two probabilities are pretty close. If she scores only a 5, she will have to compete again, so Lei should try to do the harder dive, and win the round now. OR: Lei has a better chance of doing the pike perfectly, so she should do that, as she has a better chance of staying in the competition.

Lesson 3.3, page 62

1. $\frac{60}{10\,000}$ or 0.006
2. $\frac{66\,924}{752\,538\,150}$ or 0.000 088 93...
3. $\frac{6}{720}$ or 0.008...
4. a) $\frac{540}{1\,404\,000}$ or 0.000 384...   b) $\frac{600}{1\,757\,000}$ or 0.000 341...
5. $\frac{15}{126}$ or 0.119...
6. $\frac{1}{151\,200}$ or 0.000 006 61
7. a) $\frac{24}{11\,880}$ or 0.002 0...   b) $\frac{24}{24\,024}$ or 0.000 99...
8. 1:11

Lesson 3.4, page 66

1. a) non-mutually exclusive   c) mutually exclusive
   b) mutually exclusive   d) non-mutually exclusive
2. a) $P(A \cup B) = \frac{13}{16}$ c) $P(A \cup B) = \frac{28}{36}$ or $\frac{7}{9}$
   b) $P(A \cup B) = \frac{16}{20}$ or $\frac{4}{5}$ d) $P(A \cup B) = \frac{14}{16}$ or $\frac{7}{8}$
3. a)

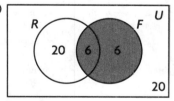

   b) non-mutually exclusive
   c) $P(R \cup F) = \frac{32}{52}$ or $\frac{8}{13}$ or 0.615...
4. a) 33.4%   b) 30.9%
5. B.   6. A.
7. 0.2

Lesson 3.5, page 70

1. a) independent   b) $\frac{1}{16} = 0.0625$ or 6.25%
2. a) dependent   b) $\frac{12}{2652} = 0.004\,52...$ or about 0.5%
3. a) $\frac{95}{165} = 0.575...$ or about 57.6%
   b) $\frac{40}{95} = 0.421...$ or about 42.1%
4. 0.318... or about 31.3%
5. 0.7925 or 79.25%
6. 0.411... or about 41.2%
7. 0.823... or about 82.4%
8. $\frac{2}{3} = 0.666...$ or about 66.7%
9. a) 0.65 or 65%   b) 0.35 or 35%

Lesson 3.6, page 74

1. a) independent   b) dependent   c) independent   d) independent
2. a) $\frac{1}{25}$ or 0.04   c) $\frac{1}{12}$ or 0.083...
   b) $\frac{21}{90}$ or 0.233...   d) $\frac{16}{144}$ or 0.111...
3. a) independent   b) $\frac{1}{6} = 0.166...$ or about 16.7%
4. a) dependent   b) $\frac{1}{6} = 0.166...$ or about 16.7%
5. a)

    Red Die   **Green Die**

    $P(\text{point}) = \frac{1}{2}$ $\begin{cases} P(\text{point}) = \frac{1}{3} \\ P(\text{no point}) = \frac{2}{3} \end{cases}$

    $P(\text{no point}) = \frac{1}{2}$ $\begin{cases} P(\text{point}) = \frac{1}{3} \\ P(\text{no point}) = \frac{2}{3} \end{cases}$

   b) $\frac{1}{6} = 0.166...$ or about 16.7%   c) 0.5, or 50%
6. e.g., The spinner has 8 equal areas, and only 1 area is red.
7. C.   8. A.   9. B.   10. C.   11. A.
12. a) $\frac{5}{64} = 0.078...$ or about 7.8%   b) 0   c) $\frac{1}{8} = 0.125$ or 12.5%...
13. a) $\frac{1}{36}$ b) $\frac{7}{18}$ c) $\frac{11}{18}$

Chapter 3 Test Prep, page 78

Q1: • The odds in favour of an event A with <u>probability</u> $P(A)$ are expressed as a <u>ratio</u>, $P(A):1 - P(A)$ or $P(A):P(A')$.
   • The odds <u>against</u> the same event A are expressed as $1 - P(A):P(A)$ or $P(A'):P(A)$.
   • If the odds in favour of an event A are $m:n$, its probability is $P(A) = \dfrac{m}{m+n}$.

Q2: • If events A and B are <u>mutually exclusive</u>, then the probability of either of them occurring is $P(A \cup B) = P(A) + P(B)$.
   • If the events are <u>not mutually</u> exclusive, then $P(A \cup B) = P(A) + P(B) - P(A \cap B)$.

Q3: • Two events are <u>dependent</u> if the <u>probability</u> of one depends on the <u>probability</u> of the other.
   • The <u>conditional</u> probability that Event B will occur, given that Event A has occurred, is $P(B|A) = \dfrac{P(A \cap B)}{P(A)}$.
   • The probability that both events will occur is $P(A \cap B) = P(A) \cdot P(B|A)$.

Q4: • If two events are independent, then the <u>probability</u> of one event does not affect the <u>probability</u> of the other.
• $P(B \mid A) = P(B)$ and $P(A \mid B) = P(\underline{A})$
• $P(A \cap B) = \underline{P(A) \cdot P(B)}$

Chapter 3 Test, page 79

1. B.   2. A.   3. D.   4. B.   5. B.
6. A.   7. C.
8. a) 40%   b) 3 : 2   c) 3 : 22
9. 3 : 1   10. 66.7%
11. a) $\dfrac{7}{64}$ b) $\dfrac{22}{64}$ c) $\dfrac{23}{64}$
12. 0.45 or 45%   13. no; e.g., odds in favour are 12 : 8 or 3 : 2
14. a) no   b) 0.165... or 16.5%

1–3 Cumulative Test, page 82

1. B   2. A   3. C   4. D
5. D   6. B
7. a) 20   b) 9   c) 11
8. a) 14 776 336   b) 1 413 720
9. 495
10. a) $\dfrac{1}{4}$ b) $\dfrac{19}{78}$
11. a) e.g., A = {Regina, Calgary, Edmonton, Vancouver, Victoria}
   b) e.g., B = {4, 8, 12, 16, 20}
12. a)

	1	2	3	4
1	2	3	4	5
2	3	4	5	6
3	4	5	6	7
4	5	6	7	8

b)

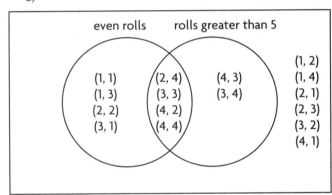

c) 4   d) $\dfrac{6}{16}$ or $\dfrac{3}{8}$

13. a)

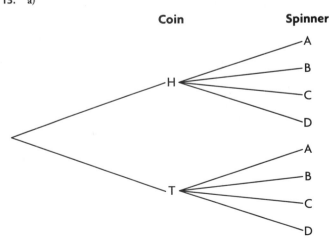

b) 8
c) $\dfrac{1}{8}$
14. a) 7! = 5040   b) $\dfrac{7!}{2!} = 2520$ c) $\dfrac{7!}{3!2!} = 420$
15. $n = 4$
16. 0.25
17. a) 0.000 016 3...
   b) 0.000 000 000 006 29...
18. a) $\dfrac{3}{124\,750}$ or 0.000 024 0...
   b) $\dfrac{246\,512}{249\,500}$ or 0.988...
   c) $\dfrac{2982}{249\,500}$ or 0.011 9...

Chapter 4

Getting Started, page 88

1. a) iv)   b) ii)   c) v)   d) vii)   e) iii)   f) i)   g) vi)
2. a) $\dfrac{3}{8}$ b) $\dfrac{2}{3}$ c) $\dfrac{1}{6}$ d) $\dfrac{16}{5}$ or $3\dfrac{1}{5}$
3. a) $\dfrac{8}{7}$ or $1\dfrac{1}{7}$ b) $\dfrac{14}{15}$ c) $\dfrac{1}{2}$ d) $\dfrac{5}{12}$
4. a) $x = 0$ or $x = -4$ b) $x = \dfrac{2}{3}$ or $x = -\dfrac{2}{3}$ c) $x = 3$
5. a) $x = \dfrac{7}{20}$ b) $x = 2$ or $x = -7$
6. $4\dfrac{1}{6}$ in.²

[rectangle: width $1\dfrac{1}{3}$ in.; split into $\dfrac{7}{8}$ in. and $2\dfrac{1}{4}$ in.]

7. e.g., To determine how many $\dfrac{1}{8}$ portions there are in $2\dfrac{5}{8}$ pizzas, you have to divide $2\dfrac{5}{8}$ by $\dfrac{1}{8}$. This means that you are determining how many times $\dfrac{1}{8}$ goes into $2\dfrac{5}{8}$.
8. a) $\dfrac{103}{342}$ km/min   b) 18.1 km/h

Lesson 4.1, page 90

1. a) e.g., $\dfrac{x^2}{x^2 + 25}$ c) e.g., $\dfrac{y + 2y^2}{2y}$
   b) e.g., $\dfrac{x^2 - 4x}{5x^3}$ d) e.g., $\dfrac{2x - 4}{x}$
2. a) e.g., t = time for journey, in hours; speed = $\dfrac{60}{t}$ km/h, $t > 0$
   b) e.g., t = time for journey, in hours; speed = $\dfrac{150}{t}$ km/h, $t \neq 0$
   c) e.g., t = time for journey, in hours; speed = $\dfrac{20\,000}{t}$ leagues/h, $t \neq 0$
   d) e.g., b = height of beanstalk; rate of growth = $\dfrac{b}{20}$ mm/day, $b > 0$
3. a) none; e.g., $\dfrac{8x - 4}{6x^2 + 2}$
   b) $x = 2$, $x = -3$; e.g., $\dfrac{4x - 8}{4x^2 - 24}$
   c) $x = -5$, $x = 5$; e.g., $\dfrac{2x - 10}{2x^2 - 50}$

d) $x = 1, x = -2$; e.g., $\dfrac{x}{6x^2 - 6x}$

e) $x = -1$; e.g., $\dfrac{x^2}{2x^3 + x^3}$

f) $x = -3, x = 4$; e.g., $\dfrac{4x^2 + 12x}{4x^3 - 48x}$

4. B.   **5.** C.   **6.** A.

7. **a)** e.g., $\dfrac{1}{60x - 30}, x \neq \dfrac{1}{2}$

b) $x > \dfrac{1}{2}$; e.g., so the newer machine harvests a row in a positive amount of time

8. e.g., **a)** $\dfrac{7}{t - 20}$

b) $t = 20$; e.g., Division by zero is not defined.

c) $t \neq 20$

Lesson 4.2, page 94

1. **a)** $x \neq 0, x \neq \sqrt{2}$; $\dfrac{3}{2(2 - x^2)}$ **c)** $x \neq 3, -3$; $\dfrac{1}{x - 3}$

b) $x \neq 0$; $\dfrac{x + 2}{7x}$ **d)** $x \neq -6$; $\dfrac{1}{x + 6}$

2. **a)** $\dfrac{-4}{3y^2}, y \neq 0$ **c)** $4y^2, y \neq 0$ **e)** $\dfrac{3x^2}{4}, x \neq 0$

b) $\dfrac{-5}{4x^2}, x \neq 0$ **d)** $\dfrac{9s}{4}, s \neq 0$ **f)** $\dfrac{37s^3}{(s + 2)}, s \neq -2$

3. **a)** $\dfrac{7x^2}{6(3x + 1)}, x \neq -\dfrac{1}{3}$ **c)** $\dfrac{x + 1}{x - 3}, x \neq 3$

b) $\dfrac{9}{x^2 + 1}, x \neq 0$ **d)** $\dfrac{6}{3x - 1}, x \neq -2, x \neq -\dfrac{1}{3}$

4. **a)** $\dfrac{-5}{4x^2}, x \neq 0$ **c)** $\dfrac{35}{11x}, x \neq 0$ **e)** $\dfrac{8}{5t}, t \neq 0$

b) $\dfrac{4}{-3r}, r \neq 0$ **d)** $\dfrac{3x^2}{4}, x \neq 0$ **f)** $\dfrac{11u}{-5}, u \neq 0$

5. **a)** $\dfrac{4 - x}{x + 8}, x \neq 0, x \neq -8$ **d)** $\dfrac{7x^2}{x - 5}, x \neq 0, x \neq 5$

b) $\dfrac{3}{x}, x \neq -\sqrt{\dfrac{1}{2}}, x \neq \sqrt{\dfrac{1}{2}}$ **e)** $\dfrac{7x + 1}{3x + 2}, x \neq -\dfrac{2}{3}$

c) $\dfrac{2x(3 - x)}{(2 - x)}, x \neq 0, x \neq 2$ **f)** $\dfrac{x + 2}{x - 4}, x \neq 0, x \neq 4$

6. **a)** $\dfrac{8}{2x^2 + 1}, x \neq 0$ **c)** $\dfrac{x + 2}{x - 4}, x \neq 0, x \neq 4$

b) $\dfrac{-4}{3x^2}, x \neq 0$ **d)** 1, none

7. B.   **8.** D.   **9.** A.   **10.** C.

11. 2.625 mg/L

Lesson 4.3, page 98

1. **a)** $x = 5, x = \dfrac{1}{2}$ **b)** $x = 0, x = 1, x = -4$ **c)** none

d) $x = -2, x = 0, x = 3$

2. **a)** $\dfrac{1}{9x^2}, x \neq 0$ **b)** $128x, x \neq 0$ **c)** $\dfrac{-x}{6}, x \neq 0$ **d)** $\dfrac{3x}{2}, x \neq 0$

3. **a)** $\dfrac{6x^2}{3x - 1}, x \neq -2, x \neq \dfrac{1}{3}$ **c)** $\dfrac{(x - 4)(x + 2)}{x(2x - 1)}, x \neq \dfrac{1}{2}$

b) $\dfrac{4x^4}{2x + 1}, x \neq -2, x \neq -\dfrac{1}{2}$ **d)** $\dfrac{4x(x - 2)}{x - 5}, x \neq 5, x \neq -3$

4. **a)** $\dfrac{5(2x - 1)}{3(x + 2)(x + 5)}, x \neq -2, x \neq -5, x \neq \dfrac{1}{2}$

b) $\dfrac{8x}{x + 5}, x \neq \dfrac{3}{2}, x \neq -5$

c) $\dfrac{(5x - 2)(x - 1)}{(x + 1)(x + 2)} \ x \neq -2, x \neq -1, x \neq 1$

d) $4x, x \neq -2, x \neq -1$

5. **a)** $\dfrac{1}{2(4x + 1)}; x \neq -5, x \neq \dfrac{1}{4}$

b) $\dfrac{x}{2}, x \neq -7, x \neq 0$

c) $\dfrac{9(x + 7)(x + 1)}{2(x - 3)(x - 1)}, x \neq 0, x \neq 1, x \neq 3$

6. $\dfrac{9(x + 7)(x - 1)}{2(x - 3)(x + 1)}, x \neq -1, x \neq 0, x \neq 1, x \neq 3$

7. **a)** $3, \dfrac{1}{4}$ **b)** none   **c)** $-2, 0, 2$ **d)** $2, 0, -4$

8. e.g., Fatouma thought that $(x + 6)$ and $(x + 3)$ are common factors, but they are not.

$$\dfrac{2x(x + 6)}{3x(x - 2)} \div \dfrac{(x - 3)}{3(x - 2)}$$

$$= \dfrac{2x(x + 6)}{3x(x - 2)} \cdot \dfrac{3(x - 2)}{(x + 3)}$$

$$= \dfrac{2x(x + 6)}{3x(x - 2)} \cdot \dfrac{3(x - 2)}{(x + 3)}$$

$$= \dfrac{2(x + 6)}{(x + 3)}$$

Lesson 4.4, page 102

1. **a)** $2x^2(x - 2)$ **b)** $24x^3$ **c)** $x(2x - 1)$ **d)** $(x - 3)(x - 1)(x + 1)$

2. **a)** $x \neq 0, 2$ **b)** $z \neq 3, x \neq -3$ **c)** $x \neq 0$ **d)** $x \neq 1, x \neq -1, x \neq 3$

3. **a)** $2x, x \neq 0$ **c)** $\dfrac{-5y - 3}{y(y + 2)}, y \neq 0, y \neq -2$

b) $\dfrac{7x - 2}{x + 1}, x \neq -1$ **d)** $\dfrac{9z - 1}{z^2(z - 1)}, z \neq 0, z \neq 1$

4. **a)** $\dfrac{-19a + 20}{10a^2}, a \neq 0$ **c)** $\dfrac{6(11x + 2)}{11x}, x \neq 0$

b) $\dfrac{27y^2 - 18y + 1}{6y^2}, y \neq 0$ **d)** $\dfrac{2b^2 - 9}{6b}, b \neq 0$

5. **a)** $\dfrac{2(x + 1)}{(x - 2)(x + 2)}, x \neq 2, x \neq -2$

b) $\dfrac{x + 3}{3(x + 6)}, x \neq -6$

c) $\dfrac{3x(3x - 1)}{(3x + 2)(3x - 2)}, x \neq \dfrac{2}{3}, x \neq -\dfrac{2}{3}$

d) $\dfrac{-x(x^2 + 2x - 1)}{2(x - 2)(x + 2)}, x = 2, x \neq -2$

6. **a)** $\dfrac{-2x^2 + 5x - 3}{(x - 3)(x + 3)}, x \neq 3, x \neq -3$

b) $\dfrac{3x^2 + 9x - 5}{(5x - 3)(4x + 5)}, x \neq \dfrac{3}{5}, x \neq -\dfrac{5}{4}$

c) $\dfrac{2x^3 - 6x^2 + 19x + 18}{(2x^2 - 3)(4x + 3)}, x \neq \dfrac{3}{2}, x \neq -\dfrac{3}{4}$

7. B.   **8.** A.   **9.** D.

10. $\dfrac{2x}{3x + 2} - \dfrac{2x + 1}{x + 1} = \dfrac{2x(x + 1)}{(3x + 2)(x + 1)} - \dfrac{(2x + 1)(3x + 2)}{(3x + 2)(x + 1)}$

$$= \dfrac{2x^2 + 2x}{(3x + 2)(x + 1)} - \dfrac{6x^2 + 7x + 2}{(3x + 2)(x + 1)}$$

$$= \dfrac{2x^2 + 2x - 6x^2 - 7x - 2}{(3x + 2)(x + 1)}$$

$$= \dfrac{-4x^2 - 5x - 2}{(3x + 2)(x + 1)}, x \neq 1, x \neq -\dfrac{2}{3}$$

Lesson 4.5, page 106

1. a) $x \neq 2$; $x = -4$ **c)** $x \neq 0$; $x = 4$
    b) $x \neq 3$; no solution   **d)** $x \neq 2$; $x = 4$

2. a) $v =$ original speed, in kilometres per hour; $\dfrac{100}{v - 20}$; $v > 20$

    b) $t =$ original time for distance, in metres per second; $\dfrac{2t}{150}$; $t > 0$

    c) $t =$ time for Bobby to complete the job, in minutes; $\dfrac{150}{2t}$; $t \neq -5$, $t > 0$

3. a) $x \neq 2$; $x = 5$; $\dfrac{5 + 7}{5 - 2} = 4$

    b) $x \neq 2$; $x = 3$; $\dfrac{3 + 5}{3 - 2} = 2(3) + 2 = 8$

4. a) $x \neq 0, -2$; $x = 3$, $\dfrac{6}{3(3) - 2(3)} + \dfrac{2}{2(3) + 4} = \dfrac{3(3) + 2}{5} = \dfrac{11}{5}$

    b) $x \neq 0, 3$; $x = 7$; $\dfrac{7 + 2}{7 - 3} - \dfrac{7 + 3}{7} = \dfrac{3(7) + 2}{4(7)} = \dfrac{23}{28}$

    c) $x \neq -4, \dfrac{4}{3}$; $x = 2$; $\dfrac{5}{3(2) - 4} - \dfrac{4}{2 + 4} = \dfrac{4(2) + 3}{6} = \dfrac{11}{6}$

    d) $x \neq 1, 2$; $x = 3$; $\dfrac{3 - 4}{3^2 - 4} + \dfrac{8}{3 - 1} = \dfrac{3}{10}$

5. a) $-1, -\dfrac{1}{7}$ **b)** $x = 7$

6. a) $1, -1, -\dfrac{7}{2}$ **b)** $x = 4$

7. about 175 min

Chapter 4 Test Prep, page 110

Q1: • A rational expression is undefined for values of the <u>variable</u> that make the <u>denominator</u> equal to <u>zero</u>. These are called <u>non-permissible</u> values.

Q2: • The <u>greatest</u> common <u>factor</u> (<u>GCF</u>) of the numerator and denominator is <u>1</u>.
   • The <u>non-permissible</u> values are stated, based on the denominators be<u>fore</u> the expression was <u>simplified</u>.

Q3: Both processes involve the following steps:
   • <u>Factor</u> the <u>numerators</u> and <u>denominators</u>, if possible.
   • Identify all <u>non-permissible</u> values and write them as restrictions.
   • <u>Multiply</u> the numerators and multiply the <u>denominators</u>. Write as a <u>single</u> rational <u>expression</u>.
   • <u>Simplify</u> using <u>common</u> factors.
   • Write the product, stating the <u>restrictions</u> on the <u>variable</u>.

Q4: The <u>LCD</u> is the product of all the <u>common</u> factors and all the unique <u>factors</u> of the <u>denominators</u>. It is not always the <u>product</u> of <u>all</u> the factors.

Q5: • An extraneous root is a root of the equation that is a non-permissible value. It <u>is not</u> a valid solution of the equation.
   • An inadmissible solution <u>is</u> a valid solution of the equation, but is ruled out by the <u>context</u> of the problem.

Chapter 4 Test, page 111

1. A.   **2.** B.   **3.** D.   **4.** A.   **5.** D.   **6.** A.

7. a) e.g., $\dfrac{6x^2 + 3x}{4x^2 + 4x + 1}$; $-\dfrac{1}{2}$ **b)** e.g., $\dfrac{y^2 + 2y^3}{2y^2}$; 0

8. a) $\dfrac{-7}{4x^2}$; 0 **b)** $\dfrac{x + 6}{2}$; $0, -4$ **c)** $x + 4$; 5 **d)** $\dfrac{1}{5x}$; 0

9. a) $2, \dfrac{3}{4}$ **b)** none

10. a) $\dfrac{(3x - 2)(2 - x)}{(2x + 5)(x - 6)}$; $0, -\dfrac{5}{2}, 6$ **c)** $\dfrac{18}{4 - x}$; $0, 4$

    b) $\dfrac{15}{2x(3 - 2x)}$; $0, -3, \dfrac{2}{3}$

11. a) $0, -\dfrac{1}{2}$ **b)** 4

12. a) $-\dfrac{3}{4}, -\dfrac{2}{5}, -16$ **b)** 4

13. $\dfrac{4x}{6x + 5} - \dfrac{x + 4}{x - 2} = \dfrac{(4x)(x - 2)}{(6x + 5)(x - 2)} - \dfrac{(x + 4)(6x + 5)}{(x - 2)(6x + 5)}$

Step 1: Multiply each term by 1.

$= \dfrac{4x^2 - 8x}{(6x + 5)(x - 2)} - \dfrac{6x^2 + 11x + 20}{(x - 2)(6x + 5)}$

Step 2: Simplify the numerators.

$= \dfrac{4x^2 - 8x - (6x^2 + 11x + 20)}{(6x + 5)(x - 2)}$

Step 3: Combine the numerators.

$= \dfrac{4x^2 - 8x - 6x^2 - 11x - 20}{(6x + 5)(x - 2)}$

Step 4: Change the sign.

$= \dfrac{-2x^2 - 19x - 20}{(6x + 5)(x - 2)}$, $x \neq -\dfrac{5}{6}$, $x \neq 2$

Step 5: Cannot simplify further.

14. about 230 min

Chapter 5

Getting Started, page 114

1. a) ii)   **b)** vi)   **c)** v)   **d)** iii)   **e)** i)   **f)** iv)

2. a) $y = \dfrac{1}{3}x - 1$ **b)** $y = -\dfrac{1}{2}x + 4$ **c)** $y = -3x + 4$ **d)** $y = 4x - 3$

3. a) maximum: 4; vertex: (2, 4); axis of symmetry: $x = 2$; opens down; y-intercept: -3
    b) minimum: 4; vertex: $(-1, 4)$; axis of symmetry: $x = -1$; opens up; y-intercept: 7

4. a) parabola, opening up, with vertex at $(5, -3)$, minimum value of -3, y-intercept of 7
    b) e.g., decreasing linear function, y-intercept of 5
    c) e.g., parabola, opening down, maximum value of 27, y-intercept of 24
    d) e.g., constant linear function, with y-intercept of -2

5. a) quadratic; e.g., the function has a minimum point, so it is not linear, and it appears to be symmetric around the point $(2, -3)$
    b) neither; e.g., it looks like the function has a maximum point at or near $(0, 4)$, which linear functions do not have, but the function is not symmetric about this point, so it is not a quadratic
    c) linear; e.g., these points all lie on a straight line with slope -2 and y-intercept 3

Lesson 5.1, page 116

1. a) cubic polynomial function   **c)** not a polynomial function
    b) linear polynomial function

Lesson 5.2, page 118

1. Graph A: 1; 2; II, IV, negative; $\{x \mid x \in R\}$, $\{y \mid y \in R\}$; none; linear; iii)
    Graph B: 1; -1; II, IV, negative; $\{x \mid x \in R\}$, $\{y \mid y \in R\}$; 2; cubic; i)
    Graph C: 1; -2; III, I, positive; $\{x \mid x \in R\}$, $\{y \mid y \in R\}$; 2; cubic; iv)
    Graph D: 1; 2; III, I, positive; $\{x \mid x \in R\}$, $\{y \mid y \in R\}$; none; linear; ii)

2. a) e.g., $f(x) = -2x^2 + 2x + 4$ **c)** e.g., $f(x) = 4x^3 - 3$
    b) e.g., $f(x) = -4x - 2$ **d)** e.g., $f(x) = 2x^3 - x + 5$

3. a) 2; -3; 1; 0, 1, or 2; 1; III, IV; $\{x \mid x \in R\}$; $\{y \mid y \leq$ maximum, $y \in R\}$; 1
    b) 3; 4; 34; 1, 2, or 3; 34; III, I; $\{x \mid x \in R\}$; $\{y \mid y \in R\}$; 0 or 2

4. a) e.g., The degree of the function is 1, so the graph is a line. The leading coefficient is positive, so the graph extends from Quadrant III to Quadrant I. The constant term is -390.8. The graph has one x-intercept and one y-intercept. The domain is $\{x \mid 1920 \leq x \leq 2008, x \in I\}$. The range is $\{y \mid y > 0, y \in I\}$.

b) e.g., No; according to the equation, a male born in 1000 would live for −156.9 years, which does not make sense. This graph should be used only to estimate life expectancy for Canadian males born from 1920 to 2008.

Lesson 5.3, page 122

1. e.g., **a)** $f(x) = -0.101x + 257.366$ **b)** 54.38 s
   c) The estimated time is 0.12 s less than the actual time.
2. e.g., **a)** $f(x) = -0.063...x + 1.859...$ **b)** $0.90/L   **c)** $13 500
3. e.g., **a)** $f(x) = -0.38x + 433$ **b)** $243.00   **c)** 193 parkas
4. D.
5. I entered the data into my calculator, with number of horses as the independent variable and area as the dependent variable. I used the regression feature on my calculator to determine the equation of the line of best fit for the data. The equation is $f(x) = 145.211...x + 86.107...$. I graphed the equation and the scatter plot of the data. According to the equation, if $x = 15$, then the value of $f(x)$ is 2264.287.... The stable should have 2264 ft^2 for 15 horses.

Lesson 5.4, page 126

1. e.g., **a)** The population appears to have grown in a quadratic curve from 1871 to 2001. The leading coefficient of the equation will be positive.
   b) $f(x) = 1.537...x^2 - 5736.200...x + 5\ 355\ 423.403...$
   c) about 33 930 000 people
   d) about 40 260 000 people
2. e.g., **a)** The ball appears to go up in a quadratic curve, and then descend as part of the same curve. The leading coefficient of the equation will be negative.
   b) $f(x) = -9.521x^2 + 42.546x + 12$
   c) 59.008 m
   d) 4.7 s
3. e.g., **a)** At first, the bacteria's mass grows quickly, then less quickly, then quickly again. The growth appears to represent a cubic function with a positive leading coefficient.
   b) $f(x) = 0.023...x^3 - 0.233...x^2 + 1.257...x + 2.442...$
   c) about 18.9 g
4. e.g., **a)** $f(x) = -3.879...x^2 - 2.698...x + 24.999..$

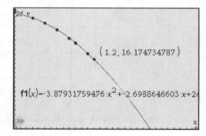

   b) about 16.17 m
5. e.g., **a)** The points bend twice, like a cubic function with a positive leading coefficient.

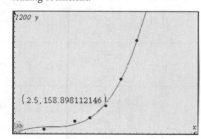

   b) $f(x) = 37.133...x^3 - 132.674...x^2 + 165.256...x - 5.243..$
   c) 58.9 cm^3
6. e.g., **a)** $f(x) = 0.006x^2 + -0.006x + 5$ **b)** 23.36 m
7. e.g., **a)** The data points curve upward. They appear to represent a quadratic function with a positive leading coefficient.

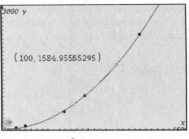

b) $f(x) = 0.163...x^2 - 0.742...x + 23.797...$ **c)** 1585 s
8. e.g., **a)** The data points curve upward. They appear to represent a quadratic function with a positive leading coefficient.

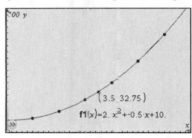

b) $f(x) = 2x^2 - 0.5x + 10$ **c)** 32.8 min

Chapter 5 Test Prep, page 131

Q1: Possible types of ranges for polynomial functions are $\{y \mid y \in R\}$, $\{y \mid y \leq max, y \in R\}$, and $\{y \mid y \geq min, y \in R\}$. A range such as $\{y \mid min \leq y \leq max, y \in R\}$ does not match a polynomial function.

Q2: • The maximum number of x-intercepts is equal to the degree of the function.
• The maximum number of turning points is equal to one less than the degree of the function.
• A quadratic function always has one turning point. A cubic function may have zero or two turning points.

Q3: • Linear and cubic functions with a negative leading coefficient extend from Quadrant II to Quadrant IV.
• Quadratic functions extend from Quadrant II to Quadrant I when the leading coefficient is positive, and from Quadrant III to Quadrant IV when it is negative.
• Linear and cubic functions with a positive leading coefficient extend from Quadrant III to Quadrant I.

Q4: **A1:** To create a graphical model, create a scatter plot.
   A2: To create an algebraic model, use linear, quadratic, or cubic regression to determine the equation of the line or curve of best fit.

Chapter 5 Test, page 132

1. B.   **2.** A.   **3.** D.   **4.** C.
5. horizontal, straight line; 0, 1; II, I; $\{x \mid x \in R\}$; $\{y \mid y = 3, y \in R\}$; 0; constant, linear
6. **a)** 1; 14; 3; 1; 3; II, I; $\{x \mid x \in R\}$; $\{y \mid y \in R\}$; 0
   b) 3; 9; −1; 1; −1; III, I; $\{x \mid x \in R\}$; $\{y \mid y \in R\}$; 1
7. e.g., $6010
8. e.g., **a)** $f(x) = 0.004x^2 - 0.004x + 2$ **b)** 24.20 m
9. **a)** cubic polynomial function   **b)** quadratic polynomial function
10. e.g., I plotted the points on a graph using technology, and they appeared to form a straight line. A linear regression gave the equation $f(x) = -0.00112x + 12.24$. 6000 packets would cost $5.52 each. $6000 \times \$5.52 = \$33\ 120$, so the manager should expect to pay $33 120 for 6000 packets.
11. e.g., **a)** At first, the bacteria's mass grows quickly, then less quickly, then quickly again. The growth appears to represent a cubic function with a positive leading coefficient.
   b) $f(x) = 0.12x^3 - x^2 + 13x + 5$
   c) about 58.02 g

12. e.g., I ran a quadratic regression function. The function $f(x) = 0.5x^2 - 0.5x + 2$ models the data, where x is the day of the week. According to the equation, Kendall will solve Friday's puzzle in 12 min.

4–5 Cumulative Test, page 136

1. D   **2.** A   **3.** B   **4.** C   **5.** D

6. $a = \dfrac{20}{9}, a \neq 0$

7. $y = -5$

8. 2

9. 3

10. **a)** e.g., $\dfrac{2y}{1}$

b) e.g., $y = -4$

c) e.g., for $y = 0$, $\dfrac{2(0)^2 + 8(0)}{0 + 4} = \dfrac{0}{4} = 0$

for $y = 0$, $\dfrac{2y}{1} = \dfrac{2(0)}{1} = 0$

11. **a)** $x \neq 0, -\dfrac{6}{x^2}$

b) $n \neq 2, -2, \dfrac{3}{n + 2}$

12. **a)** $8x^2, x \neq 0$ **b)** $5b^8, b \neq 0$ **c)** $\dfrac{5}{8y^5}, y \neq 0$

13. **a)** $6, a \neq -3, 3$ **b)** $2y, y \neq -\dfrac{3}{5}, \dfrac{3}{5}$

14. **a)** $\dfrac{15x - 2}{10x^3}, x \neq 0$ **b)** $\dfrac{3y^2 + y}{(y + 5)(y - 2)}, y \neq 5, 2$

15. $x \neq -5, 5; x = -15$ or $x = 1$

16. Ted: 105.25 min; Cam: 95.25 min

17. domain: $x \in$ R; range: $y \in$ R; intercepts: $x = -5, -4, 3, y = -6$; end behaviour: graph extends from Quadrant III to Quadrant I

18. **a)** end behaviour: graph extends from Quadrant II to Quadrant I; 1 possible turning point; 2 possible x-intercepts; y-intercept: $y = -12$; domain: $x \in$ R; range: $\{y \mid y \geq -16, y \in$ R$\}$

b) end behaviour: graph extends from Quadrant II to Quadrant IV; 2 possible turning points; 3 possible x-intercepts; y-intercept: $y = 1$; domain: $x \in$ R; range: $y \in$ R

19. **a)** $y = 9.8x + 59$ **b)** about \$177   **c)** the 15th month

Chapter 6

Getting Started, page 140

1. **a)** iii)   **b)** v)   **c)** iv)   **d)** ii)   **e)** vi)   **f)** i)

2. **a)** $\{x \mid x \in$ R$\}$; $\{y \mid y \in$ R$\}$ **c)** $\{x \mid x \in$ R$\}$; $\{y \mid y \in$ R$\}$
b) $\{x \mid x \in$ R$\}$; $\{y \mid y \leq -3, y \in$ R$\}$ **d)** $\{x \mid x \in$ R$\}$; $\{y \mid y \geq -5, y \in$ R$\}$

3. **a)** decreasing
b) increasing when $x < 0$, decreasing when $x > 0$
c) increasing
d) decreasing when $x < 1$, increasing when $x > 1$

4. **a)** e.g., $\{n \mid n \in$ N$\}$ **b)** e.g., $\{t \mid t \geq 0, t \in$ R$\}$

5. **a)** e.g., $\{c \mid c \geq 9, c \in$ N$\}$ **b)** e.g., $\{h \mid -50 \leq h \leq 20, h \in$ R$\}$

6. **a)** $3, -3; -27$ **b)** $3; 0.75$ **c)** $0, 1; 0$ **d)** none; 3

7. **a)** $y = -\dfrac{3}{4}x + 3$

b) yes; e.g., the vertex of the graph of $y = \dfrac{3}{16}(x - 4)^2$ is at $(4, 0)$, which is the only x-intercept; substituting $x = 0$ gives a y-intercept of $(0, 3)$

Lesson 6.1, page 142

1. **a)**

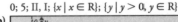
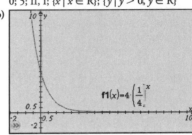

0; 5; II, I; $\{x \mid x \in$ R$\}$; $\{y \mid y > 0, y \in$ R$\}$

b)

0; 4; II, I; $\{x \mid x \in$ R$\}$; $\{y \mid y > 0, y \in$ R$\}$

2. B.

3. **a)** 0   **b)** 0.5   **c)** II, I   **d)** $\{x \mid x \in$ R$\}$ **e)** $\{y \mid y > 0, y \in$ R$\}$

Lesson 6.2, page 144

1. **a)** Yes, because the consecutive y-values increase by the same ratio of $2:1$.
b) No, because the consecutive y-values do not increase by the same ratio.
c) Yes, because the consecutive y-values decrease by the same ratio of $1:4$.

2. **a)** yes, because consecutive y-values increase by the same ratio, $2:1$; y-intercept $= 3$; function is increasing
b) no, because consecutive y-values do not increase by the same ratio

3.

	Number of x-intercepts	y-intercept	End Behaviour	Domain	Range
a)	0	3	from Quadrant II to Quadrant I	$\{x \mid x \in$ R$\}$	$\{y \mid y > 0, y \in$ R$\}$
b)	0	2	from Quadrant II to Quadrant I	$\{x \mid x \in$ R$\}$	$\{y \mid y > 0, y \in$ R$\}$
c)	0	4	from Quadrant II to Quadrant I	$\{x \mid x \in$ R$\}$	$\{y \mid y > 0, y \in$ R$\}$
d)	0	5	from Quadrant II to Quadrant I	$\{x \mid x \in$ R$\}$	$\{y \mid y > 0, y \in$ R$\}$

4.

	Function	Number of x-intercepts	y-intercept	End Behaviour	Domain	Range
a)	$y = 2.5(5)^x$	0	3	from Quadrant II to Quadrant I	$\{x \mid x \in$ R$\}$	$\{y \mid y > 0, y \in$ R$\}$
b)	$y = 14(0.4)^x$	0	2	from Quadrant II to Quadrant I	$\{x \mid x \in$ R$\}$	$\{y \mid y > 0, y \in$ R$\}$
c)	$y = 3\left(\dfrac{1}{3}\right)^x$	0	4	from Quadrant II to Quadrant I	$\{x \mid x \in$ R$\}$	$\{y \mid y > 0, y \in$ R$\}$
d)	$y = 3.1\left(\dfrac{1}{4}\right)^x$	0	5	from Quadrant II to Quadrant I	$\{x \mid x \in$ R$\}$	$\{y \mid y > 0, y \in$ R$\}$
e)	$y = 20(2.1)^x$	0	20	from Quadrant II to Quadrant I	$\{x \mid x \in$ R$\}$	$\{y \mid y > 0, y \in$ R$\}$
f)	$y = 10(0.5)^x$	0	10	from Quadrant II to Quadrant I	$\{x \mid x \in$ R$\}$	$\{y \mid y > 0, y \in$ R$\}$

5. **a)** e.g., The base is 7. It is increasing, because $b > 1$.

b) e.g., The base is $\frac{3}{4}$. It is decreasing, because $0 < b < 1$.

6.

	Function	y-intercept	Base	Increasing or Decreasing
a)	$y = 5(2)^x$	5	2	increasing
b)	$y = 6\left(\frac{1}{3}\right)^x$	6	$\frac{1}{3}$	decreasing
c)	$y = 5(6)^x$	5	6	increasing
d)	$y = 25\left(\frac{1}{7}\right)^x$	25	$\frac{1}{7}$	decreasing
e)	$y = 20(1.8)^x$	20	1.8	increasing
f)	$y = (0.4)^x$	1	0.4	decreasing

7. A.

8. **a)** increasing, because $b > 1$ **b)** decreasing, because $0 < b < 1$

Lesson 6.3, page 148

1. **a)** e.g., 0.42 and 1.74   **b)** e.g., 0.14, 0.43

2. **a)** $x = 2$ **b)** $x = \frac{1}{2}$

3. **a)** $x = -3$ **c)** $x = 2$

b) $n = -4$ **d)** $x = -\frac{7}{2}$

4. **a)** $x = -0.666...$ **b)** $x = -0.2$

5. (0.8, 3.7)

6. **a)** 30 years   **b)** 79.4%   **c)** 99.7 years

7. **a)** $t = 18$

b) e.g., The population of bacteria will grow to 87 500 in 18 h.

8. **a)** $21 258   **b)** about 6.6 years

c) e.g., Yes, it is possible if you know the date on which the car was bought. For example, if the car was bought on January 2, 2012, then it will be worth $18 000 about 6.6 years after that, or about July 2018.

Lesson 6.4, page 153

1. **a)** exponential growth, because the y-coordinates increase by the same ratio, $2.5:1$; $f(x) = 2(2.5)^x$

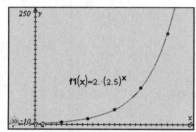

b) neither, because the y-coordinates increase in a linear fashion.

c) exponential decay, because the y-coordinates decrease by the same ratio, $\frac{1}{3}:1$; $f(x) = 63\,423\left(\frac{1}{3}\right)^x$

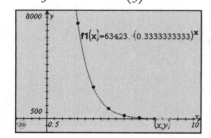

2. **a)**

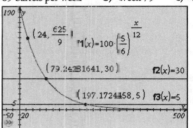

b) $f(x) = 5.150...(1.018...)^x$ **c)** 4 070 000   **d)** 2017

3. e.g., **a)** $f(x) = 1.569...(1.020...)^x$ **b)** 92.4

c) My value was 1.1 greater than the actual value.

4. **a)** $5.475...(1.135...)^x$ **b)** $\approx 817\,000$ **c)** 2012

5. **a)** 69 barrels per week   **b)** Week 79   **c)** Week 197

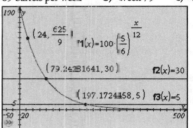

Lesson 6.5, page 157

1. **a)** I: $2000; II: $3500

b) I: 6% interest, compounded annually; II: 2.5% interest, compounded annually

c) I: $2676.45; II: $3959.93

d) I: 12 years; II: 6 years

2. **a)** $A = 4000(1.053...)^n$ **b)** $4118.04

3. e.g., $78.22

4. **a)** 73 months

b) $28 825.71; e.g., There are 72.064...payments of $400 each. $(72.064...)(400) = 28\,825.705...$

5. **a)** 2.5%   **b)** $3000; e.g., because $f(0) = 3000$ **c)** $3394.20

6. **a)** B.   **b)** C.

7. **a)**

Time (end of year)	2	3	4	5	6	7
Value of Equipment ($)	40 000	34 000	28 900	24 565	20 880	17 748

e.g., I multiplied by 0.15 and subtracted. I recorded each value to the nearest dollar, but did not round during my calculations.

b) $A(t) = 55\,363.321...(0.85)^t$ **c)** $10 899.62

Chapter 6 Test Prep, page 162

Q1: An exponential function of the form $f(x) = \underline{a}(\underline{b})^x$, where $a > 0$, $\underline{b} > 0$, and $b \neq \underline{1}$,
- has $\underline{0}$ x-intercept(s) and 1 y-intercept(s)
- extends from Quadrant $\underline{II}$ to Quadrant $\underline{I}$
- has domain $\{x \mid x \in R\}$ and range $\{y \mid y > 0, y \in R\}$

Q2: • The value of a is the y-intercept of the graph of the function.
- The value of b in the exponential function determines whether the function increases or decreases. The function increases when $\underline{b > 1}$. The function decreases when $\underline{0 < b < 1}$.

Q3: **A1:** Algebraically: write both sides of the equation as powers of the same base (if possible). If $a^m = a^n$ with $a > 0$, $a \neq 1$, and m, $n \in R$, then $\underline{m = n}$.

A2: Graphically: Enter the equation as a system of equations on a graphing calculator, and then determine the point(s) of intersection. The x-coordinate of this point is the solution of the equation.

Q4: • If a scatter plot of the data appears to follow an exponential curve, you can use exponential regression to determine the exponential function that models the data.
- You can make predictions by reading values from the curve of best fit or by using the equation of the exponential regression function.

Chapter 6 Test, page 163

1. D. 2. B. 3. C. 4. a) B. b) A. 5. a) C. b) D.
6. a) 0 b) 4 c) II, I d) $\{x \mid x \in \mathbb{R}\}$ e) $\{y \mid y > 0, y \in \mathbb{R}\}$
7.

	Function	y-intercept	Base	Increasing or Decreasing
a)	$y = 7(3)^x$	7	2	increasing
b)	$y = 4\left(\dfrac{1}{3}\right)^x$	4	$\dfrac{1}{3}$	decreasing
c)	$y = 6(2)^x$	6	6	increasing

8. a) 29 years b) 62.0% c) 67.3 years
9. a) $12.376...(1.020...)^d$ b) 15.8 cm
10. a) $2.406...(1.106...)^x$ b) $362 billion; $3 billion less
    c) $491 billion; $168 billion more
11. Graph A represents an exponential function because it has no x-intercepts and 1 y-intercept, and extends from Quadrant II to Quadrant I; Graph B does not represent an exponential function because it has two x-intercepts.
12. a) increasing, because $a > 0$ and $b > 1$
    b) decreasing, because $a > 0$ and $0 < b < 1$
13.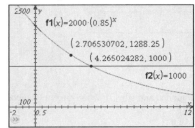

a) Week 4 b) Week 2
14. a)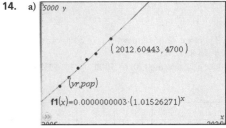

b) $f(x) = 0.000\ 000\ 000\ 271(1.015...)^x$
c) 5 265 120; e.g., I substituted $x = 2020$ into my function from part b).
d) e.g., in the second half of 2012; I identified the point of intersection of the regression function and $y = 4700$.
15. a) $f(x) = 11\ 999.911...(1.039...)^x$ b) $16 422.63

Chapter 7

Getting Started, page 168

1. a) ii) b) iv) c) iii) d) v) e) i)
2. a) e.g., $\{t \mid t \geq 0, t \in \mathbb{R}\}$ b) e.g., $\{n \mid n \in \mathbb{N}\}$
3. a) e.g., $\{V \mid V \geq 0, t \in \mathbb{R}\}$ b) e.g., $\{A \mid A \geq 5000, A \in \mathbb{R}\}$
4, 5. a) $x = -2.25, y = 9$ b) $x = 2, y = 24$ c) $x = 0$ or $2, y = 0$
6. a) $\{x \mid x \in \mathbb{R}\}, \{y \mid y > 0, y \in \mathbb{R}\}$ b) $\{x \mid x \in \mathbb{R}\}, \{y \mid y > 0, y \in \mathbb{R}\}$
7. a) increasing b) decreasing
8. a) $x = 4$ c) $x = -\dfrac{1}{2}$
   b) $x = -\dfrac{3}{2}$ d) $x = 2$
9. a) 5730 years b) 42.9% c) 15 700 years

Lesson 7.1, page 170

1.

	x-intercept	Number of y-intercepts	End Behaviour	Domain	Range
a)	1	0	from Quadrant I to Quadrant IV	$\{x \mid x > 0, x \in \mathbb{R}\}$	$\{y \mid y \in \mathbb{R}\}$
b)	1	0	from Quadrant IV to Quadrant I	$\{x \mid x > 0, x \in \mathbb{R}\}$	$\{y \mid y \in \mathbb{R}\}$

2.

	Function	x-intercept	Number of y-intercepts	End Behaviour	Domain	Range	Increasing or Decreasing
a)	$y = -4 \log x$	1	0	from Quadrant I to Quadrant IV	$\{x \mid x > 0, x \in \mathbb{R}\}$	$\{y \mid y \in \mathbb{R}\}$	decreasing
b)	$y = 13 \ln x$	1	0	from Quadrant IV to Quadrant I	$\{x \mid x > 0, x \in \mathbb{R}\}$	$\{y \mid y \in \mathbb{R}\}$	increasing
c)	$y = 20 \log x$	1	0	from Quadrant IV to Quadrant I	$\{x \mid x > 0, x \in \mathbb{R}\}$	$\{y \mid y \in \mathbb{R}\}$	increasing
d)	$y = -10 \ln x$	1	0	from Quadrant I to Quadrant IV	$\{x \mid x > 0, x \in \mathbb{R}\}$	$\{y \mid y \in \mathbb{R}\}$	decreasing

3. e.g., i) goes with c) because it is in logarithmic form and goes from Quadrant IV to Quadrant I; ii) goes with a) because it is in logarithmic form and goes from Quadrant I to Quadrant IV; iii) goes with b) because it is in exponential form and its y-intercept is 1.
4. a) Yes, it represents a logarithmic function; e.g., It extends from Quadrant I to Quadrant IV; it has no y-intercept; the x-intercept is 1; the domain is $\{x \mid x > 0, x \in \mathbb{R}\}$; the range is $\{y \mid y \in \mathbb{R}\}$.
   b) No, it does not represent a logarithmic function; e.g., It extends from Quadrant II to Quadrant I; it has a y-intercept; it has no x-intercept; the domain is $\{x \mid x \in \mathbb{R}\}$; the range is $\{y \mid y > 0, y \in \mathbb{R}\}$.
5. C. 6. A.
7. a) P-intercept: 100, no t-intercepts; $\{P \mid P > 0, P \in \mathbb{R}\}$, $\{t \mid t \in \mathbb{R}\}$; increasing; at $P = 100$, $t = 0$; e.g., the full amount of the sample at time $t = 0$
   b) about 30 years; e.g., I graphed the equations $y = -96.336 \log \dfrac{x}{100}$ and $y = 50$, then I determined their point of intersection.

Lesson 7.2, page 174

1. a) $x = 6^y$ b) $x = 12^y$
2. e.g., The equation $y = \log_b b$ is just another way of writing $b = b^y$. The only value of y for which this equation is true is 1. So, it must be that $\log_b b = 1$.
3. a) $y = \log_3 x$ b) $y = \log_4\left(\dfrac{1}{16}\right)$ c) $y = \log_5 x$ d) $y = \log_2 1024$
4. a) 1.18 b) 1.56 c) 2.71 d) 3.58
5. a) 2 b) 4 c) 4
6. a) $y = 2.477...$ b) $y = 2.484...$ c) $y = 0.920...$
7. a) 3 b) 5 c) -4
8. a) $\log_{\frac{1}{2}} 5 > \log_{\frac{1}{2}} 7$ c) $\log_{\frac{1}{4}} 4 = \log_{\frac{1}{5}} 5$
   b) $\log_3 5 > \log_5 3$ d) $\log\left(\dfrac{1}{16}\right) = \log 4^{-2}$
9. a) 10^6 or 1 000 000 times c) 10^3 or 1000 times
   b) 10^2 or 100 times d) $10^{2.6}$ or about 398 times
10. 2.5 times

Lesson 7.3, page 178

1. a) $\log_4 5 + \log_4 6$ b) $\log_a c + \log_a d$
2. a) $\log_2 (5 \cdot 4)$ b) not possible, because the bases are different
3. a) $\log_4 42 - \log_4 31$ b) $\log_5 d - \log_5 c$
4. a) $\log_3\left(\dfrac{14}{13}\right)$ b) $\log_4\left(\dfrac{25}{4}\right)$
5. a) $\log_6 36 = 2$ c) $\log 0.01 = -2$
   b) $\log_3 3 = 1$ d) $4 \log_2 2 = 4$

6. a) $\log_2 32 = 5$ c) $\ln\left(\dfrac{20}{3.5}\right) \doteq 1.74$

   b) $2\log 6 \doteq 1.56$ d) $\log_2 2 = 1$

7. yes, e.g., $\log_3 49 = \log_3 7 + \log_3 7$

8. e.g., a) $\log_2 16 + \log_2 4$; $\log_2 128 - \log_2 2$
   b) $\log_5 13 + \log_5 13$; $\log_5 338 - \log_5 2$
   c) $\log_4 36 + \log_4 6$; $\log_4 432 - \log_4 2$
   d) $\log_3 7 + \log_3 7$; $\log_3 98 - \log_3 2$
   e) $\log_4 12 + \log_4 12$; $\log_4 288 - \log_4 2$
   f) $\log_6 343 + \log_6 7$; $\log_6 4802 - \log_6 2$

9. a) $2\log_2 8$ c) $3\log_4 6$ e) $2\log_4 12$
   b) $2\log_5 13$ d) $2\log_3 7$ f) $4\log_6 7$ or $2\log_6 49$

10. a) $2\log 2.5 = 0.79$ b) $4\log_2 2^5 = 20$

11. D.   **12.** A.

13. agree; e.g., $\log_x 14 - \log_x 1 = \log_x\left(\dfrac{14}{1}\right)$, or $\log_x 14$;

   $\log_x 14 + \log_x 1 = \log_x(14 \cdot 1)$, or $\log_x 14$

Lesson 7.4, page 182

1. a) $x = 1.661$ b) $x = 2.087$
2. a) $x = 1.5$ b) $x = 0.368$
3. a) $x = -3.585$ b) $x = 0.333$ c) $x = 2.059$
4. a) $\dfrac{\log 40}{\log 4}$; 2.661 c) $\dfrac{\log 1000}{\log\left(\frac{1}{6}\right)}$; -3.855

   b) $\dfrac{\log\left(\frac{3}{8}\right)}{\log 2}$; -1.415 d) $\dfrac{\log 400}{\log 0.2}$; -3.723

5. a) $x = 0.73$ b) $x = 6.13$
6. 8 years
7. a) $x \doteq 4.17$ b) $x \doteq 18.34$
8. 13 days
9. D.   **10.** A.
11. 19 quarters; 3 years and 9 months
12. 21 years
13. 1298 days; 3.6 years

Lesson 7.5, page 186

1. $y = 0.036\ldots + 23.871\ldots\ln x$; x-intercept: 1, no y-intercepts; graph extends from Quadrant IV to Quadrant I; domain $\{x \mid x > 0, x \in R\}$, range $\{y \mid y \in R\}$; increasing

2. a)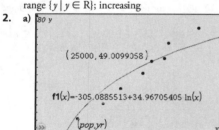
$(25000, 49.0099058)$
$f1(x) = -305.0885513 + 34.96705405\ln(x)$
(pop, yr)

   b) $t = -305.286\ldots + 34.986\ldots\ln P$; P-intercept $= 1$, no t-intercept; graph extends through Quadrant I; domain $\{P \mid P > 0, P \in N\}$, range $\{t \mid t \in R\}$; increasing
   c) 1989

3. a)
$(40000, 24.6474552)$
$f1(x) = -558.5206333 + 55.03332928\ln(x)$
(pop, yr)

   b) $t = -558.520\ldots + 55.033\ldots\ln x$; P-intercept $= 1$; no t-intercept; graph extends through Quadrant I; domain $\{P \mid P > 0, P \in N\}$, range $\{t \mid t \in R\}$; increasing
   c) 2021

4. 15 years; 21 years
5. 10 years

Chapter 7 Test Prep, page 190

Q1: A logarithmic function of the form $f(x) = a\log x$ or $f(x) = a\ln x$, where $a \neq 0$,
   • has $\underline{1}$ x-intercept(s) and $\underline{0}$ y-intercept(s)
   • extends from Quadrant IV to Quadrant I if $a \geq 0$, or from Quadrant I to Quadrant IV if $a \leq 0$
   • has domain $\{x \mid x > 0, x \in R\}$ and range $\{y \mid y \in R\}$

Q2: • The logarithmic function $y = \log_b x$ is equivalent to the exponential function $x = b^y$.

Q3: A1: Product Law of Logarithms: $\log_b mn = \log_b m + \log_b n$
   • Quotient Law of Logarithms: $\log_b\left(\dfrac{m}{n}\right) = \log_b m - \log_b n$
   • Power Law of Logarithms: $\log_b m^n = n\log_b m$
   A2: The laws of logarithms can be used when all the terms have the same base.

Q4: • You can use one of these three methods:
   - If possible, write both sides of the equation with the same base, set the exponents equal to each other, and solve for the unknown.
   - Take the logarithm of each side and solve for the unknown.
   - Use graphing technology, using systems of equations strategies.
   • You can evaluate any logarithm with base b, using the change of base formula $\log_b x = \dfrac{\log x}{\log b}$

Q5: • Use logarithmic regression to determine the equation of the curve of best fit.

Chapter 7 Test, page 191

1. C.   **2.** B.   **3.** C.   **4.** C.   **5.** D.

6.

	Function	x-intercept	Number of y-intercepts	End Behaviour	Domain	Range	Increasing or Decreasing
a)	$y = -6\log x$	1	0	from Quadrant I to Quadrant IV	$\{x \mid x > 0, x \in R\}$	$\{y \mid y \in R\}$	decreasing
b)	$y = 12\ln x$	1	0	from Quadrant IV to Quadrant I	$\{x \mid x > 0, x \in R\}$	$\{y \mid y \in R\}$	increasing

7. a) 3   b) 2   c) 3
8. a) 4   b) 5
9. a) 1.6   b) 3.2
10. 13 years
11. 38 years
12. e.g., a) $\log_4 11 + \log_4 11$ b) $\log_4 242 - \log_4 2$ c) $2\log_4 11$
13. 100 times as loud
14. $x \doteq 3.13$
15. 8 years

Chapter 8

Getting Started, page 194

1. a) iii)   b) iv)   c) v)   d) i)   e) v)   f) ii)
2. a) 0.978   c) 0.208
   b) 0.438   d) -0.899
3. a) $y = 1.259\ldots(1.079\ldots)^x$ b) e.g., 1.52 million
4. a) $\{y \mid y \in R\}$ b) $\{y \mid y \geq -3, y \in R\}$ c) $\{y \mid 1 \leq y \leq 2, y \in R\}$

5. a)

x	0°	10°	25°	40°	55°	70°	85°	90°
sin x	0	0.17	0.42	0.64	0.82	0.94	0.99	1
cos x	1	0.98	0.91	0.77	0.57	0.34	0.09	0

b) e.g., The value of sin x increases from 0 to 1, increasing more slowly as the value of x increases.

c) e.g., The value of cos x decreases from 1 to 0, decreasing more quickly as the value of x increases.

6. a) 9.4 **b)** 14.0 **c)** 5.3

Lesson 8.1, page 196

1. e.g., **a)** 0.4 **b)** 4
2. e.g., **a)** 20° **b)** 160° **c)** 211° **d)** 348°
3. e.g., **a)** 45° **b)** 200° **c)** 420°
4. e.g., **a)** 6.7 **b)** 12.5
5. e.g., **a)** 1.7 **b)** 4.7 **c)** 6.4
6. B. **7.** A.
8. e.g., 410°; 7.1
9. Patty travelled about 10 m farther.

Lesson 8.2, page 200

1. a) $y = \cos x$ **c)** neither; has no x-intercepts
b) neither; amplitude is greater than 1 **d)** neither; period is 720°

Lesson 8.3, page 202

1. a) $\{y \mid -4.5 \le y \le 3.5, y \in R\}$; 4 **b)** $\{y \mid -4 \le y \le 2, y \in R\}$; 3
2. a) $y = 1$; 2 **b)** $y = -2$; 4
3. a) 120° **b)** 3
4. a) $\{y \mid -9 \le y \le 1, y \in R\}$; $y = -4$; 5; 180°
 b) $\{y \mid -2 \le y \le 8, y \in R\}$; $y = 3$; 3; 5
5. $\{x \mid 0 \le x \le 2.2, x \in R\}$; $\{y \mid -9 \le y \le 4, x \in R\}$; $y = -2.5$; 6.5; 0.5
6. a) e.g.,

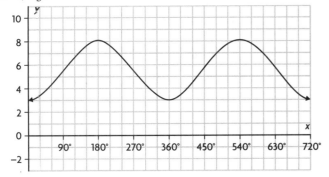

b) e.g.,

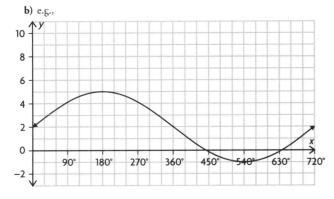

c) e.g.,

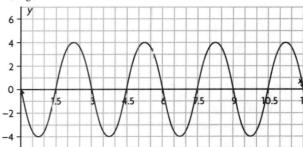

d) e.g.,

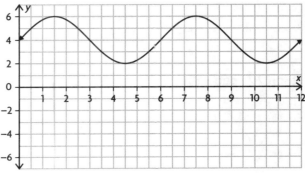

7. B.
8. e.g., A and B have the same midline equation: True: A graph with a maximum of 3 and a minimum of −3 and a graph with a maximum of 2 and a minimum of −2 have the same midline equation, $y = 0$.

A and B can have the same amplitude: True: A graph with a maximum of 4 and a minimum of 0 and a graph with a maximum of 5 and a minimum of 1 have the same amplitude, 2.

A and B can have the same midline equation and the same amplitude: False: Two graphs can only have the same midline equation and amplitude if they have the same maximum and minimum values.

Lesson 8.4, page 208

1. c), a), b)
2. c), a), b)
3. a), b), c)
4. a) 45° to the right **b)** 180° to the left **c)** 90° to the right **d)** none
5. a) $y = 2$ **b)** $y = -6$
6. a) 7; $\{y \mid -7 \le y \le 7, y \in R\}$ **b)** 15; $\{y \mid -13 \le y \le 17, y \in R\}$
7. a) 30° to the right **b)** 90° to the left **c)** 4.5 to the right
 d) 4 to the left
8. A.
9. a) amplitude 3; midline $y = -1$; range $\{y \mid -4 \le y \le 2, y \in R\}$;
 period 60°; translation 45° to the right
b)

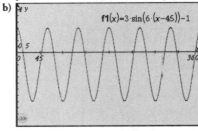

Lesson 8.5, page 212

1. 54.8%; 95.2%
2. 35.6°; 26.1°
3. 42.3%; 97.2%
4. B. **5.** D.

6. about 5.8 °C; e.g., I graphed the data for each community on a scatter plot, and the points appeared to follow a sinusoidal pattern. I did a sine regression to determine equations that fit the points on each scatter plot. Then I used interpolation to predict the average temperature on April 1 for each location, and determined the difference.

Chapter 8 Test Prep, page 216

Q1: In radian measure, 1 is equivalent to about $60°$ and π is equivalent to $180°$. A complete revolution, or $360°$, is 2π in radian measure.

Q2:
- Both graphs are periodic with period $360°$ or 2π in radian measure.
- Both graphs have domain $\{x \mid x \in R\}$ and range $\{y \mid -1 \le y \le 1, y \in R\}$.
- Both graphs have amplitude 1 and midline $y = 0$.

Q3: Sinusoidal functions have graphs the same shape as the graph of a sine function. For any sinusoidal function:
- The period is the horizontal distance between consecutive maximum values or consecutive minimum values.
- The midline has equation $y = \dfrac{\text{maximum value} + \text{minimum value}}{2}$.
- The amplitude is the positive vertical distance between the midline and either a maximum or a minimum value.

Q4: $y = a \sin b(x - c) + d$ and $y = a \cos b(x - c) + d$, where
- a is the amplitude
- b is the number of cycles in $360°$ or 2π, so the period is $\dfrac{360°}{b}$ or $\dfrac{2\pi}{b}$
- c gives the horizontal translation of the graph of $y = \sin x$ or $y = \cos x$
- $y = d$ is the equation of the midline

Q5: Use sinusoidal regression to determine the equation of the curve of best fit.

Chapter 8 Test, page 217

1. D. **2.** C. **3.** B. **4.** A. **5.** A.
6. B. **7.** C.
8. a) 1.3 b) 8.4 c) 150° d) 240°
9. 3; π
10. $\{y \mid 0 \le y \le 4, y \in R\}$; $y = 2$; 2; 2π
11. 45° to the right; 4; $\{y \mid -2 \le y \le 6, y \in R\}$; $y = 2$; 180°
12. 98.9%; 44.0%
13. e.g., 315°; 5.5
14. $y = \cos x$
15. 2; $y = 1$; $\{y \mid 0 \le y \le 4, y \in R\}$; 120°
16. a) amplitude 2; midline $y = 1$; range $\{y \mid -1 \le y \le 3, y \in R\}$; period 90°; translation 45° to the right
b)

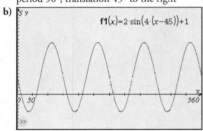

$f1(x)=2\cdot\sin(4\cdot(x-45))+1$

17. about 5.3 °C; e.g., I graphed the data for each community on a scatter plot, and the data points appeared to follow a sinusoidal pattern. I did a sine regression to determine equations that fit the points on each scatter plot. Then I used interpolation to predict the average temperature on April 1 for each location, and determined the difference.

6–8 Cumulative Test, page 222

1. B **2.** D **3.** C
4. C **5.** C. **6.** B
7. 4 **8.** 3 **9.** 2
10. 6.5 h
11. a) 3.81 b) −1.70
12. $y = -6$

13. a) 0 b) $y = 6$ c) extends from Quadrant II to Quadrant I
d) $\{x \mid x \in R\}$ e) $\{y \mid y > 0, y \in R\}$ f) increasing

14.

	Number of x-Intercepts	y-Intercept	End Behaviour	Domain	Range	Increasing or Decreasing
a)	0	4	extends from Quadrant I to Quadrant I	$\{x \mid x \in R\}$	$\{y \mid y > 0, y \in R\}$	increasing
b)	0	2	extends from Quadrant II to Quadrant I	$\{x \mid x \in R\}$	$\{y \mid y > 0, y \in R\}$	decreasing

15. a) domain: $\{x \mid x \ge 0, x \in R\}$ range: $\{y \mid y \ge 550, y \in R\}$
b) $y = 550$; the purchase price of the coin in 2000
c) e.g., i) $3800 ii) third quarter of 2007

16. a) $x = 2$ b) $x = 1$ c) $x = -1$ d) $x = \dfrac{3}{4}$

17. a) $x = 1.15$ b) $x = -4.27$

18. a) $f(t) = 1500(1.06)^t$
b) $a = 1500$, the initial investment; $b = 1.06$, the multiplier between consecutive values of t
The value of the investment at the end of each year is 106% of what it was at the start of the year.
c) The investment doubles near the end of the 11th year ($t = 11.895...$).

19 a) $x = 1$, no y-intercept, the graph extends from Quadrant IV to Quadrant I, $\{x \mid x > 0, x \in R\}$, $\{y \mid y \in R\}$, increasing
b) $x = 1$, no y-intercept, the graph extends from Quadrant I to Quadrant IV, $\{x \mid x > 0, x \in R\}$, $\{y \mid y \in R\}$, decreasing

20. a) $\log_6 320 \approx 3.22$ b) $\log_8 16 = \dfrac{4}{3}$

21. e.g., a) $y = -13.888... + 43.753... \ln x$
b) 104.6 cm
c) 5.4 weeks

22. range: $\{y \mid -7 \le y \le -1, y \in R\}$; period: π; amplitude: 3; equation of midline: $y = -4$

23. amplitude: 4; period: 120°; equation of the midline: $y = 5$; domain: $\{x \mid x \in R\}$; range: $\{y \mid 1 \le y \le 9, y \in R\}$; horizontal translation: 20° to the right

24. e.g., a) $y = 18.496... \sin (0.469...x - 1.708...) + 0.770...$
b) about −0.6 °C
c) from about the middle of May to the middle of August

1–8 Cumulative Test: Exam Prep, page 228

1. C **2.** B **3.** A **4.** C **5.** A
6. C **7.** C **8.** D
9. a) 20 b) 15 c) 2
10. 60
11. $\dfrac{36}{752\ 538\ 150}$
12. 1; 3 **13.** $x = 0$ **14.** 5 **15.** $x = 1$ **16.** 180°
17. a) no
b) $A \cup B = \{1, 2, 3, 4, 5, 6, 7, 8, 9, 10, 11, 12, 13, 14, 15, 16, 17, 18, 19, 20\}$
c) $n(B) = 11$
d) $n(A \cap B) = 1$
18. 23
19. $n^2 + 11n + 30$
20. a) 150 b) 315 c) 115
21. 45 360
22. $n = 5$
23. Yes. $P(\text{Amy wins a point}) = \dfrac{15}{36}$; $P(\text{Jeff wins a point}) = \dfrac{15}{36}$
24. a) independent b) mutually exclusive c) dependent
25. $\dfrac{5}{12}$
26. $\dfrac{x^2 - 3x}{4(x - 4)}, x \ne -5, -4, 2, 0$

27. $\dfrac{2x+1}{(x+2)(x-2)}$, $x \neq -2, 2$

28. $x = 1, x \neq 0, x \neq -5$

29. domain: $\{x \mid x \in R\}$; range: $\{y \mid y \in R\}$; intercepts: $x = -4, -1, 2$, $y = 4$; end behaviour: graph extends from Quadrant II to Quadrant IV

30. **a)** end behaviour: graph extends from Quadrant II to Quadrant IV; possible turning points: 0; possible x-intercepts: 1; y-intercept: $y = 3$; domain: $\{x \mid x \in R\}$; range: $\{y \mid y \in R\}$
b) end behaviour: graph extends from Quadrant III to Quadrant I; possible turning points: 2; possible x-intercepts: 3; y-intercept: $y = -8$; domain: $\{x \mid x \in R\}$; range: $\{y \mid y \in R\}$

31. e.g.,

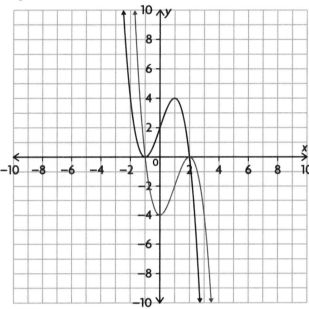

32. **a)** $y = -4.900\ldots x^2 + 10.000\ldots x - 0.000\ldots$
b) about 0.6 s and 1.5 s
c) 4.9 m

33. **a)** 0   **b)** $y = 5$ **c)** extends from Quadrant II to Quadrant I
d) $\{x \mid x \in R\}$ **e)** $\{y \mid y \geq 0, y \in R\}$ **f)** decreasing

34. $x = 0.577\ldots$

35. 23.2 days

36. **a)** $\dfrac{3}{2}$ **b)** -2

37. **a)** $\log_3 125\,000 \approx 10.68$ **b)** $\log_5 3 \approx 0.68$

38. range: $\{y \mid 2 \leq y \leq 0, y \in R\}$; period: $360°$; amplitude: 2; equation of midline: $y = 4$

39. amplitude: 2; period: π; equation of midline: $y = -3$; domain: $\{x \mid x \in R\}$; range: $\{y \mid -5 \leq y \leq -1, y \in R\}$; horizontal translation: 2 units to the left

40. **a)** $y = 40.041\ldots \sin(0.682\ldots x - 3.031\ldots) + 34.731\ldots$
b) from about early September to the middle of April

Notes

Notes

Notes

Notes